AMERICAN CRISIS,
SOUTHERN SOLUTIONS

ALSO IN THIS SERIES

Where We Stand: Voices of Southern Dissent (2004)

American Crisis, Southern Solutions

From Where We Stand, Peril and Promise

ぐう

EDITED BY ANTHONY DUNBAR
FOREWORD BY RAY MARSHALL
AFTERWORD BY DAN CARTER

WITH ESSAYS BY

JASON BERRY ᶝ CHARLES J. BUSSEY ᶝ DANNY DUNCAN COLLUM

DOUG DAVIS ᶝ LESLIE W. DUNBAR ᶝ GLENN FELDMAN

FRYE GAILLARD ᶝ J. DREW LANHAM ᶝ LAUGHLIN MCDONALD

GENE R. NICHOL ᶝ DANIEL H. POLLITT ᶝ WADE RATHKE

JANISSE RAY ᶝ ELLEN G. SPEARS ᶝ SUSAN FORD WILTSHIRE

NEWSOUTH BOOKS
Montgomery | Louisville

NewSouth Books
P.O. Box 1588
Montgomery, AL 36102

Library of Congress Cataloging-in-Publication Data

American crisis, southern solutions / edited by Anthony Dunbar.
p. cm.
ISBN-13: 978-1-58838-228-3
ISBN-10: 1-58838-228-1
1. United States—Politics and government—21st century. 2. Southern
states—Politics and government—21st century. I. Dunbar, Anthony P.
JK275.A43 2008
973.93—dc22

2007051492

Design by Randall Williams
Printed in the United States of America

I believe there are more instances of the abridgement of the freedom of the people by gradual and silent encroachments of those in power than by violent and sudden usurpations.

JAMES MADISON
SPEECH TO THE VIRGINIA RATIFYING CONVENTION
JUNE 16, 1788

Contents

Foreword... RAY MARSHALL 9

Introduction.............................ANTHONY DUNBAR 18

Hope from Southern Voices .... CHARLES J. BUSSEY 27

To Rescue Our Heritage....................... DANIEL H. POLLITT 40

Education and Economic Justice .... GENE R. NICHOL 70

Politics and Religion...........................LESLIE W. DUNBAR 78

Towards Home... J. DREW LANHAM 96

The Tupelo Solution .... DANNY DUNCAN COLLUM 110

Can a Third World Town Be Saved? ....JASON BERRY 123

Hospitality or Exile? ....SUSAN FORD WILTSHIRE 152

Labor's Failure in the South .... WADE RATHKE 169

On Human Rights & Immigration ....DOUG DAVIS 190

Reducing Environmental Burdens............ ELLEN G. SPEARS 200

Dixie Reaches the Boiling Point .... JANISSE RAY 212

"Ballot Security"............................LAUGHLIN MCDONALD 224

Lessons from the Bayou............................FRYE GAILLARD 234

Our Appointment with Destiny .... GLENN FELDMAN 244

Afterword.. DAN CARTER 255

Notes 263

Acknowledgments 280

FOREWORD

RAY MARSHALL

The contributors to this volume see in some of the policies of the current administration the worst aspects of Southern history: growing inequality of wealth and income, which threatens national unity and the American ideal of equal opportunity for all; a tendency to rationalize inequality and elite privileges as in the public interest; a doctrinaire commitment to "free market" forces, another way to strengthen constituents with the most market power; paying lip service to democracy and limited government, while using the power of the state to favor the advantaged and to deny citizens the most basic personal freedoms; and using real and imagined external threats as an excuse to limit constitutional freedoms and to expand the unilateral use of military power, thus strengthening our real enemies and damaging America's image as a champion of peace, democracy, and human rights.

The contributors to this book believe, in addition, that some of the South's worst values have been exported through national political processes to the rest of the country. The political power of Southern whites was enhanced during the first half of the twentieth century by the disenfranchisement of minorities and many poor whites, Senate rules which favored incumbency and seniority and enabled a minority to thwart the will of a majority, and electoral rules that give inordinate power to rural states and areas. Democrats first used race as the basis of their political power. Since the mid-1960s race has been used by Republicans as their base of power.

A principal reason why the United States has lagged behind other democratic industrial countries in creating social safety nets and adopting fundamental worker rights and protections is the extent to which the South has shaped national policy. For example, a basic principle of all democratic countries, and of U.S. foreign policy, is the proposition that free and democratic countries require free and democratic worker organizations. Despite this principle, American workers have less power in the workplace and in society than their counterparts in any other major industrialized country, including Canada. Moreover, low union density has more to do with U.S. policies than with workers' desire for representation. Polls show that a majority of non-union workers would join unions if they could.[1] These polls also show that 90 percent of union members would keep their unions. If these nonunion workers could freely gain representation, union density would be three to four times what it actually is.

The basic reason millions of American workers who would like union representation are unable to get it is workers' fear of employer retribution if they join or support unions. Because of the absence of effective remedies for employer violations of the National Labor Relations Act, together with the law's pro-employer bias, employers and their consultants have taught workers that they—not the federal government—ultimately have the power to determine whether or not workers are allowed to bargain collectively.

In 1977–78, when the Carter administration tried to strengthen workers' rights to organize and bargain collectively, our bill passed the house by almost a hundred-vote majority and we had fifty-eight solid votes for passage in the Senate. But we could not muster the

RAY MARSHALL was U.S. Secretary of Labor in the Carter administration. He holds the Audre and Bernard Rapoport Centennial Chair in Economics and Public Affairs at the LBJ School of Public Affairs at the University of Texas.

sixty votes needed to break a filibuster. Even though nineteen out of twenty-six Southern senators were Democrats, we got only one vote from the South—Jim Sasser of Tennessee. In fact, we got many more Republican votes from non-Southern states than we did from Southern Democrats.

The Republicans' "Southern Strategy," especially as practiced by President Reagan, further weakened support for workers and civil rights. Reagan's strategy included thinly disguised racist appeals to whites and weakening unions by breaking the Professional Air Traffic Controllers strike, officially sanctioning employers' growing anti-union tactics. Reagan, who understood that the civil rights acts of 1964 and 1965 had made Republicans out of most Southern whites, played to this sentiment by telling an audience in Philadelphia, Mississippi—near where three civil rights activists were murdered in 1964—that the 1965 Voting Rights Act "humiliated" the South.

A similar appeal was made by Reagan during his 1976 campaign, with his frequent references to apocryphal Cadillac-driving welfare queens and "strapping young bucks" buying T-bone steaks with food stamps. Reagan's defenders protest that he was really not a racist, but his actions are more important than his beliefs; after all, discrimination is an action, not an attitude.

Workers' ability to bargain collectively is being eroded almost everywhere by globalization, automation, deregulation, and low-wage competitiveness strategies, which have now spread to the whole country. Reversing these trends would give workers more power to promote high-value-added competition and policies to moderate the negative impacts of market forces, provide a more equitable sharing of the benefits and costs of change, and strengthen democratic institutions. Bargaining rights would, in addition, give workers more protection when their jobs are outsourced, as has been the case in industries like steel and automobiles. Organized workers have demonstrated that they can contribute, as they did by helping US Steel (on whose parent Company, USX, I served as a union-nominated director) become a very productive and competitive enterprise.

Fortunately, as the contributors to this volume show, there are other, more progressive Southern voices that point the way to solutions to national and regional crises. Some of the positions advocated by progressive Southerners require strengthening constitutional guarantees, especially reaffirming the separation of powers to limit the president's usurpation of legislative responsibilities and the abrogation of individual constitutional rights. Southern Democrats understand from their history and personal experiences how important these constitutional protections are. This is particularly true of black and Hispanic Southerners, who have been able to leverage the gaps between America's grand goals and social and political realities. For example, A. Philip Randolph and his followers used the threat of a protest march on Washington to force President Roosevelt to protect the rights of blacks to work in World War II defense installations. The contradiction between the ideal of a war to make the world safe for democracy and the reality of discrimination against the employment of minorities to produce the materials to fight that war caused Randolph's strategy to succeed.

Randolph and other civil rights leaders also understood the need for the victims of oppression to lead the fight for change. "Your friends can help you," Randolph said, "but they can't save you: you have to save yourselves."

President Johnson understood this principle when he told a delegation seeking his support for the 1964 Civil Rights Act that it would be good for the country and he was for it, but he instructed them to "go and make me do it."

Thoughtful Southerners likewise understand the threat to democracy from the religious right's attempts to breach the constitutional wall separating church and state. Democratic politics is the art of compromise. It is, however, impossible to compromise religious beliefs. The founders understood that democracy and state-imposed religious beliefs cannot coexist.

Unlike most ideological conservatives, Southern progressives also understand the power of governments to improve opportunity and protect basic human and civil rights.

This attitude contrasts markedly with that of conservative Southerners who lobby to gain tariff protection, tax advantages, contracts, and other public benefits while denigrating government and extolling the virtues of free markets. Few of us who not only lived through the Great Depression and World War II, but also benefited from the GI Bill, can be persuaded that the government is the enemy. We understand that markets are important institutions to increase efficiency in the production and allocation of goods and services, but cannot produce justice, equity, technological innovation, protect the environment and workers' safety and health, or effectively produce and allocate health care, education, or public infrastructure. We understand that the fundamental issue is not the size of government but its efficiency in responding to common needs and concerns. We understand, further, that at its best government does the most for those who need help, not the rich and powerful. So, as the late Arthur Okun put it, two cheers for the market, but not three.

Progressive Southerners understand, in addition, that politicians are important people who have great power for good or ill. LBJ taught us that whether we survive on this planet is a political, not a technological or economic, issue. The challenge, therefore, is to change the political system from one responsive mainly to economic elites and make it more responsive to middle- and low-income families. Presidents Carter and Clinton demonstrated that, since the passage of the Voting Rights Act, progressive Southerners with inclusive political messages can defeat the Republicans' Southern strategy.

Southern leaders like LBJ and Martin Luther King supported the New Deal principle that we could not have sustainable, broadly shared prosperity in an interdependent society unless all major groups shared in that prosperity. Dr. King taught that political democracy without economic democracy was incomplete. It is not a coincidence that he was murdered while supporting a strike by Memphis sanitation workers.

It is equally clear that under twenty-first century conditions, broadly shared prosperity requires economic policies to moderate market tendencies that produce inequality. Southern history warns us about the dangers of a "plantation mentality," where the wealthy feel that they have little, if anything, in common with the poor, especially shared schools, churches and justice systems. Worse yet, planters considered good public schools and other services to be contrary to their predominant interests in a ready supply of low-cost, compliant labor and low and regressive tax systems. It also was common for elites to argue that since the poor are inherently inferior, they could not benefit from high quality schools. Moreover, in their rationalization, a regressive system is fair because the rich pay most of the taxes and accumulated wealth "trickles down" to low-income people.

Not surprisingly, these attitudes threaten national unity and breed class conflicts. Inequality also is accompanied by numerous social pathologies and lower-quality lives for rich and poor alike. Indeed, gross inequalities make it difficult for any country to develop sound economic and social policies. Little wonder, then, that thoughtful Southerners, like President Carter and the contributors to this book and its 2004 companion, *Where We Stand*, consider growing inequality to be America's most serious domestic challenge.

During the years between the end of the 1930s and the 1980s, New Deal policies contributed to America's longest period of sustained, broadly shared economic growth. We need to return to the more inclusive economic and political policies of that period, to include those who have been excluded from full and equitable participation in our democratic, market-oriented society. That is, *if* we want to survive in today's much more competitive globalized economy. A major challenge in this more knowledge-intensive environment is reforming our schools to eliminate the achievement gaps between more- and less-advantaged students and to provide high-quality postsecondary education opportunities to all students. This will require radical changes in our education and training policies, including the allocation of relatively more resources to poor schools and a much stronger adult education system to foster lifelong learning.[2]

To be sure, economic policies that strengthen democratic institutions and divert us from our present low-wage economic course will require much more than education and school reform, including:

- adequate social safety nets, including universal health insurance, the absence of which not only increases the costs of health care but puts many American companies at a competitive disadvantage.

- greater worker empowerment in workplace decisions, which can significantly improve productivity and quality. This means measures to strengthen workers' collective bargaining rights and to minimize the need for risky contests with their employers, and enhanced rights to participate in non-adversarial decisions to improve productivity and workplace safety. Worker participation on corporate boards of directors could strengthen business performance, cause companies to take longer-time perspectives, provide a modest check on corporate executive compensation unrelated to performance, and moderate corporate tendencies to outsource work to other countries without well-supported economic reasons.

There is abundant evidence that worker involvement can improve workplace decisions, especially crucial safety and health practices.

- processes to enable displaced workers to move to new jobs without excessive losses of income. Positive "adjustment" policies would reduce workers' resistance to a more open and expansive global trading system, which could benefit people everywhere.

- adequate minimum and prevailing wage measures both to create incentives for work and also to limit company strategies to compete by lowering wages. This is how employers have dealt since the 1970s with workers with high school degrees or less, and since 2000 with college graduates who do not have postgraduate professional degrees.

The U.S. needs to develop much better foreign policies based on an understanding of common global interests, deeper understandings of other peoples, and much more collegial approaches to international problems.

President Carter often warned us about the dangers of the political temptation to initiate military adventures for partisan political advantage. He argued that Americans should be known, without equivocation, as the leading champions of democracy and human rights.

The United States also should take the lead in protecting the global environment. It is in our self-interest to use our resources and the access to the American market to leverage Mexico and other developing countries to reform their political and economic institutions, to provide good jobs for their people, and to promote political and public safety institutions to reduce crime and corruption. Part of this foreign economic policy regime should be labor and environmental standards that are transparent, fair, and enforceable. FDR taught us that we could not have real prosperity unless all major groups shared in that prosperity. In today's globalized world, this doctrine applies to the international as well as the domestic economy. Let's hope that progressive Southern voices can be as influential in the twenty-first century as reactionary voices were in the twentieth. ≈

INTRODUCTION

ANTHONY DUNBAR

This book speaks not only to the South's role in driving America away from its best principles, but also to new directions this country's leadership should take, based upon some lessons Southerners have learned through their own hard times.

The South has been blamed for many things—extending slavery, starting the Civil War, Jim Crow, inattention to poverty, bad public schools. Who can say it isn't so? Now the South can justifiably be blamed not only for its historical flaws but also for exporting its peculiar style of politics, religion, economics and entertainment—its very public life—to the far-flung corners of the republic. The South's impact upon the national agenda and America's buccaneering role in the world has been astonishing.

On the redeeming side, there also came from the South a civil rights movement that gave the country some of its finest examples of courage. In the South we have seen determined people firmly grasp the fundamental institutions of democracy, with the result that millions of new voters have come on board in the last decades and thousands of contenders have emerged for elected offices in towns so small that many Americans might wonder why anyone would care who ran them. From the South has come not just hip-hop from Atlanta's 'hoods, but new explorations of jazz and roots music. Not just rampant environmental destruction but also community-based oversight that has achieved solutions business people and regular citizens might live with. The South has given us examples of rebuilding after disasters—be they ferocious hurricanes or, looking to history, General Sherman's "swath of destruction." These personal human achievements stand in dramatic contrast to the bumbling, indifference, or actual enmity of government. And from the South comes a tradition of outspoken, if not always immediately successful, resistance to misguided power, in the pragmatic spirit of keeping the cause alive for another day. This volume suggests that in many ways the Southern experience points the way toward solutions—some seen dimly, but some quite clear—to the most critical problems America faces, and to some of the turmoil America has left in its wake in the world today. In many ways, it is an optimistic book.

One aspect of the Southern experience, however, deserves special mention because it illustrates how snake oil salesmen, properly cleaned up and educated at good schools, can sell useless and dangerous products while making you glad you spent your money. Look back into history. A century or more ago, in parlors a generation removed from the Civil War, this was known as the "New South." This strange philosophy was traced in considerable detail by Paul M. Gaston, one of the people who inspired this volume, in *The New South Creed, A Study in Southern Mythmaking*. It was espoused by influential scribes and entrepreneurs, notably Henry W. Grady, an owner of the *Atlanta Constitution*, who believed in what is now called diversified agribusiness (though few of its proponents actually toiled in the fields) and the wonders that might be wrought from an infusion of capital (though they had very little of it) with which the fields might be turned into factories.

Their vision was a new and prosperous South emerging from the ashes of the Civil War and the Klan terrorism of Reconstruction. But the dream was not grounded in reality. The New-Southers were entranced by the "marketplace" but lacked any fear of monopoly, oligarchy, or environmental costs. They were blithely unconcerned about the pervasive poverty of real Southerners or the obstacles poverty presented to overall progress. They discounted Southern racism, and the toll it took on lofty intangibles such as the human spirit and practical matters such as public schooling. And, consequently, their ideals did not match the South's true condition and were temporarily discarded as topics of lively public debate. It would take World War II, desegregation, and decades of national prosperity before capital would finally find a home in the South, and blossom, and prevail.

And in prosperity the New South concepts, speaking as they did to the aspirations, though not the assets, of the common man, resurfaced. Unconcerned about the growing imbalance between rich and poor, and the citizens left behind, the New South Creed now drives not just the South but, through the stealth of Southern politicians, it has amassed fans enough to march steadily across the United States. This is one of the reasons why one whistles past Dixie at his peril. The attitudes and voting biases assembled in the ascendant South are now pretty much common everywhere. But does excessive consumption and fast profit measure the success of a society when not everybody is enjoying the bounty?

Four years ago a number of the contributors to this book published *Where We Stand: Voices of Southern Dissent.* It sought to give expression to writers who stood for a progressive tradition in Southern thinking and who were alarmed—angry might be the better word—about the forces driving the United States into Iraq and dividing neighbors at home. They spoke as redeemers, too, but not quite like the Redeemers of the 1870s who sought to rid the South of the Republican Party for its promotion of black enfranchisement. The *Where We Stand* writers instead leaned toward ridding

---

ANTHONY DUNBAR is a Lillian Smith Award-winning writer, editor, and attorney, and is the author of seven novels and several nonfiction books. He lives in New Orleans.

the country of an administration that has neglected the principles of enfranchisement, perfect union, and equality of citizenship.

The contributors to the first volume looked ahead toward a coming day when the power of guns and money will be harnessed and when the poor of many nations will believe that their advancement and our democratic ideals are compatible. As former President Jimmy Carter wrote in his foreword:

> The rich and powerful can be tempted to suppress the poor in order to keep them from trying to take what is ours. Democracy, peace, and human rights suffer under such conditions. You can see this in the South, in Georgia, in Plains. You can see this in the conduct of the United States today.

It seems less lonely to present this indictment in 2008. Another presidential election is upon us, another watershed year in a tumultuous new century. People are beginning to sense the sweet smell of change in the breeze. Yet it is not enough now to protest the failures of administration policies and the lack of imagination and compassion at the top. The more difficult task is pointing out the path, and that is what the writers of this book try to do.

An overall observation is that a certain breed of Southerners has been remarkably successful in influencing the course of human events. These include a formidable lot of Southern congressmen and senators as well as popular preachers who have networked their pulpits into a potent and powerful special interest group. It is upon this foundation that the national administration has stood to advance, though not proclaim the true name of, its philosophy. The hallmarks of that philosophy seem strangely familiar to students of the South's history. In addition to an underlying faith that market forces will cure all ills, there is the idea that the immediate needs of the poor and the dispossessed can be overlooked because they are irrelevant. There is the axiom that racial inequality, since it is contra-policy, does not exist. There are the beliefs that saying something with conviction makes it real ("America is doing everything it can to help Katrina victims"), that the will of God underlies one's personal ideas, that business counts more than values or science, that immigration in the abstract is good but that the available immigrant population is bad, and that cash flow proves a civilization superior.

These core values of the "New South" failed to work in Dixie, and the essays that follow argue that they are not working for the United States today. Recognizing the special contribution the South has made to spreading this troubling way of thinking, we search for light to shine upon the road.

CHARLES J. BUSSEY, in the introductory essay, reminds us of Southern voices, past and present, who have called upon Americans to reach high to achieve the country's promise of equality and respect for human welfare.

Drawing upon the lessons the South has learned from the repressions of the past, DANIEL H. POLLITT writes about the war in Iraq, the abuses of our prisoners, and the United States Constitution.

GENE R. NICHOL points out the extent to which higher education is increasingly available only to the children of wealthy families, and the steps some institutions, including his own College of William and Mary, have taken to close the gap.

Politicians of all stripes clothe themselves in religion, and churches to their peril reach out for political power. LESLIE W. DUNBAR's thoughtful essay calls upon church and state to take a good look at each other and step back.

DREW LANHAM bears personal witness to the dramatic loss of land experienced by African Americans in the South and the commitment it takes to resist the pressure.

A special person is portrayed in DANNY DUNCAN COLLUM's "The Tupelo Solution," about a north Mississippi small-town paper and its founding editor, George McLean, both examples of courage, truthfulness, and civic leadership in contrast to the timidity and detachment of national megamedia.

Hurricane Katrina's mark on New Orleans will be lasting. JASON BERRY tells the story of a city failed by its politicians, and he finds hope in the energy of the young, the resilience of culture, and the possibility that average people might stand up and lead.

SUSAN FORD WILTSHIRE writes about how today's excluded—by reason of their sexuality—are changing society in the tradition of the Southern Freedom Riders, Gandhi, and the last play of Sophocles.

Recent efforts by organized labor to break into the Southern workplace have been little-chronicled. Organizer WADE RATHKE portrays the campaigns, the obstacles, and his vision of a Southern workplace model as exportable as that Southern business model, Wal-Mart.

DOUG DAVIS looks at immigration from a business owner's perspective and asserts that the lessons of the civil rights struggle teach us to stop talking about "aliens" and welcome the willing into our communities.

ELLEN G. SPEARS explains how the burdens of our toxic environment fall unfairly upon the poor, how the Voting Rights Act provides a model for legislative redress, and just as important, how Southerners have shown the power to get their towns cleaned up.

The stunning impact of global warming has hit the South hard. Southerners have done more than their share to cause this crisis, but JANISSE RAY highlights the efforts of Florida's Republican Governor Charlie Crist to address the problem on a state level, and she provides a prescription for national change.

LAUGHLIN McDONALD takes proponents of "ballot security" and of the partisan "oversight" of voting to task for ignoring the lessons learned in the South since *Brown v. Board of Education* about the need for stringent laws to protect this most important of civil rights.

The personal service, dedication to neighbors, and self-sacrifice of a small-town doctor on the Alabama coast seems so out of step with mainstream health care delivery in America today that it merits this inspiring profile: **FRYE GAILLARD** tells about Regina Benjamin, M.D., of Bayou La Batre.

GLENN FELDMAN explores the harsher South and how the "Southern way" of emotional, super-patriotic, and pietistic politics overtook the nation. The essay also expresses the hope that Southerners steeped in civil rights might provide inspiration to embattled progressives elsewhere.

In his afterword, historian **DAN CARTER** reminds us that we ignore the gradual undermining of democracy and equality at our peril and that realizing the promises of freedom depends on what we do in the months ahead. ❧

AMERICAN CRISIS,
SOUTHERN SOLUTIONS

Hope from Southern Voices

These Speak to Me

Charles J. Bussey

A few years back writer John Egerton talked about the "wonderful irony" it would be if America's problems could be solved by Southerners. That got me thinking—maybe we need to hear Southern voices from the past (and present) to see us through these dark days, to point us toward solutions. As Bill Moyers is so fond of saying, "We need to tell our story."

My story, voices that inspired me to think and be concerned about those less fortunate, began at an early age. Mother graduated Ole Miss in 1940 and went immediately to New York City to live. It was an exciting time for a Southern girl who loved parties and who dated two Mississippi boys—a Columbia University philosophy graduate student and a medical student at Harvard. After about a year, maybe a little longer, her mother called and said, "Daughter, it's time to come home." She came.

Back in Mississippi she put aside her majors in French and English to take a secretarial job with a construction company and met my father, whose small business made some sales to mother's firm. Shortly thereafter, the Japanese attacked Pearl Harbor, and the world shifted gears. My parents had a quick romance. They got married in Yazoo City, and Dad joined the Army air corps despite his deferment.

After the war, and probably due in part to my father's difficult wartime experiences, my parents left Mississippi and moved to

Livingston County, Kentucky, a back-to-the-land experiment. They bought a 450-acre farm with no electricity, no running water, no telephone, and no road from Highway 60 to the old farmhouse. That was in early 1946.

It was a challenge for both of them—neither had ever lived on a farm, and mother was a city girl used to all the modern conveniences. Two years into that experiment, mother was ready to leave, but my father persuaded her that electricity would be coming soon courtesy of the Rural Electric Administration, one of Franklin Roosevelt's New Deal programs. Harry Truman, FDR's successor, and his vice president, Kentuckian Alben Barkley, had promised it; and my father was convinced that the Democratic Party liberals cared about people struggling to make it on small farms. In 1947 or 1948, my father's faith was vindicated. Family legend has mother packing her bags when one day men and trucks showed up to plant light poles across our farm.

From an early age, my father told me that a person should always take the part of the underdog. He taught this not just by words but by the way he acted and the things he did for others. I got the same from our nearest neighbor, a blind, guitar-picking farmer named Haskel Parks, who had a wife, two children, and seventy-five hard-scrabble acres. I remember sitting in the yard with Haskel while he played the guitar, talked about baseball, and told me about FDR: "I listened to all his radio talks, and by God he understood the troubles people like us have." Haskel told me about the New Deal programs like the CCC camp where he'd worked for thirty dollars a month, five dollars for him to keep and twenty-five to go home

Mississippi native CHARLES BUSSEY, a professor of history at Western Kentucky University, was a Senior Fulbright Lecturer in Denmark in 1993 and again in Norway 2003–2004. His classes include "The American South," "America: 1945 to the Present," and "The Southern Civil Rights Movement."

to the family. I learned a lot by listening to his stories.

My first political memory is at age five when in November 1948 my parents, along with most of our neighbors, took me to the county courthouse in Smithland to wait for election returns. They were convinced that Truman would win despite the odds—that he would win because he was a liberal who was for the "little man." (I realize as a historian that some of Truman's contemporaries, including Eleanor Roosevelt, had reservations about Truman's liberalism, but for my parents and our neighbors, there was no doubt.) And Truman won.

About that time, another strong voice showed up in my life— Jack Scott, now elderly and retired and living in Elizabethtown, Kentucky. Jack worked in the early 1950s for a New Deal program designed to help farmers improve the quality of their lives by using resources more effectively and enlarging their operations. He was dedicated to helping people like Haskel Parks and my father diversify their farms (in our cases, to move into dairy farming). He helped arrange realistic loans, and he was there to encourage the small farmers.

Jack later went into commercial banking, first in St. Louis, and then he opened his own bank in Elizabethtown. He never, however, deviated from his desire to help people who were overlooked by most others. Jack's commitment to liberalism has never wavered. Throughout the Reagan years, the first President Bush's term, and now through the nightmare years of George W. Bush's tenure, Jack has continued to speak against policies that favor the rich over the poor. He and his wife Alice, a retired Methodist minister, have taken strong antiwar positions since 2003 and are beacons of light for dark times.

Those are Southern "voices" which spoke to me in my younger years, but there are other voices which speak to us all.

When I was seven years old, my mother read me William Faulkner's acceptance speech of the 1950 Nobel Prize for literature in Stockholm, Sweden. That makes sense only in context. As an Oxford girl, Mother often went to the Faulkner home for cookouts and would plead with "Mr. Bill" to tell a story. Oxford attorney Phil Stone and his wife Emily, early mentors and Faulkner supporters, were close family friends, and my grandparents lived across the street from Faulkner's sister-in-law Dorothy Oldham. (Sometimes, if Dorothy was in a good mood or had sipped a couple of whiskies, she would invite me over to shoot off fireworks, much to my parents' dismay!)

Over the years, I read Faulkner's Nobel speech many times and took to heart his words:

> Our tragedy today is a general and universal physical fear
> so long sustained by now that we can even bear it. There are no
> longer problems of the spirit. There is only one question: When
> will I be blown up? . . . [But] I believe that man will not merely
> endure: he will prevail. He is immortal . . . because he has a soul,
> a spirit capable of compassion and sacrifice and endurance.

Despite Faulkner's flaws, that statement will stand the test of time. It is a testimony of hope, of conviction that humankind will somehow make it through dark days.

If we look to Southern voices from the past and present, we can find the tools to combat the anti-historical, foolish, and wicked ways of George Bush, Dick Cheney, Alberto Gonzales, Condi Rice, and the whole gang.

I recently re-read George Washington's "Farewell Address" and thought how sad that our current President gives no indication of ever having read it. Washington told us that

> The nation which indulges toward another [nation or
> individual] a habitual hatred . . . is . . . a slave. It is a slave to
> its animosity . . . Hence, frequent . . . bloody contests . . . The

government sometimes . . . adopts through passion what reason
would reject . . . The peace often, sometimes perhaps the liberty,
of nations, has been the victim.

Think about those remarkable words from the first president
of the United States, and consider that not only did the architects
of the current crisis in Iraq and the Middle East avoid military
service, they probably were also never aware of this advice from
our first commander in chief. Review the tapes or transcripts of the
television appearances and speeches of Bush, Cheney, Wolfowitz,
Rice, and Rumsfeld during the run-up to the Iraq War, and note
how clearly President Washington's words from 1796 indict these
ignorant people.

Hear, too, James Madison, Washington's fellow Southerner, who
said, "If Tyranny and Oppression come to this land, it will be in
the guise of fighting a foreign enemy." Read as well his comments
about the dangers of war which include these remarkable words:
"[War stirs] the strongest passions and most dangerous weaknesses
of the human breast; avarice, vanity, the . . . love of fame, are all in
conspiracy against the desire and duty of peace."

Madison concluded, "In no part of the Constitution is more
wisdom to be found, than in the clause which confides the question of war and peace to the legislature, and not to the executive
department . . . The trust and temptation would be too great for
any one man."

Nineteenth-century Southerners likewise offer advice and hope.
I think first of Frederick Douglass who escaped slavery and moved
North to become one of the great voices of wisdom and hope. His
words still resonating in today's atmosphere, Douglass said in 1848,
"We have been accustomed . . . to hear much talk about 'Christian
America, and Infidel France.' I want to say . . . that I go for that
infidelity . . . which strikes the chains from the limbs of our brethren;
and against that Christianity which puts them on . . ."

Likewise, Douglass taught us that "Power concedes nothing without demand, it never has and it never will." Those are words every American patriot should have burned on her heart. As he spoke on July 4, 1852, before he became a key advisor to Abraham Lincoln, Douglass said:

> What, to the American slave, is your 4th of July? I answer; a day that reveals to him, more than all other days of the year, the gross injustice and cruelty to which he is the constant victim . . . There is not a nation on the earth guilty of practices more shocking and bloody than are the people of the United States at this very hour.

Followed by:

> Allow me to say . . . notwithstanding the dark picture I have this day presented, of the state of the nation, I do not despair of this country."

Douglass found hope and encouragement in the Declaration of Independence, "the great principles it contains, and the genius of American Institutions, [and] my spirit is . . . cheered."

Southerner Mark Twain, in his willingness to dissent from a war for empire, the Spanish-American War of 1898, offers words of hope to us who dissent from this one.

> It was a time of great and exalting excitement. The country was up in arms, the war was on, in every breast burned the holy fire of patriotism; the drums were beating, the bands playing, the toy pistols popping, the bunched firecrackers hissing and spluttering; on every hand and far down the receding and fading spread of roofs . . . a fluttering wilderness of flags . . . [and] the pastors preached devotion to flag and country . . . [and beseeched God's] aid in our good cause.

It was in that atmosphere that Twain wrote his remarkable "The War Prayer," perhaps the most powerful anti-war statement in American history.

Moving into the twentieth century, I call your attention to Arkansas Senator J. William Fulbright. Certainly he was a flawed individual—think about his unfortunate stance on civil rights— but he produced a book in the mid-1960s that should be required reading for every politician in Washington today. His voice in *The Arrogance of Power*, resounds today and simply must be heard. Fulbright, a Southern Democrat, challenged Democratic President Lyndon Johnson over the Vietnam War. First, he explains clearly that dissent in America is patriotic. "To criticize one's country," Fulbright wrote, "is to do it a service and pay it a compliment." For "in a democracy dissent is an act of faith . . . Criticism . . . is more than a right; it is an act of patriotism . . ." Our current administration—especially with the voices of the president, the vice president, and Karl Rove—has perverted the traditional idea of dissent. The Bush team says, "If you're not with us, you're on the side of terrorists."

Second, saying God is on our side is close to blasphemy. It is dangerously arrogant to assume that America is God's chosen country and can do as it will without "a decent respect for the opinions of mankind." President Bush commented at the National Cathedral shortly after 9/11 that it is "America's responsibility" to "rid the world of evil." What unbelievable arrogance! Listen to Fulbright: "We are not God's chosen Savior of mankind but only one of mankind's more successful . . . branches, endowed by our creator with the same capacity for good and evil, no more and no less, than the rest of humanity." America is powerful, but as Fulbright wrote, "Power tends to confuse itself with virtue, and a great nation is susceptible to the idea that its power is a sign of God's favor!"

Fulbright's words from the mid-sixties are even more poignant today:

America is now at that historical point at which a great nation is in danger of losing its perspective on what exactly is within the realm of its power and what is beyond it. Other great nations, reaching this critical juncture, have aspired to too much and, by over extension of effort, have declined and then fallen . . . America is showing signs of that arrogance of power which has . . . destroyed great nations in the past.

One Southerner has asked, "Can the American state . . . be disciplined?" Yes, it can, and the Southern civil rights movement has much to teach us today as we who love America try to discipline our nation gone wrong.

Most people, I suspect, think about Martin Luther King, Jr., when anyone mentions civil rights. No wonder! His words moved a nation and speak directly to today's difficult times. Unfortunately, most people today connect King only with the August 1963 "I Have A Dream Speech." Those were fine words and needed to be spoken. But if those are the only King words people know, we liberal Southerners fail in "telling our story." He wrote and spoke other words with a sharp edge.

King's rightly famous "Letter From A Birmingham Jail" is a classic reminder what American ideals have promised to all people. That letter shamed many white Americans into realizing that black Americans had been denied social, political, and economic justice. Today, however, in the midst of our never-ending misadventure in Iraq, with the Bush administration's efforts to scare Americans by equating dissent with treason, and the growing gap between the rich and the poor, Americans need also to hear King's 1967 Easter Sermon at Riverside Church in New York City.

"We are," he said one year before his death, "at the moment when our lives must be placed on the line if our nation is to survive its own folly. Every man [and woman] of human conviction must decide on the protest that best suits his [or her] conviction, but we must all protest." When I hear those words today, I am reminded that it is imperative for those of us who love our country, who are patriotic, to do all in our power to bring America back to her ideals. As King said, "We can no longer afford to worship the god of hate or bow down before the altar of retaliation. The oceans of history are made turbulent by the ever-rising tides of hate. History is cluttered with the wreckage of nations and individuals that pursued this self-defeating path of hate." More directly to the point, perhaps more pertinent today than then, King said, "This madness must stop."

There are so many inspiring voices dating from the Southern civil rights movement—Diane Nash, John Lewis, Robert Moses, and Julian Bond as examples—who are still working today for the "beloved community" of their youthful ideals. Those young people, who brought to America the two most important pieces of legislation of the twentieth century—the Civil Rights Act of 1964 and the Voting Rights Act of 1965, which make American democracy possible—told us then and tell us today what we need to know to make change. The iconic John Lewis, now a multi-term congressman from Georgia, started his civil rights career in Nashville as a teenager. Still in his twenties in 1968, but already a veteran of the movement and the poster child for nonviolence, Lewis returned to Nashville and spoke at Vanderbilt University. He called his talk "Human Rights—A Final Appeal to the Church" and said: "Woe unto the political leaders who listen to the voices of expediency and act in the interests of a Great Consensus, rather than do what is right." He was speaking truth to power, prophecy. We who love America need Lewis's courage, persistence, and words today to force our political leaders to stop the Iraq War and to enact legislation creating a more equitable economic system in America.

Jimmy Carter, another Southerner, has from the early seventies tried to teach America by word and deed how to create a more humane world. Carter has a strong, almost intuitive, sense of the distinction between what scholar Christopher Lasch called Hope and Memory versus Optimism and Nostalgia. The former reflect a distinct and positive way of looking at both the past and the future while the latter reflect a negative way of viewing time and history. Hope requires hard choices and, together with Memory, demands a realistic view of the past and future. Optimism and Nostalgia, on the other hand, do the opposite. To Lasch they promote the attitude that there are unlimited resources for people to exploit and that the past was perfect. In my mind the ideas are personified by Bush and Cheney. President Carter obviously understands the concept. In his presidential inaugural, Carter saw it as his duty to educate the people in the realities of the new age of limits. "We have," he said, "learned that more is not necessarily better, that even our great nation has its recognized limits, and that we can neither answer all questions nor solve all problems." He promoted "the common good" and human rights as opposed to policies that focused fed on human greed. He understood that if luxury, avarice, and wealth were the driving forces in our society, democracy was threatened.

I first learned about Jimmy Carter in 1974 when I read an article by Hunter Thompson in *Rolling Stone*. Carter had decided to run for president (when he first told his mother, Lillian, she allegedly said: "Of what?"). In May 1974, then-Governor Carter gave a re-markable speech at a University of Georgia Law Day ceremony at which a portrait of former U.S. Secretary of State Dean Rusk was being dedicated. Carter introduced Teddy Kennedy, the featured speaker, and completely upstaged the Massachusetts senator.

Opening with a joke, Carter quickly turned serious. In speaking about crime, he noted that he was not a lawyer, but "I read a lot and I listen a lot," and he indicated that much of his "understand-ing about the proper application of criminal justice and the system of equities is from Reinhold Niebuhr." That got some attention. Further, Carter said, another "source of my understanding about what's right and wrong in this society is from a friend of mine, a poet named Bob Dylan." He mentioned several of Dylan's songs and then, according to Thompson's article, ". . . railed and bitched about a system of criminal justice that allows the rich and privileged to escape punishment for their crimes and sends poor people to prison because they can't afford to bribe the judge." Carter spoke without a text but from "a page and a half of scrawled notes in his legal pad." Overwhelmed by the speech, Thompson understood correctly Carter's compassion and quest for justice and that for Carter, Dylan's music must be understood from the biblical perspective of the prophetic commands to seek justice.

Carter's was a controversial presidency beset by problems not of his making: the oil shortage, ever-rising interest rates, and finally the Iranian hostage crisis. America's good presidents (Washington, Lincoln, FDR) have all tried to educate the public—so did Carter. He clearly understood that if better stewardship or natural resources were not implemented, environmental disaster would result. He tried to teach Americans not only about human rights but also tried to foster a way of life which involved planning for the future. He's still working at that!

In a 1987 interview, the former president said that a few months after losing to Ronald Reagan, he and Rosalynn decided to set their objectives high and try to do more than if he'd won the 1980 election. And they have. This story is an example of Carter's sense of Hope and Memory—rather than wallowing in the "damned" present and yearning for a "perfect" past, Carter moved into the uncertain future with hope.

Carter's consistent work as one of the few public figures to stand up to the Bush administration after 9/11 is our model. In 2002 he recognized the "un-American" nature of holding prisoners at Guantanamo Bay, that the neo-cons were "trying to realize long-pent-up ambitions under the cover of the proclaimed war against terrorism." And, he stated unequivocally, "a unilateral war with

Iraq is not the answer." Iraq, he said, has become an obsession of our political leaders.

Bill Moyers, who came to the national scene from Texas with President Lyndon B. Johnson in the 1960s, is another Southerner providing us with sage advice and encouragement to speak. He wrote recently that the Republicans have hoodwinked America with their story and their values which "come from the Gilded Age, devised by apologists for the robber barons." Their idea is that the rich have "the freedom to accumulate wealth without social or democratic responsibilities and the license to buy the political system right out from under anyone else . . ." But—and here's where you and I come in—". . . we have a story of equal power. It is that the promise of America leaves no one out." Let's tell it!

Today's young people will hear the story. For example, Zach Hunter is a fifteen-year-old Virginian who founded "Loose Change to Loosen Chains," a student-run effort to raise money to free the twenty-seven million slaves in the world today. He credits Martin Luther King, Jr., as his inspiration. King "empowered a whole race," young Hunter wrote, "to carry out a peaceful revolution and that was really what he led, a peaceful revolution and that's what we're basically trying to do."

I personally like John Edwards, because I think he takes strong ethical positions on issues I care about: anti-Iraq War, pro-universal health care, pro-labor, and concern for the poor. I said in a talk to Blount County, Tennessee, Democrats that Edwards has the potential to be a "Southern FDR." That might be dreaming, but no one can say the man does not speak up. Coming from a working-class family, he speaks directly to the need to strengthen unions in America. He put it this way: "The difference between being unionized and not is the difference between poverty and not." After so many years of anti-union voices speaking to Americans, it is refreshing to hear Edwards—he says it consistently and not just to union groups. He announced his campaign from New Orleans' Ninth Ward, and the plight of those living in poverty is an issue that animates him. He has called it "the moral issue of our time."

Hannah Arendt once wrote in an essay, "Women for Dark Times," the following:

> That even in the darkest of times we have the right to expect some illumination, and that such illumination may well come less from theories and concepts than from the uncertain, flickering, and often weak light that some men and women, in their lives and their works, will kindle under almost all circumstances and shed over the time span that was given them on earth . . .

I believe that she is absolutely right. These are my Southern voices, past and present. ❧

To Rescue Our Heritage

The Constitution and the Sword

Daniel H. Pollitt

"A frequent recurrence to fundamental principles is absolutely necessary to preserve the blessings of liberty." — Article 1, Section 35, Declaration of Rights, North Carolina State Constitution

During the Civil War, President Lincoln issued a proclamation that persons "guilty of any disloyal practice affording aid and comfort to rebels" would be subject to "martial law and liable to trial and punishment by courts-martial or military commission." A Democrat named Milligan (who had lost the race for governor of Indiana) was convicted by a military commission of conspiring to free some eight thousand Confederate prisoners, raid the arsenals, and wage war from within. He was sentenced to death. He appealed to the federal courts for relief. The Supreme Court held that even rebels of this kind could not be tried by the military when the civilian courts were open for business, and wrote that the Constitution

> "is a law for rulers and people, equally in war and in peace, and covers with the shield of its protection all classes of men at all times and under all circumstances. No doctrine, involving more pernicious consequences, was ever invented by the wit of man than that any of its provisions can be suspended during any of the great exigencies of government." *Ex parte Milligan*, 71 U.S. 2 (1866)

The Bush administration turns a blind eye to this, our legal heritage, and has cut to the bone many of our hard-won Constitutional protections. The pernicious consequences are worldwide. Let's count some of the Bush rendings and ravages of our Constitutional heritage.

I. THE POWER OF THE SWORD

In December 2002, after the attack of September 11, 2001, President Bush lifted the long-time ban on assassination, thereby giving the CIA blanket authority to kill al-Qaeda leaders wherever they might be found.[1]

President Woodrow Wilson put it in these words:

> Once lead these people into war and they'll forget there
> ever was such a thing as tolerance. To fight you must be brutal
> and ruthless. And the spirit of ruthlessness and brutality will
> enter into the very fiber of our national life, infecting Congress,
> the courts, the policeman on the beat, the man in the street.[2]

Using dubious pretexts and outright lies concerning Iraq's alleged weapons of mass destruction, its hand-in-glove relations with al-Qaeda terrorists, that the people of Iraq would welcome our troops with flowers and open arms, that the Iraqi oil would pay for it all, and the ugly specter of a mushroom cloud just over the horizon, President Bush persuaded Congress to expand the war in Afghanistan to a war for regime change in Iraq. Bush dangled the prospect of a new nation—peaceful, united, stable, and secure, guiding the path for democratic government in the Mideast.

With "shock and awe," our military quickly toppled the government of Saddam Hussein. President Bush posed on a battleship in semi-military gear before a large placard trumpeting "Mission Accomplished."

But the mission, built on a shifting sand of falsehoods, was not accomplished. Iraq split into a Kurdish north, bordering Turkey; a Sunni west, bordering Syria; and a Shiite east, bordering Iran. The religious factions are at war, and Baghdad witnesses ever-growing atrocities. The body bags bring our troops home in increasing number. Our armed forces are strained to the limit. The country is war weary. Bush's ratings are at a phenomenal low; and the country voted the Democrats to power in Congress to end the war.

Bush's reaction was to enlarge the war, to give superior firepower one more chance. Bush wanted a "surge" of twenty-five thousand more troops to clamp down on the mounting internecine civil war in Baghdad. On February 8, he asked Congress for another $100 billion to carry the war through September.

The more things change, the more they stay the same. In 1846, the Mexican War was going badly with mounting casualties. President Polk accused Congress of placing the troops in jeopardy by dragging its feet on funding. Congress responded with a resolution condemning the Mexican war as "unconstitutionally begun" (President Polk had lied to Congress that Mexican troops had spilled American blood on American soil).[3]

As in the 1846 our current legislators have begun to react. Congressman John Murtha, who holds the purse strings in the House, threatened to block troop replacements unless they are well-trained, well-armed, and well-rested (none are).

Senator Hillary Clinton proposed that Congress repeal the

DANIEL H. POLLITT is Kenan Professor of Law, Emeritus at the University of North Carolina at Chapel Hill. A graduate of Wesleyan University and Cornell Law, he served in World War II as a Marine Infantry Officer (twice wounded). He has served on the Southern Regional Council, on the board of the American Association of University Professors, and on the national boards of the ACLU and Southerners for Economic Justice. He has litigated and published widely in the areas of labor law, civil liberties, and civil rights.

authority it gave the president in 2002 to invade Iraq, to take effect on October 11, the fifth anniversary of the original vote. Robert Byrd, the senior senator, joined in this proposal; he had led a failed effort in 2000 to put a one-year limit on the president's war authority.[4]

John Edwards, another presidential aspirant, agreed with the Clinton-Byrd proposal, but thought it to be inadequate. He recalled the 1971 congressional resolution that repealed the earlier Tonkin Gulf resolution (authorizing use of force in Vietnam) and noted that the war in southeast Asia went on for another three years. Edwards suggested Congress simply use its power of the purse to cut off all war money.

The Democratic Congress gave the requested money, but with "benchmarks" requiring progress: toward ending the internecine blood-letting; cleansing the death squads from the organized militia; resolving the dispute over sharing the oil wealth; and so on. If progress was not made on these issues, our troops would be withdrawn.

President Bush vetoed the spending bill with a pen given him by the father of a fallen Marine. He warned that an early exit from Iraq was a "prescription for chaos and confusion," would turn that country into a "cauldron of chaos," and "impose impossible conditions on our Commanders."[5]

Underneath it all, the White House objects to congressional "micromanagement" of troop levels and deployment as undermining the authority of the president as commander-in-chief.

The president and Congress are at loggerheads as to who can leash the dogs of war.

Bush asked a sympathetic audience who should make such decisions, "the Congress or the Commander." His rhetorical answer: "As you know, my position is clear. *I'm the Commander guy.*"[6] (emphasis added)

President Bush got the clean bill he wanted. But he is wrong, wrong with his claim to be the *Commander guy*. That authority lies in Congress, as evidenced by the language of the Constitution, the words of our Founding Fathers, and a history stretching back to our beginning.

A. The Constitution

The Constitution clearly gives primacy to Congress. It states broadly that "The Congress" shall have the power to "provide for the common Defense." Then in no uncertain terms it lodges in Congress the power to "declare War"; to "raise and support Armies"; to "provide and maintain a Navy"; to "make Rules for the Government and Regulations of the land and naval Forces"; to "provide for calling forth the Militia"; and to appropriate money to that use for a term no longer than two years.

If there could be any doubt that the Constitution lodges the power of the sword in Congress, it is easily dispelled by a glance at what the Founding Fathers had to say.

B. The Founding Fathers

At state conventions called to ratify or reject the proposed Constitution, the Founding Fathers emphasized again and again that the power of the sword is lodged in Congress.

Alexander Hamilton in New York noted that "the Power of the President as Commander in Chief is much inferior to the Power of the King" whose authority "extends to the declaring of war and raising and regulating of fleets and armies"—all of which by the Constitution would appertain to the legislature.[7]

James Wilson in Pennsylvania explained: the Constitution "will not hurry us into wars, it is calculated to guard against it," it will "not be in the power of a single man to involve us in such a distress; the important power of declaring war is vested in the legislature at large."[8]

Pierce Butler in South Carolina said "it was improbable that a single member of the Convention would have signed his name to the Constitution if he had supposed that the instrument might be construed as authorizing the President to initiate a war."[9]

Thomas Jefferson, serving as ambassador to France, wrote his friend James Madison praising the Founders' "effectual check to the Dog of war by transferring the power of letting him loose from the Executive to the Legislative body, from those who are to spend to those who are to pay."[10]

James Madison replied: the Constitution supposes "what the History of all Governments demonstrate, that the Executive is the branch of power most interested in War, and most prone to it." The Constitution accordingly, "with studied care, vested the question of war in the Legislative."[11]

Years later Abraham Lincoln, as a first-term member of Congress, voted against President Polk's unauthorized war in Mexico, and explained to his law partner that the Constitution gives the "war-making power to Congress" because "Kings had always been involving and impoverishing their people in wars." The "Constitutional Convention," continued Lincoln, considered this "the most oppressive of all kingly oppressions," and resolved to so frame the Constitution that "no one man should hold power to bring this oppression upon us."[12]

C. Executive Action: Early and Late

Our early presidents complied with the Constitution, its letter and spirit. In 1798, French ships of war "hovered on the coast of the United States" committing "depredations on the vessels belonging to our citizens." President John Adams delayed action until he obtained congressional authority and approval to order U.S. ships to the ready.[13]

Similarly, when North African Barbary pirates attacked our merchant vessels in 1801, President Thomas Jefferson refused to permit our ships of war to take offensive measures "without the sanction of Congress."[14] But there were aberrations from this policy. President Polk ordered American troops into disputed territory and ignited a war with Mexico. When the bands first began to play, Congress gave instant approval. But as casualties mounted, Congress resolved that the war "had been unnecessarily and unconstitutionally begun by the President,"[15] our first congressional authorization followed by repeal and censure.

President McKinley dispatched five thousand American troops to China as part of an international expeditionary force to quell the Boxer Rebellion.[16] In 1950 President Truman sent eighty-three thousand troops to Korea as part of a United Nations international expedition, all without congressional authority. This set a pattern.

In 1958, President Eisenhower sent fourteen thousand troops to Lebanon;[17] in 1960, President Kennedy mounted the Bay of Pigs invasion of Cuba, and sent fifteen thousand "military advisors" to Vietnam. President Johnson requested and received a Gulf of Tonkin Resolution from Congress authorizing his use of force in Vietnam, but did not think it necessary. President Nixon denied a need for congressional resolutions to continue the conflict.

D. The War Powers Resolution

Again, as in the 1846 Mexican War, when casualties in Vietnam mounted to over fifty thousand, America had had enough. Congress sought to regain its power of the sword with the 1973 War Powers Act.[18] It authorizes the president, as commander-in-chief, to commit the armed forces into hostile situations in three situations: (1) a declaration of war, (2) specific statutory authority, and (3) a national emergency created by attack upon the United States, its territories or possessions, or its armed forces.

In every possible instance, the president must "*consult*" with Congress before taking action; and *report* to Congress within forty-eight hours when armed forces are introduced into situations where imminent involvement in hostilities is clearly indicated. Thereafter, the president must withdraw all troops *within sixty days* unless Congress (1) declares war, (2) specifically authorizes the use of armed forces, or (3) extends the sixty-day period.

Presidents have honored the War Powers Resolution mainly in the breach. President Carter sent the ill-fated military expedition to rescue U.S. Embassy hostages in Iran without compliance with the law, on advice by White House counsel that "rescue operations" were not covered.[19]

President Ford in 1975 ordered immediate retaliation and invasion of Cambodia to free the crew of the freighter *Mayaquez*. Eighteen Marines and twenty-three airmen lost their lives, all unnecessarily, as the crew had been released prior to the incursion.[20]

President Reagan was the greatest scofflaw. He sent troops into El Salvador in 1981, then to Nicaragua, Grenada, and the Persian Gulf. In each situation, members of Congress turned to the courts for redress, arguing that the unilateral presidential action deprived them of their rights under the War Powers Act to "participate in the decision to declare war." In each situation the lower courts refused to take jurisdiction, generally on the theory that the case raised "political" issues best decided by the political process.[21] This is not always the case. The Supreme Court has acted on these issues.

E. The *Flying Fish* and the Steel Seizure Case

In cases both early and late, the Supreme Court has held that it is the Congress that controls the war powers.

During the hostilities between the United States and France at the turn of the eighteenth century, Congress passed a series of annual acts to suspend commercial intercourse between the two countries. The Non-Intercourse Act of 1799 authorized the seizure of any American-owned ship "bound or sailing *to any port* within the territory of the French Republic" (emphasis added). The president was authorized to enforce this act, and he sent instructions to captains of American armed vessels "to be vigilant that vessels or cargoes really American, but covered by Danish or other foreign papers, and bound to, *or from* French ports, do not escape you." Captain Little, commander of the frigate *Boston*, captured the *Flying Fish*, a Danish vessel based at St. Thomas (a Danish possession). It had carried a cargo of provisions to Jeremie (a French possession), and was on its way home with a load of coffee. As the *Boston* drew nigh, the crew of the *Flying Fish* threw the ship's log and other papers overboard. The master was American, and Captain Little had reason to believe the *Flying Fish* was American-owned. He seized the ship. Chief Justice John Marshall ruled in 1804 that the *Flying Fish* must be returned to its owners, and Captain Little must pay damages resulting from the seizure. Captain Little had obeyed the president's instructions to seize vessels bound *to* or *from* French Ports; but Congress had only authorized seizure of ships *bound to* French ports. The presidential instructions could not transgress the limitations imposed by Congress.[22]

The issue again reached the Supreme Court during the Korean War in the *Steel Seizure* case, when the United Steel Workers of America threatened to strike when the steel companies balked at the proposal for a "union shop" (agreement requiring all those represented by the union to pay union dues). Truman could not let a strike jeopardize the flow of significant munitions. He seized the steel mills, and authorized the "union shop" agreement. The steel companies challenged the president's authority and won. Congress had rejected "seizure" as a means of dealing with "national security" labor disputes, and the president could not shortcut the method authorized by Congress (sixty-day injunction against the strike with continuing negotiations).[23]

Most recently, the court held that the president must follow congressional guidelines regarding tribunals for the trial of detainees in Guantanamo.[24] The War Powers Act does not give the president a blank check, wrote Justice O'Connor.

F. Examples of Congressional Authority

History confirms that Congress controls the war powers. There are other examples of congressional control that did not reach the Supreme Court. In 1974 during the Vietnam War, Congress gave the president six months to reduce military personnel to four thousand troops.[25]

In 1983, Congress required the president to get its approval for any substantial increase in the troop level in Lebanon.[26]

In 1983, Congress used its *power of the purse* and passed the Boland Amendment putting a cap on the amount of money available to the CIA or the Defense Department "for the purpose of supporting military operations in Nicaragua by any nation, group, organization, movement, or individual."[27] Cut off from appropriated funds, the White House sold arms to Iran and used the proceeds to support the "contras" fighting the government in Nicaragua. This led to a Senate investigation, indictments of high government officials (mostly for perjury), and presidential pardons.

In 1999, the House voted to bar President Clinton from sending ground troops to Yugoslavia without congressional approval, and defeated a proposal supporting President Clinton's policy of air strikes.[28]

In short, Bush is not the "*Commander guy.*" Congress has the authority to unsheathe the sword, or to return it to its scabbard.

Congress can, and should, end the carnage in Iraq, and soon. Sixty-four percent of Americans want our troops out of Iraq. Sixty-five percent of Iraqi people want the occupation to end, and half of them see nothing wrong in killing Americans. A majority of Iraq parliamentarians signed on to a bill asking us to leave.

What's more, despite the bluster from the White House, seventy-two percent of our troops in Iraq say the war should be ended in one year, and twenty-nine percent of that number say "immediately." Only twenty-three percent backed the president's position that they should stay as long as necessary.[29]

We should leave. There are many reasons.

Listen to Wayne Muller tell of his son's homecoming with his Marine unit after eight months' hard duty in Ramadi:

> The men in the unit were met with cheers, tears and hugs from family and friends. Banners were everywhere. A huge black banner stood out. Under the caption "Heroes Live Forever" were the names of twelve who were not coming home, who had been killed in Iraq.
>
> I knew the harsh realities of war but this banner hit home. Then I noticed many young men in civilian clothes. They had shorts on, smiles on, and prosthetic legs. There were several scattered about the crowd. I know, we all knew, but no one wanted to say anything.
>
> All of a sudden I felt a tap on my shoulder. My son Danny had found me. To say I cried was an understatement. I had to let him go to his other family members and his wife. When he left me, my eyes went back on the big black banner . . .
>
> I noticed my son Danny and the Marines of Charlie Company (they lost four from their company) approach a family. A father whose son never made it home handed each a personalized ball cap. I watched my son hug him.
>
> The day was coming to an end. As I walked to my truck I turned around to look at the big black banner just one more time. It would soon be taken down . . .
>
> At least ten people at work asked me about the homecoming. Every darn one of them said the same thing, "You don't look happy."

I'm not. Someone please tell me why our young men and women are dying. I want this war to end. Thank you for praying for my son while he was in harm's way. Don't forget to keep all the others in your prayers.[30]

To answer Wayne Muller, there is no good reason why our young men and women are dying. We must end the war.

But we should not turn our backs on the chaos we created. In the vernacular, "we broke it, we own it." It is our moral obligation to fix it, as best we can.

We must divert the money we now spend on war into efforts to make Iraq whole once again. This is not only the moral thing to do, it is by far the most practical path for our own security. We can kill Osama bin Laden (if we can find him) and all his cohorts, but authorities on the Mideast say this is like slapping at mosquitoes and ignoring the swamp.[31]

Bitterness and anger thrive on the pain of the maimed, the orphaned, the widowed. Those bombed out of their homes do not look favorably on the bombers.

Gunpoint liberation is not the answer, at least on its own. We have tried economic reconstruction, countless millions spent on no-bid contracts to Halliburton, Blackwater, and the others, which failed. Because we are the enemy, the occupiers.

We should assemble neighboring nations in a regional Marshall Plan, giving generous financial support but leaving "hands on" functions to others.

While we're at it, we should enlarge existing attacks on malaria, AIDS, TB and other medical scourges.[32] We should be "good Americans." This would protect us from terrorists' attacks far more than would our killing Osama bin Laden.

II. GUANTANAMO: OUR OWN DEVIL'S ISLAND

The U.S. Naval Base at Guantanamo Bay is forty-five square miles of land and water along the southeast coast of Cuba. We seized it from the Spanish during the Spanish-American War for a naval "coaling station." With Cuban independence, we entered into a lease agreement in 1903, providing that we exercise "complete jurisdiction and control . . . and may continue to exercise such control permanently."

Guantanamo basks under a relentless Caribbean sun in a parched scrub-land pockmarked by cactus trees and populated primarily by iguanas and land crabs. We lease it for four thousand dollars a year although Fidel Castro refuses to cash the rent checks.

No longer necessary for refueling, we were about to give it up when lawyers in the White House and Justice Department decided it was a perfect place to store War on Terror prisoners. Guantanamo is in Cuba, they rationalized, under the sovereignty of Castro, hence the U.S. courts lack jurisdiction should the prisoners ever seek legal redress.[33]

Detention pens were prepared: eight-by-ten-foot wire mesh cages with tin roofs, concrete slabs, and a pad to sleep on.

The first twenty prisoners arrived on January 20, 2002, and by September there were almost six hundred, from forty-three countries. Construction continues, toward the planned two thousand inmates.[34]

When complaints were made about the harsh primitive conditions, the response from Vice President Dick Cheney was that it's "better than they deserve." He called the prisoners "the worst of a very bad lot." Defense Secretary Donald Rumsfeld agreed they were "among the most dangerous, best-trained, vicious killers on the face of the earth."[35]

But are they? Certainly not all, maybe not any. The CIA

segregates the few "high value" captives from the rest in secret prisons around the world, and a few within a special "holding and interrogation" center at Guantanamo.[36]

Who are the others, those who are not "high valued"? We have some scant knowledge.

A. Who They Are

The first three released from Guantanamo were Afghan men turned over to Afghan officials. They complained of confinement for days at a time in sweltering cells, denied contact with the outside for eleven months. The endless isolation had worn them out.

One, a shriveled old man, partially deaf, was unable to answer simple questions. His faded mind kept failing him.

The second old man said he was ninety years old, walked with a cane, said "enough questions" and stared impassively out the window.

The third was younger, in his fifties. He fought with the Taliban but said he had no choice—Taliban soldiers conscripted him. He was captured by an Afghan warlord, who told the Americans he had ten "senior Taliban officials."

"They came and took ten strong-looking people. Only one was a Talib." The released former prisoner said he was a victim of lies and circumstances, and complained of confinement in the small cells with only two fifteeen-minute breaks a week for exercise. The temperature in his cell was stifling.[37]

At the other end of the age scale were three young boys, one thirteen, the others around fifteen. The youngest was sold by a warlord to the Americans, sent to Bagram Prison near Kabul, interrogated daily for several months, and sent to Guantanamo for eleven more months. One of the boys said he was kicked by American soldiers at Bagram, once so badly in the stomach that it still pained when he got to Cuba several months later. They were released, when the Red Cross expressed concern about holding juveniles at Guantanamo. The oldest boy said he was told "you were wrongly detained."

They were kept apart from the adult prisoners, taught to read and write their native language, Pashto, and once went on a picnic with their guards.[38]

Then there are the twelve Kuwaitis: teachers, engineers, students, according to leave-of-absence documents signed by their employers. They spent their vacation as charity workers assisting refugees of Afghanistan's harsh regime when they were caught up in the chaos of the war. Attempting to flee across the Pakistani border, they fell into the hands of warlords who "sold" them to U.S. troops. Their parents filed suit on their behalf seeking their release, or in the alternative, a trial where they can prove their innocence.[39]

They have won the support of top Kuwaiti officials, who retained the old-line law firm of Shearing and Sterling to represent them. Thomas Wilner of the firm took their case all the way to the Supreme Court. The Kuwaiti minister of state for foreign affairs compared the twelve to American Peace Corps Volunteers, and asked for visitation rights and a trial. He told the American authorities: "We think people are innocent until proven guilty."[40]

We did not release the Kuwaitis, but after diplomatic negotiations, we released citizens of Great Britain, Germany, France, Australia, and others: eighty-three in 2003; one hundred fourteen in 2004; fifty-four in 2005.[41]

Apparently, the prisoners are not the "worst of a bad lot," at least not most of them.

In December of 2006, we sent eighteen prisoners home: seven Afghan prisoners, six to Yemen, three to Kazakhstan, one each to Libya and Bangladesh. Sixteen Saudi Arabians had been sent home earlier, and eighty-five others of various nationalities were designated for release.[42]

B. Torture

Word of torture spread out with the release of prisoners. Three British Muslims reported "they suffered beatings, saw guards throw Qurans into the toilet, were forced to watch videotapes of prisoners who had allegedly been ordered to sodomize each other, and were chained to a hook in the floor while strobe lights flashed and heavy metal music blared."[43]

They had been arrested while traveling to Pakistan for the marriage of one of the three. Sold to the Americans, they suffered starvation, beatings, abusive interrogations, and months of solitary confinement.

These stories, and the many others like them, are substantiated by neutral sources: the Red Cross, the FBI, former soldiers stationed at Guantanamo, even videos.

The Red Cross found physical and psychological abuse: "Humiliating acts, solitary confinement, temperature extremes, use of forced positions."

A frequent complaint of prisoners was that some of the female interrogators baited their subjects with sexual overtures. General Miller, in command of intelligence operations there until he moved on to Abu Ghraib outside Baghdad, said that female interrogators had proved to be among the most effective.[44]

The Supreme Court pierced the numbing darkness of Guantanamo on June 28, 2004, with a ray of hope. It held that the government could detain "enemy combatants" until hostilities end, and defined "enemy combatants" as "members of a force hostile to the United States who engage in an armed conflict against the United States." On the bright side, it held that detainees had a right to challenge their unfavorable status: to receive notice of the factual basis for their classification and a fair opportunity to rebut the government's factual assertions, all before a neutral decision-maker, and with the aid of counsel. It is possible, wrote Justice O'Connor for the Court, that constitutionally adequate hearings could be held "by an appropriately authorized and properly constituted military tribunal that observed due process."[45]

C. Combatant Status Review Tribunals

The government grudgingly complied, but only in very small part. Within a month the process had begun. Gordon E. England, the Secretary of the Navy in charge of the project, established Combatant Status Review Tribunals, three panels of three officers each, and hoped to move seventy-two detainees a week through the procedures. All the detainees were notified and about 95 percent asked to participate.[46]

Hope quickly turned to despair. A review of an early hearing tells the story:

> Each day, several shackled detainees are marched by their military guards into a double-wide trailer behind the prison camp's fences and razor wire to argue before three anonymous military officers that they not belong here. One, a twenty-seven-year-old Yemeni, spent more than an hour on Saturday trying to convince the panel that he was not a member of al-Qaeda, had never fought against the United States, and should never have been detained at Guantanamo.
>
> The Yemeni, a scraggly-bearded man bound hand and foot, sat in a low chair, his shackles connected to a bolt in the floor. Inside the small harshly lighted room, he alternated between pleading his case and angrily criticizing the process as unfair. Although he spoke Arabic that had to be translated by a woman who sat beside him, there was no mistaking his contempt for the panel members who sat on a raised platform about ten feet away and whose questions he ridiculed frequently.
>
> An officer not on the panel acted as sort of a prosecutor in assembling the charges, while yet another acted as the detainee's personal representative to explain the proceedings but not to

serve as a defense lawyer. All the officers had their nametags covered by tape.

Like detainees at all the hearings, the Yemeni was given an unclassified summary of the charges, but the evidence to support the most serious accusations is classified and was considered in a closed session after he was taken back to his cell."

This process is in response to but is a far cry from the type of hearing required by the Supreme Court in the *Hamdi* decision.

As of November 8, 2004, final judgments have been passed on one hundred and four detainees: one detainee was released; the rest were found to be unlawful combatants and properly in prisons.[47]

The matter does not end should a Combatant Status Review Panel rule in favor of a detainee. There are "do-overs," as critics call them. If Pentagon officials disagree with the results of a hearing, they order a second one, or even a third, until they approve of the finding.[48]

Why go through this charade of a mock due process? Senior military officials suggest an informal expectation: that after the detainees are found to be enemy combatants by the Combatant Status Review Tribunals (thus justifying their initial captivity), they will go before an Annual Administrative Review Board to determine if they remain a threat. If not, they are released (a solution to the diplomatic demands of foreign countries for the release of their nationals, plus the desire to cut down on the number of detainees).[49]

The Administrative Review Boards act like parole boards for those determined to be unlawful combatants after earlier rounds by the Combatant Status Review Tribunals. The proceedings are similar in that the serious evidence used to determine a detainee's fate is classified and the detainees are not told of it. *New York*

Times reporter Neil Lewis told of a hearing of a Sudanese prisoner whose panel heard the prisoner out, then reconvened after the prisoner was led back to his cell to hear the classified evidence supporting the charges against him.[50]

The *New York Times* editorialized that "the tribunals are, in fact, kangaroo courts that give the inmates no chance to defend themselves, allow evidence that was obtained through torture, and can be repeated until one produces the answer the Pentagon wants."[51]

Of the first sixty-four detainees scheduled for hearings, thirty-nine have declined to attend. They have no faith in American-style justice.

D. Mental Health, Hunger Strikes and Suicides

The Pentagon admits regularly using physical and psychological abuse on the detainees to obtain information: sleep deprivation, "stress positions" for hours on end, stripping them naked, etc. This drives the detainees mad (literally) and to retaliate as best they can with hunger strikes, and even suicide.

As the poet W. B. Yeats once wrote:

> He has chosen death:
> Refusing to eat or drink, that he may bring
> Disgrace upon me; for there is a custom,
> An old and foolish custom, that if a man
> Be wronged, or think that he is wronged, and starve
> Upon another's threshold until he die,
> The Common People, for all time to come,
> Will raise a heavy cry against that threshold,
> Even though it be the King's.

Abused, tormented, humiliated, told over and over there was no end to the travail, it is small wonder that many of the traumatized detainees went around the bend. Simply put, we drove them crazy. Within half a year, Captain Albert Shimkus, who runs the hospital, said fifty-seven prisoners were treated for mental illness. He added that with the uncertainty over their fate, "mental health problems could be expected to increase."[52] And they did. By the following year "about one in five detainees were being medicated for clinical depression."[53] And a $1.7 million psychiatric wing is under way.[54] A Red Cross spokesman said "the uncertainty the detainees faced was a major factor in the high incidence of clinical depression."[55]

For the others, the only protest available is, as Yeats wrote, "Refusing to eat or drink that he may bring Disgrace upon me." And there were hunger strikes a plenty.

The first began shortly after the camp opened, in March 2002. It began when a guard knocked a turban from the head of a praying prisoner. The Marine commander ordered that prisoners be allowed to wear turbans, and all but a handful ended the strike. The handful continued to refuse meals to protest their *detention*. They were hospitalized and force-fed a thick fluid, rich in nutrients—like a milk shake.[56]

As years went by with no relief in sight, the number of strikes and strikers increased. In June 2005, there was a "widespread" strike over the amount and quality of the drinking water. In July, more than one hundred eighty Afghans refused to eat, protesting mistreatment.[57] In September, two hundred inmates were fasting, to demand trials, better food, bottled drinking water, more reading materials, and greater religious freedoms. Deaths were expected in the fifth such protest.[58] In May 2006, a hunger strike ballooned from three to seventy-five, revealing a growing defiance. Defense layers said it reveals increasing frustration with being held for four and a half years with no end in sight.[59]

The military at Guantanamo turned to aggressive methods to deter the hunger strikes. General Craddock decided to make life more miserable for the hunger strikers, and began strapping them into what are described as "restraint chairs." The measure was seen as successful.[60] Military guards bound the men to the chairs by their ankles, waists, wrists, shoulders, and heads, and military nurses force flexible plastic tubes through their nostrils, down their throats and into their stomachs. "In goes the food."[61]

Lawyers for the prisoners protested that the doctors sometimes used excessively thick tubes (causing internal bleeding) and deliberately overfed the prisoners (causing them to defecate in their clothing). They took the case to court.[62] U.S. District Judge Gladys Kessler in Washington ordered the government to inform defense counsel within twenty-four hours of any force-feeding of a client and to provide medical records beginning a week before force-feeding began, and weekly updates.[63]

At an earlier 1975 conference in Tokyo, the World Medical Association adopted a resolution to place a ban on forced feeding. This was endorsed by the American Medical Association in 2000. In the same year, a U.S. District Court judge held that a federal prisoner could not be force fed. "I just don't think the government has put forward any compelling justification that would allow me to override a person's last, ultimate means of protesting government."[64]

This leads to suicide, another form of protest. It was announced in February of 2003 that "three more men have attempted suicide at Guantanamo . . . lifting the total to nineteen."[65] In 2005, twenty-three tried to hang or strangle themselves in a mass protest. The coordinated actions were among three hundred fifty "self harm" incidents that year. A rash of suicide attempts occurred after General Geoffrey Miller took command with instructions to get more information from the detainees.

In May of 2006, twenty-three detainees attempted suicide, and in June, three detainees hanged themselves—two Saudis and a Yemeni. The father of one of the Saudis said his son was seventeen when apprehended in Afghanistan, where he worked with Islamic charities. He also commented that hundreds of people attended a wake for his son.[66]

The Saudis were ready, willing, and able to suspect the worst from America. There was marked skepticism that the prisoners committed suicide. Many denounced the suicide claim as a fabrication, and the Kingdom's semi-official human rights organization called for an independent investigation.[67]

E. Close Gitmo Down

America's image in the Arab world is colored by an orange prison jumpsuit. The stench spreads worldwide. Gitmo must be closed. This is the near uniform view of world leaders and concerned institutions.

The Red Cross wants it closed.[68] The United Nations Human Rights Commission wants it closed.[69] The United Nations Commission Against Torture wants it closed.[70] The European Union Parliament and former United Nations Secretary General Kofi Annan want it closed.[71] The leaders of Britain, Germany, Sweden, Denmark, and other European countries want it closed.[72]

Here at home Senators John McCain, Lindsey Graham, and Maria Cantwell called on then-Defense Secretary Donald Rumsfeld to bring the prisoners to trial or send them home.[73]

More pointedly, in his first weeks as defense secretary, Robert Gates argued that Guantanamo has become so tainted abroad that it should be shut down as quickly as possible. Secretary of State Condoleezza Rice joined him in this effort. The State Department has long been concerned about the adverse foreign-policy impact of housing prisoners at Guantanamo.

Attorney General Alberto Gonzales and Vice President Dick Cheney expressed strong objections to any closing and President Bush went along with them.[74]

Since then, Senator Dianne Feinstein has introduced a bill to shut down Guantanamo and move the inmates to more conventional detention facilities for speedy trials in the time-tested procedures of the normal American legal system. The *New York Times* supports her effort to remove "an ugly stain on this country's long tradition of respect for the rule of law and an endless propaganda bonanza for America's enemies."[75]

III. EXTRAORDINARY RENDITION

In the early 1970s, the Chilean dictator Pinochet kidnapped those thought to be dangerous to his regime, and they were never heard from again. They were known as "the disappeared."

We have our own kidnapping practice—known as "extraordinary rendition." We kidnap those thought to be dangerous and whisk them away to friendly nations for questioning under torture.

How large is the program? We don't know for sure. The White House won't tell. The law requires the White House to notify the House and Senate Intelligence Committee of all intelligence-gathering activities. But the White House takes the position that the secret detention program is too sensitive to discuss with anyone but the top Republican and Democrat on each panel, who cannot share this information with anyone.[76]

A senior career officer at the CIA was fired the day after she talked about the program after it was discussed in a Pulitzer Prize winning article in the *Washington Post*. Dismissal of an agency employee over a leak is rare, perhaps unprecedented.[77]

Some in Congress estimate some three dozen senior Qaeda leaders are detained in secret sites around the world.[78] The Human Rights Watch documented sixty-three cases where detainees were sent to Egypt alone, but estimated the total number could be as high as two hundred people. Terror suspects are also held in Jordan, Morocco, Saudi Arabia, Yemen, Syria, and in Europe.[79] The European Parliament reports that the CIA had flown one thousand undeclared flights over Europe.[80] The *Washington Post* reported that one hundred or more terrorist suspects "disappeared" into the netherworld of secret prisons.[81]

How does it work?

There were a few cases covered fairly well in the press. They give us a look at what happens.

1) Maher Arar, a thirty-five-year-old Syrian-born Canadian engineer, coming home from a vacation, was apprehended at Kennedy Airport as he changed planes for Canada, taken to a dank cell in Brooklyn for eleven days, then flown to Syria for questioning under torture.[82] He was held for a year, beaten repeatedly with a metal cable, and released after Syrian officials concluded he had no connection to terrorism.[83]

His case attracted considerable attention in Canada where the practice of rendition has raised the outcry of "outsourcing torture." A commission was appointed to investigate. It reported that the Royal Canadian Mounted Police (RCMP) first took note of Arar when he joined a man named Almalki for dinner, a man under surveillance. From this, the RCMP asked Canadian customs to put Arar and his wife on a "terrorist lookout" list. From there, the RCMP asked that the United States Border Patrol be informed that Arar and his wife were "Islamic extremists suspected of being linked to the al-Qaeda movement."

This was not true, but when Arar arrived at Kennedy Airport, the FBI was there to detain and question him for eleven days before putting him on a chartered jet to Syria. There he was held for a year, beaten with a shredded electrical cable until he was disoriented. A United States official said he was sent to Syria to find out more about him and the threat he might pose.[84]

The Canadian Prime Minister apologized and offered $8.9 million in compensation.[85] The United States did not apologize and Arar filed suit for turning him over to the Syrians and the prior torture for eleven days at the Metropolitan Detention Center in Brooklyn.

The government argued first that foreign citizens who change planes at U.S. airports can legally be seized, detained without charges, deprived access to a lawyer or the courts, and even be denied basic necessities like food. If the government decides that a passenger is an "inadmissible alien," he remains legally outside the United States—and outside the reach of the Constitution—even if he is being held in a Brooklyn jail. Further, argued the government, under the separation of powers doctrine, the judiciary "should not stick their noses" in foreign affairs and national security questions. The court dismissed Arar's case on the theory it might disclose "state secrets." The case is on appeal.[86]

2) Khaled El-Masri, a German citizen of Lebanese descent, was captured on New Year's Eve, 2003, while vacationing in Macedonia. He was held for twenty-three days, kicked, hit, photographed nude, and injected with drugs, before the Macedonian authorities turned him over to seven or eight men in masks who stripped him naked, put him in a diaper and jumpsuit, drugged him and chained him spread-eagle on the floor of a Boeing 737. He was flown to Afghanistan on January 24 and held in the notorious "Salt Pit" prison. The torture continued. Mr. El-Masri joined a hunger strike, and was force fed.

After five months, he was released on direct orders of Condoleezza Rice, then the National Security Advisor. This was the first link connecting the White House directly to the program.[87]

It seems el-Masri was confused with a man with a similar name. There was uproar in Germany, a parliamentary inquiry was authorized,[88] and a German court ordered the arrest of three "ghost pilots," and ten members of the CIA rendition team on charges of kidnapping. The so-called "ghost pilots" have been identified as employees of Aero Contractors, Ltd., based in Smithfield, North Carolina. The company has flown scores of sensitive missions for the CIA.[89]

Mr. el-Masri, denied an apology, sued CIA director George Tenet and Aero Contractors, Ltd. Judge T. S. Ellis III dismissed the suit on the basis of "state secrets":

> Any admission or denial of these allegations would reveal the means and methods employed pursuant to this clandestine program and such a revelation would present a grave risk of injury to national security."

The ACLU lawyer who filed the suit argued that there was nothing secret about the program, "the whole world knows."[90] The ACLU, on behalf of three men kidnapped and flown to Morocco (two of them) and Egypt (the other) for interrogation and torture, sued a subsidiary of Boeing for providing flight plans and other services.[91]

3) Hasan Osama Nasr, also known as Abu Omar, is an imam who was on his way to his Milan, Italy, mosque for noon prayer when he was stopped by a man with a badge. Two men came from behind, forced him into a van, and drove off. It took three minutes. The CIA kidnappers made few efforts to conceal their crime. They talked frequently on cell phones that were not secure as they took Omar to the Italian-American airbase, and left behind surveillance pictures of Abu Omar himself.[92] He was flown to Ramstein Air Base in Germany, and then to Egypt. He was held for four years without charge.[93]

Released by a Cairo appeals court, Nasr said he was subjected to the worst kind of torture. The forty-four-year-old Muslim preacher showed dark circular scars on his wrists and ankles from electrical shocks. He said he has scars on other parts of his body but was embarrassed to show them.[94]

An Italian judge indicted twenty-six CIA officials for kidnapping. They have all left the country and will be tried *in absentia*. The United States will not extradite them back to Italy. The former chief of the Italian military intelligence was indicted. The possible complicity of former Prime Minister Silvio Berlusconi is one of the issues in the case.[95]

There is effort to derail the suit. But the judge answers: "It is a question of principle. Today, it's Abu Omar. Tomorrow it could be my daughter. There are fundamental human rights, and we have to respect them."[96]

This reflects the global outcry over our methods.

Meanwhile, at home, the Senate Intelligence Committee questions the continuing value of the rendition program, because of the international condemnation. Chairman John Rockefeller was concerned that the program was hurting the battle against terrorism by "alienating moderate Muslim and Arab communities around the world."

Senators Whitehouse (Rhode Island) and Feinstein (California) moved to cut off funds for the program except when the president determines "that an individual has information about a specific and immediate threat." It failed by one vote when Senator Bill Nelson of Florida joined the Republicans.[97]

Go Whitehouse and Feinstein. But bear in mind that the disappeared in Chile only saw justice when Pinochet finally was brought to heel by criminal charges in Spain.

IV. The Right to Travel

The *right to travel* is part of our liberty with roots going back to the Magna Carta. "Freedom of movement" wrote Justice Douglas "is basic to our scheme of values."[98] Here again the Bush administration turns its back on our tradition of freedom with a "No Fly List."

The FBI and other intelligence agencies collect names of

terrorist suspects and deliver the list to the Transportation Security Administration, which in turn passes it on to the airlines. Airlines then check the passengers against the No Fly List and bar them from flight if they match. The system is ineffectual to detect real terrorists as the government withholds the names of suspects (the most dangerous?) because the information is classified.[99] And what would prevent an effective terrorist from using an alias as he boards the plane?

Who is caught in this wide, but loose, net?

A number of peace activists have missed flights because of the list, as have members of the military on their way to risk their lives on our behalf. Staff Sgt. Daniel Brown was on a terror watch list and delayed as he went to fight in Iraq, and when he came back. The other Marines in his unit waited at the destination because "We don't leave anybody behind."[100]

Senator Ted Kennedy was blocked from boarding airplanes on five occasions in March 2004. Airline supervisors eventually overruled the ticket agents. Kennedy disclosed this at a Senate hearing, and Homeland Security Secretary Tom Ridge called to apologize. But days later, the senator was stopped again.[101]

Ingrid Sanden's one-year-old daughter was stopped in Phoenix,[102] as was nine-year-old James Martin at the North Carolina Raleigh-Durham airport. His mother thought it a good idea to double-check the people who get on board, but wondered if "they are going to let someone who's a real danger slip through while they're minding the kids?"[103]

Passengers can clear their names by filling out a "passenger identification verification" form. It may or may not work, but Congressman John Lewis (a formidable hero of the civil rights movement) who was stopped at least thirty-five times, says that carrying around a right-to-travel document feels suspiciously like the old apartheid South African system of passes for blacks to travel.[104]

Department of Justice inspector general Glenn Fine recently reported that the government's principal terrorist watch list is rife with errors and fails to include significant information about known terrorists. In defense, Leonard Boyle, who directs the Terrorist Screening Center, said, "When you're now talking about eight hundred thousand records, there are going to be errors as a result of human mistakes and technological glitches."[105]

Conclusion

The shock of the 9-11 attack caused a miasma of almost hysterical fear over the White House, the Congress, many of the courts, and some of our best people. Fearful people do fearsome things, as this essay depicts. But after six years of shortcutting our Constitution, it is time for a return to fundamental principles.

Thomas Jefferson has shown the way. When the Alien and Sedition Act oppressions of 1798 came to an end, Jefferson, who bore the brunt, commented: "[Should] we wander from the essential principles of our government in moments of error or alarm, let us hasten to retrace our steps and regain the road which alone leads to peace, liberty, and safety."

We must replace the sword with the plowshare. We must end torture, the dark secret prisons, kidnapping, Guantanamo. In short, we must return to the rule of law embraced in our Constitution.

As President John Kennedy said, "I am certain that after the dust of centuries has passed over our cities, we too will be remembered not for victories or defeats in battle or in politics, but for our contribution to the human spirit." America needs to learn what the South has learned. Ours was a lawless and violent place where blacks could be jailed, interrogated, tortured and disappeared with virtual impunity, in the name of popular social values and generally in contravention of written law. As the victims and the disaffected gained sufficient power to make themselves heard, one reaction was greater repression. The other response was to bring the victims and the disaffected within the Constitution.

Which course has reflected greater credit on the United States of America? ❧

Education and Economic Justice

Poverty and Higher Education

Gene R. Nichol

Five years ago, in the landmark case of *Grutter v. University of Michigan*, Justice Sandra Day O'Connor wrote that law schools "represent the training ground for a large number of the nation's leaders . . . [and] the path to leadership must be visibly open" to all segments of society. In a powerful way, that statement broke new ground. It recognized that more is at stake in our affirmative action battles than the quality of the classroom experience, vital as that is. The graduates of the nation's strong universities enjoy a disproportionate access to opportunity and authority in the private and public sectors of our economy. Selective universities and professional schools constitute distinctive pipelines to our principal corridors of power. The processes designed to channel these remarkable resources, Justice O'Connor reminded, must be patently open to us all.

The Michigan case, of course, explored the accessibility of selective higher education when it comes to race. The justices concluded, thankfully, or beyond thankfully, that universities need not be agnostic about the effective integration of their halls. Given changes in personnel, we can hope it stays that way. But what if we were to cast Justice O'Connor's question more broadly? What if we asked about the diversity of selective student bodies on the basis of class or economic status?

It is now increasingly well understood, and broadcast, that

the great institutions of American higher education—as well as their vital professional schools—are seemingly constructed on a foundation of economic advantage. That slewed foundation, sadly, is bad and getting worse. We frequently behave in ways that widen, rather than narrow, the breach. And that breach cannot be squared—and this is my simple point in this brief essay—with the promise of America.

The facts.

The Educational Testing Study of four years ago, surveying the student cohorts at the 146 most selective American universities, found that about 3 percent of the students came from families in the bottom economic quartile; 9 percent from the bottom half; and a whopping 74 percent from the top quarter. Similarly, another study two years ago determined that if you seek a college degree by the age of twenty-four, and if you come from a family with an annual income of $90,000 or more, your chances are one in two of graduating.

On the other hand, if you hale from a family making $35,000 a year or less, your odds are one in seventeen. One in seventeen. At the more selective universities apparently about one student in twenty-five is a low-income, first-generation collegian. As if wisdom, intellect, drive, ambition, virtue, and worth, were somehow hereditary.

Last year's Education Trust study concludes that our "highest-achieving low-income students actually go directly on to college at rates about the same as our lowest-achieving students from wealthy families." We have, reportedly, "less mobility [in this country] than we did twenty years ago [and] less than in most other developed countries." As Larry Summers has written, "increasing disparity based on parental position has never been anyone's definition of the American dream."

And we're all, apparently, playing our parts. Diminished state support has led to higher tuition rates at public universities. Federal

Pell grants pay a much lower percentage of university tuition than three decades ago. State governments have increased non-need-based financial aid by far greater percentages than need-based aid.

Even the Spellings Commission—apparently launched with an agenda to bring some version of "No Child Left Behind" to higher education—even the Spellings report found that "persistent financial barriers" unduly limit access to our universities. A "troubling and persistent gap between the college attendance rates of low-income Americans and their more affluent peers" constrains meaningful opportunity. "Too many students are discouraged from attending college . . . or take on worrisome debt burdens" to do so. The playing field is badly askew.

And maybe most disheartening, and closest to home for a university president, the U.S. Department of Education has reported that the lion's share of the last decade's university institutional financial aid increases have gone to students in the top economic quartile. The Lumina Foundation Report of a few years ago came to the same conclusion about tuition discounting by private universities—now those in the top quarter get more, on average, than those at the bottom. Without fanfare or even perhaps transparency, traditional notions of financial aid have been turned on their heads.

As one commentator has put it: "While institutions are unlikely to admit to this, improving their standing in the annual *U.S. News & World Report* ranking of colleges and universities is a powerful incentive to shift their own internal grants toward merit aid. The higher the entering students' test scores . . . the higher the ranking in *U.S. News*." We are apparently willing to let the artificial standards of a popular news magazine outpace our actual commitment to equal opportunity and public obligation.

GENE R. NICHOL is president of the College of William & Mary. He is a constitutional lawyer by training and was formerly dean of the law school at the University of North Carolina.

Finally, and saddest, there is my own particular neighbor-hood—the great public universities of America. The flagships. The research-extensive publics. The historic gateways to democratic opportunity—gateways that carry the promise that no matter your background or pedigree—that if you work hard, excel in school, you too can press your dreams by attending your state's flagship public university. Opening doors, lifting hearts, changing lives.

As, again, the Education Trust's study last year revealed—and as those of us who toil in the public vineyards have long known—that compact has been quietly altered.

How we spend our own institutional financial aid dollars can dwarf many of the allocations from other sources. The Education Trust concluded that over the last decade "even as the number of low-income and minority high school graduates in their states grows . . . [the flagships] are becoming disproportionately whiter and richer."

In 2003, public research universities spent $257 million of their institutional aid dollars on students from families making more than $100,000 per year. They spent only $171 million on students from families making $20,000 or less. The number for the $100,000-plus families had risen by more than $200 million from eight years before. The figure reported for families making under $40,000 rose, over the same time frame, by just $75 million.

So now, at the public research flagships, a category into which (with some adjustments) one would put my own institution, students coming from families making over $100,000 a year, on average, get $3,800 in institutional aid. That figure is higher, on average, than low- or middle-income students receive. High-income, high-achieving students are four times more likely to go to flagships than high-achieving, low-income students.

Smaller percentages of low-income students enroll at public flag-ships than twenty or thirty years ago. In the last decade, Pell-eligible students rose from 29 to 35 percent of all university attendees. At public flagships, they fell from 24 to 22 percent, and we increased institutional grants to low-income students by 29 percent and to the wealthiest by 186 percent. It is as if even the great publics no longer believed in the very core of their missions. Placing these disconcerting patterns together, connecting the immensely unpleasant dots, it is increasingly crucial to ask whether we will continue to be satisfied—particularly at the most accomplished levels of the academy—with educating for privilege. And whether that can be squared with who we are. Lincoln thought that the central idea of our nation was that the weak would gradually be made stronger and, ultimately, all would have an equal chance. The central idea. Barbara Jordan claimed that removing barriers to opportunity—barriers arising from race, from sex, from economic condition, is "indigenous to the American ideal." But what was central to Lincoln, or indigenous to Jordan, has become alien to us.

Pondering these matters, I was reminded of the statement Lyndon Johnson made more than forty years ago in his famous address at the University of Michigan: "Poverty must not be a bar to learning, and learning must offer an escape from poverty." In a different context, Johnson put it far more personally: "Tell them that the leadership of your country believes it is the obligation of your nation to provide and permit and assist every child born in these borders to receive all the education that he can take."

To me, that nudges toward the crux of it. First, because no child here in Virginia, or in the rest of the nation, chooses the neighborhood, the community, the school district, the higher education system, or the family into which she is born. Our religions teach that all children are equal in the eyes of God. But we fund our schools—and frequently open our gates to opportunity—as if we didn't believe it.

Second, I've long loved Johnson's phrase "all the education he could take." This is personal, perhaps because it is exactly the way my father would have put it. "Boy, you need to get all the education you can stand." Reminding us, as all first-generation collegians know, that we are no better, no smarter, no tougher, no more worthy, no more committed than our parents or their parents—or all the generations before them—who never had the opportunity of a college education. The difference, of course—as Neil Kinnock once put it, is that we have been given a "platform upon which [to] stand," a platform consisting of excellent, accessible, life-altering higher education.

So, for me, I am much taken with programs like the pathbreaking Carolina Covenant, Access UVA, and our own Gateway program at William and Mary. Programs offering to meet the entire need of students coming from families making $40,000 a year or less, through a combination of grants and work study, without loans. My hat is off, as well, to the marvelous and growing efforts at many of the nation's most accomplished private universities— Harvard, Princeton, Yale—sometimes going even farther than the programs of the publics can manage. Though the most elite privates will hardly offer a broad-ranging solution. I read recently that there are more Pell-eligible students at Berkeley than in the entire Ivy League.

I have been interested to see, as well, steps like those by Tony Marx at Amherst to build economic disadvantage more powerfully into the admission process. Money is far from the only causal factor creating disparities like the ones I have outlined, as William Bowen's work has shown. Amy Gutmann has written, for example, that only 4.5 percent of the students scoring over 1200 on the SAT come from families in the bottom economic quartile.

Under constitutional law as I understand it—which is not completely unschooled—there is no legal hurdle to employing economic status as a factor in admission decisions, in order to achieve a more diverse, and a more instructive, student body. I have little doubt that there will be political objections, small and large, to such efforts. But the constitutional tremors of racial affirmative action law are not triggered by economic diversity sought as a goal in its own right.

These are heartening starts, essential starts—starts that call for expansion, modification, renewal, and support. Starts that are expensive and challenging and that require movement beyond the poorest students into the middle classes. They are starts, as well, that will lead down false trails, and reveal missteps, and that will require even greater efforts to make the promise of equality real. But they are essential efforts if we are to be anything like what we claim to be. If we are to close the massive gaps, the growing gaps, between what we say and what we do. But we have surely faced larger challenges before. Climbing uphill to achieve the work of democracy is in our DNA.

It is also surely fair to say that the denial of meaningful opportunity to poorer students is but a component of a set of much larger problems—larger betrayals of the command of equal justice. Denials that we've gotten used to—that have become commonplace—betrayals from which we have chosen to simply turn our gaze away. We've gotten used to things we should never have gotten used to. And we've apparently been satisfied.

But how can we be satisfied? When the richest nation on earth, the richest nation in human history, allows almost thirty-seven million of its citizens to live in stark, unrelenting poverty? A quarter of black Americans. A fifth of Latinos. Almost one in five of our children, as if any theory of justice or virtue could explain the exclusion of innocent children from the American dream.

And how can we be satisfied, when forty-seven million Americans have no health care coverage of any kind? Leaving us alone among the industrial nations in failing to provide some form of universal coverage. When, as Dr. King proclaimed, inequality in access to health is the most pernicious discrimination of all?

And how can we be satisfied when, fifty years after the majestic phrases of *Brown v. Board of Education*—all over the country schools are rapidly re-segregating. Removing meaningful racial integration from our national agenda. Ignoring Thurgood Marshall's claim before the Supreme Court that these "infant appellants are asserting the most important secular claims that can be put forward by children"—the right to be "treated as entire citizens of the society into which they have been born."

And how can we be satisfied when in Virginia and across much of the country we allow there to be rich and poor public schools—not just private schools, mind you, but rich and poor public schools. As if it were thought acceptable to treat some of our children as second- and third-class citizens. Our religions teach that all children are equal in the eyes of God. We operate our schools as if we didn't believe it.

And how can we be satisfied when even in our political system it remains necessary to pay in order to play. Barney Frank told me once that we're the only people in the world who believe that our elected officials can walk up to total strangers, ask them for thousands of dollars, get it, and be completely unaffected by it. Achieving a state of "perfect ingratitude."

And how can we be satisfied when our legal system leaves so many priced out of the effective use of the civil justice system. Study after study shows that at least eighty percent of the legal need of the poor goes unmet. The circumstance for the near-poor is almost as bleak. Making a mockery of the "equal justice" carved on so many of our courthouse walls.

The frank truth is that if the exclusions and indignities of American poverty are right, then the Constitution is wrong.

If the debilitations of those locked at the bottom are acceptable, then our scriptures are wrong.

If these denials of equal citizenship and equal dignity are permissible, then we pledge allegiance to an illusion, not to a foundational creed. ❧

Politics and Religion

Can They Get Along? Should They Try?

Leslie W. Dunbar

Since the 2006 congressional elections, Democrats have looked forward hungrily to 2008. They believe that the presidency and more congressional seats are in prospect. I hope for that, too.

Ask ourselves, though, what have past Democratic victories meant? What would a victory in 2008 mean, beyond ridding the nation—and world—of a group of wretched spirits who have governed us these first years of the twenty-first century? Much else, I think; such as, most importantly, greater care for our surrounding natural environment—for knowing that the Earth is in balance, in Mr. Gore's phrase—and for deepened concern for our and the world's majority people, i.e., the poor.

But at age eighty-six, I have had plenty of time and occasions to be disappointed in my sunny anticipation of oncoming national elections. Somehow saddest of all for me was that of 2002, on the heels of the bitter political crime of 2000—made as bad as it was by the Supreme Court—perhaps because I had to be aware that I might not be around to see a better one. I correctly surmised at the time that the 2002 election meant a near lawless government that would be listing still more to the greed of the rich, and still more to killings of foreign peoples. And I could see no probable change ahead in my years.

Well. As I've aged my temper has grown shorter. The election of

2004 was another horror. It seemed a mark of the utter disintegration of both the public's patriotism and intelligence. The congressional elections of 2006 seemed to promise that that might not be so. Hope arose again.

But the three largest faults of modern American politics, faults rooted in our national history and our civil religion, have been and are still our embracing of militarism, oligarchy, and racism. Little in the Democratic Party's recent past or its present character encourages belief that electoral victory in 2008 will reach to the first two of those cancerous faults. Nor that it will do a whole lot more than might the Republicans on racism, which since the great reforms of the 1950s, 1960s, and 1970s is not a cause of difficult partisan issues to be confronted but a vast field of social and economic blights, diseases, and potholes which demand fixing. Some of these we can hardly comprehend except foggily and consequently know but poorly how to fix. The crass imbroglio in Jena, Louisiana, in late summer 2007, brought on by raw prejudiced behavior of some of our youngsters, showed this.

The United States' "security" budget for the Pentagon—and the many other like-minded agencies beyond—seems to me to be the principal cause of the unceasing wars that dominate the world. Not the *only* cause, certainly, but the chief. The Iraqi war alone is consuming more than $720 million a day, a half million a minute, according to the trust-worthy American Friends Service Committee, as of the summer of 2007. The AFSC goes on to illustrate how such sums could be better used. Add to this the expenditures for the many agencies and bureaus which in one way or another are at work "projecting our power" around the globe, and the sum is colossal. There is no limiting force to keep the sum from growing. The rest of the world's nations are complicit in this, some by lending us the money—we depend these days on other people's money—for our insatiable arming, or by buying from us, or—and this is the biggest lot of them—by accepting the deprivation that this hoggish absorption of the world's treasure imposes on them.

Swinish, too, are the lobbying and advertising by the corporate contractors for more and yet more of the public's dollars. I have in hand now a large Northrop Grumman ad published on Memorial Day 2007, ringing-the-changes on that day's meaning and claiming it for itself.[1] The military side of the military-industrial complex speaks up as well, to educate citizens "to fight and win the nation's wars."[2]

The most dangerous part of the military budget is, of course, that for nuclear weapons, and the signs are that we and the Russians, the two principal owners of them, prize still their possession. I cannot believe that there is a realistic possibility of bridling the nuclear race unless we restrain ourselves, especially as we and the other nuclear powers have inserted our might in every area of the world. Look at Iran, surrounded as it is by nuclear-armed states— Pakistan, India, Russia, Israel—and us. It is fanciful to believe that Iran will long accept that, unless the "haves" begin to moderate their arsenals.

Treaties will no more restrain Iran than they did Israel, Pakistan, or India as long as we and the European "haves" and China regard it as their inalienable right to have and enlarge and improve at will their own nuclear stores. While we loudly condemn North Korea and Iran for seeking to build nuclear weapons, we disregard our own commitment under the Non-Proliferation Treaty to move toward eliminating our stockpile of some thousands of nuclear weapons, and are actively planning to manufacture more.

Most contenders for the presidency, including the Democrats,

―――――――――

LESLIE W. DUNBAR, a native of West Virginia, was the director of the Field Foundation and the Southern Regional Council during the turmoil of the 1960s, and has been closely identified with the cause of Southern democracy. The author of several books, most recently, *The Shame of Southern Politics*, he lives in Washington, D.C.

want to make our expenditures even more gross. The political truth probably is that no person aspiring to the presidency, or likely as not to the Senate, will call upon the nation to restrain our excess; nor will those wanting to be Secretary of State or hold other high office. Nor for that matter will the editors of our most influential newspapers or big television networks.

The first of our foundational faults, our abiding militaristic habits, has a well-known history from our conquests of the nineteenth century and continuing with scarcely a pause to our present-day invasion of Iraq and Afghanistan. Most citizens excuse these warrings as being "not our fault"; experts by the dozens explain them as the responsibilities that come with our immense power.

The second, the strong drift toward oligarchy, arouses popular opposition about every other generation, and the present may be the onset of one of those periodic resistances; there are emerging rebel flags. The American norm, however, has been to believe—in defiance of a near-unanimous conviction by all western political philosophy from Plato and Aristotle to modern times—that constitutional democracy can coexist with the wealth of an oligarchic class.

In our conceit, we believe that we and our society are the exception, that our rich, the Gates and Buffets and their lesser likes, are different; that the Republic is secure in their hands, and even in the hands of those corporate officers who pay themselves enormous treasure. Is this not outright thievery, from their stockholders and from the nation's treasury in unpaid taxes? One of the encouraging developments of these years has been the growing awareness of these civic wrongs; one of the most discouraging is that they exist and increase. The *Washington Post* on July 16, 2007, counted twenty corporate officers in the District of Columbia area alone, which is in the financial minor leagues, who were paying themselves upwards of $8.2 million per year; the top fellow took $ 37.4 million.

I have not done close study, but I have read enough to predict confidently that research would show that Southerners in Congress are among the chief supporters of the legal devices allowing this. Are there signs yet of a rebirth of Southern populism?

Some of our universities and even some of our labor unions pay their executives huge compensations, though not yet on the scale of the corporations; but we used to expect better from them.[3] There is particular cause for concern in the increasing privatization of military tasks. As has been much in the news in 2007, private so-called security firms, such as Blackwater USA, DynCorp International, and the British company Aegis Defense Services LTD, Erinys, and Armor Group International, are all over Iraq and are quite costly to taxpayers. They even handle "intelligence" functions.[4] There was a time centuries ago when monarchs hired mercenary troops from whatever nations could supply them. Is the day far off if we continue fighting wars without the support of public opinion, as we now are doing in Iraq and Afghanistan, when we shall like those olden monarchs have our own mercenary army at the disposal of the White House? A navy and air force, too? It is not hard to imagine Blackwater, et al., trading on the New York Stock Exchange.

It is relevant to recount all this because we have to wonder where our churches stand. Are they insisting on truth-telling and fairness? Do they, as they call on their congregations to "support our troops," include in their support these hired hands and their corporate employers?

Religion in the Public Square Today

I want in this essay to comment on the intertwining of those deep faults—militarism and oligarchy—within our omnipresent religions and the state. I am no biblical scholar, but I know there is little explicit in the New Testament about political "values." Yet there is much about "putting politics in its place," at a non-corrupting distance from religious worship. Keeping that distance is the theme of this essay.

Earl and Merle Black have documented and explained the force of religion in partisan politics across the United States in our present time. What they document is a strong movement since the Reagan days of white Protestants into the Republican Party. This has been especially pronounced in the South and everywhere among voters who see themselves as Evangelicals. By the 2002 and 2004 elections, majorities of white Protestant men and women were Republicans. Similar if less pronounced movement has occurred among Roman Catholics. African Americans—who are mostly Protestant—Jews, and the non-Christians (who include adherents of other religions and the non-religious) are mostly Democratic. The two groups seem to be sharply defined and divided. Religion is lining up with party.[5]

The ancient tension between state and religion, or church, was over supremacy. That is finished. The state has won. Perhaps not, though, over civil religions. In the pre-Christian West, all large religions were state-connected, and Christianity soon became so. If I were a church leader I would worry that Christianity is tending toward re-cloaking itself today into the prevailing civil religion of its home countries. Fascism showed how thoroughly that can happen; Communism was another case; white supremacy in our "old South" was still another.

Emerson wisely remarked that, "Nothing is at last sacred but the integrity of your own mind." Again, "There is a crack in everything God has made."[6] To the same effect, Immanuel Kant once told us, "How indeed can one expect something perfectly straight to be framed out of such crooked wood" as our human natures.[7] He wrote those oracular words in the context of pondering why a "church is needed at all." His own example typified the struggle of his eighteenth century between orthodoxy and liberty, a struggle which continues. His book from which the above lines are quoted required a couple of years of struggle with censors—and then the death of a super-religious king (change of administration?) before it was clearly free to be read. He spoke of "the dreadful voice of orthodoxy," and it still clangs in our ears.[8]

From the Renaissance through the seventeenth and eighteenth centuries' Age of Enlightenment, and in Italy, Spain, and other Mediterranean countries for longer than that, the "cause" of liberalism was, generally speaking, the "cause" of secular state power over church power. Since the final, more or less, subjugation of church "power," the Christian churches have played several roles: as state partner, as critic, as limiting harness—but not for long centuries have the churches been a co-ruler or rival.

What of the present? In the USA? In its South? We are overflowing with churches of blindingly many descriptions. How do they and their state relate to each other?

They do so in various ways. Some principal ones are the following.

The First Amendment

"Congress shall make no law respecting an establishment of religion, or prohibiting the free exercise thereof." This revered statement stands at the forefront of the affirmation of our basic freedoms, preceding even the freedoms of speech and of press, and the right of the people to assemble and to petition for redress of grievances. These two clauses instruct the governments (federal, and later, states as well) to keep hands off the ways people choose to worship some deity, and tells governments not to impose ways of worship on anyone.

Of course, it might be said that we have, through the course of time, established a religion here: *viz.,* the creedal demands of patriotism. Referring to oneself as an atheist is not these days an especially bold act, unless maybe if one is running for political office. Referring to oneself as not a patriot would be. In past centuries, the reverse would have been more likely to put one in trouble.

Patriotism is our faith, to profess on demand.

The state now and then wants to be religion's guardian. A press release from the Attorney General on February 20, 2007, announced the "launching" of a "First Freedom Project" to strengthen religious liberty. I suppose that this is harmless, on its face, but the full text of the announcement tends to limit the project to something it terms religious discrimination against believers, and it is tempting, knowing this administration, to believe that the protection is specially for the doubters of evolution.

Probably more to be questioned is the U.S. Commission on International Religious Freedom that Congress legislated into being in 1998 to monitor the policies and practices of nations around the world. It is another example of our government's tendency to busy itself because it thinks the public, as it perceives the public, wants it to show concern. The Commission keeps a list, and revises it annually. Thus, for example, Iraq had been from 1999 to 2003 designated a country of "particular concern"; the designation was dropped after we occupied the country. It now is simply on the commission's "watch list." The State Department receives these evaluations. I think this is child's play.

The State Seeks Sometimes To Direct

The state enlists the churches, enlists religion, for its chosen purposes, as the present administration seeks to do by its so-called faith based initiatives programs. This is cynical manipulation of the religious to do the will of the political masters.

The Churches Seek Sometimes To Direct

Churches may seek to enlist the state's governing power to support their dogmas, as, for one example, the Catholic church does—joined and in places led by Protestant bodies—regarding contraception and proscription of homosexuality. There is a possible case to be made that the state does have always a responsibility to protect life, and that therefore abortion is of a different nature than other sex-related concerns. But the blanketing of woman–man and other sex-related matters under religion is almost always a threat to public peace.

Support and Blessings Are Requisitioned by the State

Religion is called upon to give solemn blessing to the state's plans, especially to its armies. Our war against Iraq, its people and land, has gone on for four and a half years, and there is no end in sight. It has been lamented and criticized by a large number of our church bodies. But probably many more of those have acquiesced, or even have approved, and there is scant evidence that the congregations whose leaders don't respond to the government's call are much swayed by the more liberal. By mid-September 2007, 3,800 of our troops had been killed, multiples of that had been seriously wounded, and who knows how many of our allies and opponents have been killed or in awful ways hurt. And as in all modern wars, the largest number of causalities has been among civilians. The United Nations said in May 2007 that two million Iraqis have taken refuge from the warring outside their country, that an equal number have been displaced inside their land. The private organization, Refugees International, estimates that the numbers are increasing by about fifty thousand each passing month.[9]

The *Washington Post* on June 26, 2007, reported the beliefs of Iraqi doctors, social workers, and teachers that what children have witnessed in these days of death-dealing and cruelty will have long-term consequences in their lives and behaviors. Who could doubt it?

I once a long time ago raised a similar warning about what impact the Southern culture of violence and racist oppression during the civil rights movement days would have on the Southern white children, as they grew up; would their moral outlook be coarsened? I think it may have been.

That same day's paper reported the opinion of one of our generals that, "It'll take years for Iraqi security forces not to require us." This is a war without end; as it goes on, the same day's paper reports on the record-breaking opium production in Afghanistan.

This war in the Mideast is a war which our government has chosen to wage for ends and purposes of its own. It is hard for me, or I should think anyone, to see how the Christian churches can justify it. But many apparently do.

In the course of the campaigning for the 2008 presidential election there has been unceasing discussion by the candidates of their religious beliefs and practices. The question should be asked of these candidates: what have they done to lead or spur on the church bodies to which they adhere to work to end the destruction our state is causing?

For my part, I welcome the endeavor coming out of the South of a movement of Baptist congregations and leaders, led at this time by former Presidents Carter and Clinton, committed to promoting "peace with justice, to feed the hungry, clothe the naked, shelter the homeless, care for the sick and marginalized, and promote religious liberty, and respect for religious diversity." This is a project outside the Southern Baptist Convention—indeed in deliberate distinction from that massive force for obliterating reason from religion. No one should underestimate the might of Baptists in the South, in or out of the Convention. It was Baptists from the South, mainly of black congregations, who once were the leading force of the civil rights movement. They had learned from the same teachings that in those days many, perhaps most, of their white brothers were spurning and distorting. This Carter–Clinton call was signed by a significant number of black churchpersons, offering guidance to their white co-religionists. It is a movement full of hope. I believe Martin Luther King, Jr., would be glad.

Religion Usually Joins the State in War-Making

Of far greater consequence than a ceremonial prayer and blessing, religion is expected by the state to support its war-making in manifold ways. Usually religion does as expected. But this testing of religious integrity does lead to occasional resistance.

The depth of resistance does come often from religious people; but not always. What is the moral/religious responsibility of an individual to correct/resist the state, to decline to obey orders which affront conscience? Is there an individual responsibility, for example, to refuse to participate in torture? Surely there is. I wonder if any of our "interrogators" are church- or synagogue-goers. Or in a broader sense, is there an individual responsibility to refuse the orders of the state or its corporations when they violate what religion, one assumes, teaches, such as the destruction of the Creation by mountain-top removal or other strip-mining, or of a pharmacist to refuse to fill a prescription for Plan-B, etc.?

One of the oldest traditions in American political life is the rightfulness of civil disobedience when the state violates outrageously its own principles or public morality. Ours is a curious time. This war has lost defenders by the millions. Its congressional or other governmental partisans decline steadily. Generals, some still on active status, voice disquiet. And, as American patriots historically have done, some young persons carry their dissent to the level of disobedience. Yet still the war goes on, and political leaders, Democrats among them, talk of increasing it.

As early as October 2006 we find more than one hundred service persons petitioning Congress. They wrote: "Staying in Iraq will not work and is not worth the price. It is time for U.S. troops to come home." Other dissents have followed. Some have led to courts-martial for alleged desertion; some to less than honorable discharge.

The protesters should be befriended by presidential candidates. That is not going to happen. But if church bodies are to be known either by their works or by faithfulness to their calling, they are obligated to set themselves apart from the state—if not by encouraging, at least by embracing the brave ones who protest the state's wanton warring. The opportunities for the churches to do so are mounting.

Keep Religion out of the Public Square

American politicians today are expected to announce their religious faith. This is too bad. It is, if an unfortunate term may be borrowed, almost un-American. I am myself a sort of Roger Williams Baptist, and his teaching was that no good and usually much ill can come from the mingling of religion and politics. It is not merely a matter of lawyers wrestling with the meaning of separation of "church" and "state"—though that is indeed important—but realization that these two omnipresent forces within humanity sicken each other when brought too close.

In fact, early Southern leaders knew this well and acted on the knowledge. Washington, Jefferson, Monroe were, if a name must be given, Deists. So too were others of the founders such as Franklin, John Adams, and—let's not forget him—Tom Paine. And whatever was Andrew Jackson?

This Deistic tradition weakened, sadly enough, in later years when evangelistic fervor ripped through the South. But even that fervor was unlike the fashionable politico-religion widely preached today. That "old-time religion that was good enough for Paul and Silas and good enough for me" had little time for politics. Its ambition was to save men's souls, one's own in the process. The fictional Elmer Gantrys and all-too-real Billy Sundays of the 1920s and the merchandisers of our later years, fashioning their vile mixture of right-wing politics with the South's always active jingoism and Philistine tendencies, have created their own kind of "New South." But farther back in time, and if we are smart, and lucky, lying ahead in time, there is another South which one can with some realism hope is finding itself today among youth throughout the region.

Religion and Morality

Religion is or should be subordinate to morality. Just as God itself cannot make two plus two equal anything but four (with the possible exception of loaves and fishes) so religion cannot redefine morality. It cannot make what is immoral to be morally right—ever as hard as the Robertsons/Falwells may try in their support of war-making and wealth. While recasting religion as but sexual police, and never mind the Sermon on the Mount.

But Christianity and Judaism are firmly with us. We are they, they are us. What do they say regarding the foundation stones of our secular political ideals: liberty, equality, fraternity? Most fundamentally, what are they saying in these modern times when the Christians of the West are probably becoming outnumbered by their fellow religionists in Africa and Asia, and when the European and North American strength they may still have is increasingly based on the poor of Latin America?

Little in fact about liberty and equality, and what there is mostly has to be inferred; an endless lot about the third: fraternity. Extending charity to the stranger, caring for the poor and weak, loving thy neighbor—over and over yet again the revered writings command fraternity. But if liberty and equality may be legislated, even though imperfectly, fraternity cannot be. (As the twentieth-century history of "Communism" well showed.) What does it require of our public, our social, life?

Perhaps, nothing; perhaps it has no meaning for us as citizens, only for us as persons. The good man and the good citizen, Aristotle noted, are not always the same. I would rather believe that at the very least fraternity—or, if preferred, call it sisterhood and brotherhood—means that as citizens as well as persons we do not willfully kill or maim our neighbor, depriving him of his life and liberty, as we do through the death penalty and war-making .

The grand democratic ideal of liberty, equality, fraternity, as does the Jeffersonian declaration of humanity's right to life, liberty, and the pursuit of happiness, has sadly left men free to kill each other in war, and in other services to the state.

Peace Is Not of Law

True, no word of our Constitution questions the state's right to take life. But no word of the Constitution restricts the death penalty to murderers, nor was it so restricted in earlier days. Now it is. Our minds and morals are capable of growth.[10] Morality has been evolving since we left behind the Classical Greek and Roman and Mosaic acceptance of slavery. Mankind's further maturing is humanity's hope, and mission.

Historically the South has of all American regions been the one most accepting of violence. And it still is, in practice. Better spirits may be pressing Southerners in new directions.

Monotheism may have its drawbacks but at least there is no God of War. When the American state calls on God to bless its warring, it has to call on the same one who for Christians preached the Sermon on the Mount, or for Jews taught through the books of Amos, Micah, and the other later Prophets. But if we have no god of war we make of the state itself a "mortal god," and regularly elevate it and its purposes above any lesser god in its way.

And for what ends do we go to war? The United States by its own choosing has fought at least six wars since the early 1980s—against tiny Grenada, small Panama, Serbia, Afghanistan, and twice against Iraq; and not so long ago, against Vietnam. Each was started by us. None was fought in self-defense (except as perceived by straining theorists). Each resulted in destruction of nature and human lives, and other peoples' cultures. Twice, in Vietnam and now in Iraq, we have been defeated by much smaller foes, as we invaded their homelands. Yet our appetite for war, unique among other wealthy nations, is still apparently ravenous. Of late we menace Iran.

Violence, by individuals or by great states, is seldom if ever over and done with quickly. It always has an aftermath. Violence begets violence as our South can attest. I believe Lyndon Johnson probably knew that as, despite torturing self-doubts, he tragically could not refrain from a warring that he knew was futile. Jimmy Carter knew that, and stayed our might. Bill Clinton probably knew that, and tried to evade it by fighting his war from the skies.

Neighbors

What moral progress there has been in human affairs is closely tied to an expanding sense of who is our neighbor. When ancient people or those of America's antebellum years enslaved persons, they had first to set them apart as lesser creatures beyond claim on their owners' moral obligations. We have only imperfectly learned to love our neighbors as ourselves. But we are better than we once were, I think. Today's all-too-many barbarous political acts all have their ancestors. Not as many of our better acts do.

Frederick Douglass, great American and great person, concluded his autobiography with a memorable assault on the hypocrisy of "the religion of this land," in thrall to Southern slave-holders, "which is, by communion and fellowship, the religion of the north."[11] We could not, thanks be, draw up the same bill of indictment today, and I suppose churches and the religion they represent have had much to do with that progress. Which is to say that religion, like all human creations, even those humans have founded on their discovery of God's truth, changes and moves, and seeks to grow better.

What would Douglass think and say of the present-day status of destitute masses around the world and the treatment of them by today's powerful and rich (who are most times the same people and institutions). Maybe our children and grandchildren will bring fuller, clearer, minds to this. If so, it will be because the spirit of fraternity has moved, and they with it.

So Where Are We Now?

I would say, though our hold may be slipping, we are where

the Republic has historically tended to be, despite the tugs of the doctrinaires. At a recognition that politics and religion are separate spheres. At all times in the Republic's history, some have sought to push it into clear identification with some variety of religion. The pressure these days is particularly strong, and the complexity of the forces doing the pushing is deep.

In post-World War II continental Europe, the strongest political forces were the Communist and Christian Democratic parties. The mass appeals of both were huge. Much was at stake in their rivalry. The United States in this Truman-Eisenhower era of 1945–1960, was actively involved in European political affairs and their outcomes. We did much wrong in that era. Chiefly, we laid down the foundation stones of our militarism despite the warning of President Eisenhower himself about the "military-industrial complex," a warning that has taken its place in copy-book rhetoric. I can't help but believe, though, that our basically non-ideological constitutional democracy was a standard that Europeans could gratefully embrace. The lesson for us should have been that democracy cannot breathe well amidst deep ideological divisions. Citizens can divide amongst ourselves over economics or foreign policies or environmental issues, even over war and peace, so long as these divisions are kept within "the limits of reason alone." But ideologies, religious as well as political, are plagues for democracies.

The United States has no prevailing religion; probably has not had since the mid-nineteenth century when Irish Catholics emerged as a coherent political group in the Northeast. Many religions abound today with their bodies of believers. Some of these religions are rich with treasure and with accretions of political influence.

I think it as imperative as ever that we recognize and require that they exist within boundaries, within which they may seek to fulfill their chosen missions. Their multiplicity is good. Often we Christians here lament that we are divided, are lacking in unity. I give thanks that we are. The medieval Roman Catholic Church was example sufficient of the destructiveness of an unchecked and all-powerful church, or any approaching that.

Religion and politics are incurable, it would seem, embedded directions of our species. So be it. They have to keep distance from each other. They can get along peacefully, even respectfully of each other, but only when apart. They corrupt and pollute each other if they become embroiled, entangled in the other's sphere. Pitfalls abound. I am, as I have already said, no biblical scholar. But I have lived all my life with the New Testament, and I think such is its clear, even emphatic, teaching (except possibly in that weird Book of Revelation).

Jews and Muslims face their own challenges. But the freedom we all seek is the freedom to serve high purposes, as we determine them to be. Religion and politics cannot be, will not be, should not be, sealed off from each other. To attempt to do that, whether by atheists or pietists, is defiance of all humanity's history, as well as human nature. We are meant to be whole in our creature-hood.

I think it altogether needful and proper for religion, as morality's special guardian, to endeavor to discipline the state, to speak truth to power, as the saying goes, when the state may lie, may erect its own gods and require obedience to them, may kill and torture for its own ends, or may encourage or even allow the strong and rich to oppress the weak and poor.

In like manner, I think that the state as the special protector of life and of civic order—protector of the possibility of there being a "good society"—has a right and perhaps a duty to correct religion when it over-reaches; when Roman Catholics, e.g., do not treat women in the spirit of equality or homosexuals in the spirit of fraternity. Or when Southern Baptists accept or condone violence against African-Americans and their homes. And the state, committed to all of its citizens' pursuit of happiness, can legitimately forbid Muslim practices that may degrade women.

As myself a white Protestant—both by birth—I relish the fraternity of the congregation and the freedom of the pulpit which allows a voice in behalf of political liberty and equality. That voice may just as well, though, come forth from atheists or from a myriad of other faiths, Buddhists, Hindus, Muslims, *inter alia*.

I hear our Democratic and Republican political leaders of late calling attention to their attachment to a faith. Possibly this is harmless, if they don't make too much of it; but only possibly. It is, as the saying goes, a slippery slope. It is especially hard to keep one's footing in a political campaign. I wish these politicians would stay off it.

The business of the politician is not to lead us toward godliness but to lead a country to be at peace and neighborly with other countries, and to lead their own countrymen to be a free and prosperous people at peace with and in mutual support of each other. Above all, to help lead a nation in the ways of fairness and justice. ⁂

Towards Home

A Search for Place and Land Ethic

J. Drew Lanham

"Conservation is a state of harmony between men and land."
— Aldo Leopold

Edgefield, South Carolina is my home. A small county in the western piedmont of the state, it's famous for producing political influence in proportions that far exceed its size. John C. Calhoun, Francis Pickens, Red Shirts, "Pitchfork" Ben Tillman, the Dixiecrats, and Strom Thurmond were all born of the "Home of Ten Governors"—and were staunch agents of the status quo, or worse. Ol' Strom's legacies, from an elderly biracial daughter, to schools and a lake bearing his name, are testament to the power of the one-time segregationist who proclaimed the immorality of race-mixing on the stump but apparently found it not so distasteful in his private life. Such hypocrisies seem to run rampant where folks claim to be God's chosen or where the "good old days" weren't so good for everyone. In a state that has led at times in nefarious races; violence, secession, oppression, segregation—Edgefield often set the pace.

So with this infamy clouding its character, how can anyone—other than a flag-waving son of the Confederacy—wax nostalgically about this place? Simply put, Edgefield was—is—home. In spite of its imperfections it is a point of origin from which I cannot escape and that I will not deny. As my home, I recognize the saving graces—can talk about and still claim it. Edgefield is a largely unmined ecological gem, sitting in a degrading and developing piedmont. Guarded westward by the Savannah River and reaching south and east into the deep sands of ancient dunes and coastal plain, Edgefield harbors a vast array of wild things and places that are often spectacular, many times sensitive and always to me, special.

Wild turkeys, Rock Shoals spider lily, Bachman's sparrows, Carolina heel splitter mussel, Cheve's Creek, relict trillium, Webster's salamanders, white-tailed deer, Christmas darters, pine woodlands, canebrakes, and backwater bottomlands. It was here and amidst these places and wild beings that I grew up in the southwestern outreaches of the county in a ragged, two-hundred acre Forest Service in-holding. A hole punched into the Sumter National Forest's Long Cane Ranger District. This was my Home Place.

My home place is a link to a Southern past that began with a young man named Harry Lanham. A slave who ultimately became my paternal great-great grandfather, he was brought South from the tobacco-tired fields of Virginia in the late 1800s by his owner, Josias Lanham, to try the new cash crop—cotton. As far as anyone knows, Harry lived and died a slave on the Home Place. After sixty-three years in bondage, some say he was buried in the Republican Baptist Church cemetery, an "honor" allegedly bestowed upon him by his owner for his "true and faithful" service. Never owning the land that he was tied to, great-great granddaddy Harry in truth had no less a right to the property than those who kept him chattel. But those who came after him got a piece of it, nurtured it, and passed it on. For Harry and those that followed him—Great-granddaddy Abram, my grandfather Joseph Samuel ("Daddy Joe"), and my father, James Hoover—to persist through turbulent times and social upheaval over a span of two hundred years is something that I am immensely proud of. That the links they worked so hard to keep intact are now severely weakened and perhaps uncoupling is a source of great sadness and shame.

And so as prodigal sons will do, a return home is often the penance for the neglect and carelessness that threatens the birthright. Memory—and a black mailbox, dented and perched precariously atop a decaying post, mark the spot—Route 1 Box 29, Republican Road. The way from there, towards home, is simple. Bear left at the black mailbox, go roughly a quarter of a mile on a sometimes muddy, often dusty, dirt road, and you'd see our house; a modest brick ranch—not spectacular, but mostly modern and comfortable. It was the place my parents, Willa Mae and James Hoover, worked hard to build, and where I spent some of the best years of my life.

Three white columns stood sentinel on the large front porch. A two-car garage, boxwood shrubs, and a mostly grass-covered yard made it the quintessential seventies house. Inside, paneled walls, red-sculpted carpeting and an eight-track hydro-phonic stereo in the living room firmly planted my family somewhere in the middle class.

Just across the pasture from my parent's house was Mamatha's house—my grandmother's place. It was a six-room cottage-like affair that was covered by a rusting tin roof. The loosely planked front porch was where she often sat in warm weather, rocking contentedly and admiring her handiwork: stones ringing a flower bed underneath an ancient arborvitae tree; the weedy yard punctuated by several large crepe myrtles and accented in early spring by little copses of lemon yellow daffodils and crisp white jonquils.

From a distance, in the complimentary light of fading sunset, with your eyes squinted just so, Mamatha's place seemed almost quaint—the little house in the big woods. Closer inspection in broad

J. DREW LANHAM grew up amidst the forests and fields on a small family farm in Edgefield, South Carolina. He is a professor of forest wildlife ecology at Clemson University and lives with his wife Janice and children Alexis and Colby in nearby Seneca, South Carolina.

daylight revealed a starker truth. The house was badly constructed with an interior of carelessly painted sheetrock walls and creaky, uneven floors covered by fading linoleum and beige threadbare carpet. The indoor plumbing was rudimentary—exposed pipes and white enamel basins—no frills. Insulation anywhere in that house had been an afterthought. It was a functional museum of the Depression-era South. No one ever called Mamatha's antique Frigidaire a refrigerator; it was an icebox. In a scary, dark and musty "lower" room that was probably someone's quick-fix idea of an addition, a coffin-sized deep freezer preserved food that was mostly older than me. Heating and cooking were fueled by wood and not by watts. The black and white cast iron stove was nineteenth-century state of the art that produced soul food feasts I yearn for even today. The floors were swept clean by wire-bound broomsedge. In the side yard between the pasture and the house stood a dilapidated log smokehouse that sometime in the not-so-distant past secured the family's meat supply. The front yard was mostly dirt with scattered islands of crabgrass, and there was a woodpile and a chicken coop. Though my father frequently offered upgrades and modernization, my grandmother either filibustered the improvements or downright refused the charity. This place, backwoods and backwards as it may have seemed, was the place I'd call home.

I SPENT MOST of my boyhood at Mamatha's place. I'd been more or less "loaned" to her to fend off her loneliness after my grandfather Daddy Joe died from long-suffering illnesses (which he attributed to poison gas attacks he endured in France during the Great War). The two houses and the space that lay between them were symbolic of the two worlds that I straddled: modern convenience and comfort versus old-time simplicity and a palpable link to the past and what has become a special legacy. I grew up during the "dawning of the Age of Aquarius," but Mamatha somehow kept me grounded in her antiquarian world of superstitions and herbal remedies. Any number of seemingly innocuous things might cause bad luck to befall me. Countless ameliorating agents if not outright cures lay just outside at the edge of the yard or in the pasture. Ghostly visits, conversations with the dead, salt over your shoulder, and poke-salad spring tonics were a part of my daily life. Most nights, Mamatha, though literate, wanted me to read the Bible to her. The odd mix of beliefs made my time at Mamatha's spooky and special.

Most days at Mamatha's house on brisk October mornings began in the small bedroom. We slept together in her ten-story cannonball bed until I was nine or ten. While she slept under several suffocating layers of hand-sewn quilts for most of the year, she seemed perpetually cold. The bedroom was heated by a rusting, ravenous Ashley heater that was never sated by its constant diet of oak and hickory harvested off the property. The heater's appetite for wood and Mamatha's thin blood meant that it often got hellishly hot in that little room. So often before daybreak when the fire was dying down, I'd have to rise and feed the Ashley dragon to make sure Mamatha didn't fall victim to the autumn chill.

Although the bedroom and the kitchen were the only two heated rooms, the demand for firewood was enormous. Back then it seemed as though tree-cutting and wood-splitting consumed too many of my boyhood days. The sylvan cycle of felling, cutting, loading, splitting, and burning seemed to never end.

THE INDUSTRY, THOUGH tedious, was really a testament to a sustainable forestry initiative that existed long before it became the Fortune 500 mantra for selling "green" lumber. Daddy's skill with an often-temperamental chain saw and his judicious choice of the next tree for sacrifice to the Ashley heater god was more art than science; a dying post oak or an ice-injured hickory from the bottom, the upper field, or some other area of the home place meant that no one stand of timber was depleted. It meant a constant supply of wood for Mamatha, and sturdy posts and rails for fence building. But we weren't the only ones benefiting from the home place timber. The hardwoods and pines provided food for the deer, turkeys, and squirrels, sheltering green canopies for the vireos and tanagers and the essential forested character of the bottoms and ridges that made the home place such a special realm.

Much of the wood fueled Mamatha's kitchen industry. Biscuits, fatback, grits and gravy, string beans and white potatoes, tomato and corn soup, yellow squash and green onions, macaroni and cheese, peach cobbler and coconut pie, molasses bread. These simple culinary delights were never rushed to the table via the impatient convenience of electricity or gas. A microwave would have been downright sinful. The slow and watchful process that my grandmother called cooking was an art form that's been lost in the rush to produce things quickly with no regard for the character imbued by time, patience, and love.

My stomach full from the feast, I would often complete my chores after breakfast with an eye on exploring the home place. Those frosty October mornings, when the blue jays' raucous calls boldly announced their pecan thievery from the giant tree by the smokehouse, are engraved deeply in my memory. Wood split and floors swept, I would set out to lay claim to the Republican Road Kingdom. There were hundreds of these boyhood explorations. Along pasture paths and through forests and fields, the days seemed infinitely long and abruptly short at the same time. I'd be gone for hours, before making an appearance at the brick ranch with my parents asking few questions as to where I'd been. Nowadays, some would call such behavior neglect. I recognize those times as the rare and priceless gifts of freedom and self-confidence. Time passed all too quickly on the home place. But those early years taught me lessons that I carry with me today.

The fields, the pastures, the creek bottom, the bobwhite, the blackberries, the barking foxes—all that and the land were mine, or so I thought. Two hundred or so acres are what I'd heard my daddy and grandmother talk about. That was the family's land. It was my boyhood kingdom. It was a place where turkeys, tanagers, and a host of other creatures dwelled—where Cheve's Creek and Dry Branch ran foamy and dark through the lower bottom and my daddy taught me to fish. It was the perfect boyhood kingdom. But like all kingdoms, its days were numbered.

MY CONNECTIONS TO the land are much deeper than my forty-two years. African Americans are linked to a centuries-old relationship that largely defines the South. Woods and water, forests and fields— we black folks have been connected with all of these things since our arrival here. Taken away from our aboriginal soil, land, and wild things—the home we knew—we suffered and adjusted and survived. First the torturous transatlantic sojourn brought us here. Upon our arrival, the oaks, the foreboding swamps, and the cotton fields, framed a different world amidst the torture of slavery. The land was not ours, but we worked it hard and bought it with sweat equity that ultimately built a region and in many ways, a nation. The beauty of our new place, of the land and the wild things that lived on it and the sustenance it produced, became evident.

I've often wondered, though, what my ancestors thought about this place as they lay awake after a day of forced labor, too tired to sleep, pondering their plight in some ramshackle cabin. Perhaps they finally fell asleep, serenaded by a mockingbird's midnight sonata, dreaming of the freedom they used to possess or could possess again. Perhaps they dreamed of new freedom and land of their own, to work as they wished.

And so, as the mockingbird sang and visions of freedom and working a piece of land they owned morphed slowly into a bitter-sweet reality where forty acres and a swayback mule were promised and then taken away, time and time again, the plight of the African Diaspora played on. Legacies of a kinship with the land ran through the sons and daughters of the slaves who once worked and then owned the land. But many have squandered, for a pittance, fortunes that could have supported generations if prudence and patience had been part of the process. Mosquito- and snake-infested sea islands, once left to the slaves because of their inhospitable environs, now sell by the square foot—for hundreds of thousands if not millions. Meanwhile up the I-95 corridor, in a hidden third world, poverty runs rampant. Non-potable water, lingering lead paint, substandard health systems, and educational inequities plague the region even amidst the selectively spreading luxury and development.

Land-wealth resides largely in white hands. Across the South, land that formerly lay in "colored" deeds now harbors exclusive gated communities that are often ironically designated as plantations. Thievery and unfair advantage are not the only reasons the land and any ethic behind it are in danger of disappearing from the African American psyche. Think about how many acres were simply abandoned by my people—left behind to languish, as the land's absentee heirs are more comfortable in the suburban and urban sprawl of some metropolis, far removed from the memories and stigma of the brutal rural South. Or how about the acreage that is simply neglected and ends up going cheaply for back taxes and pennies on the acre. The stories of loss are all too familiar to me as my family's home place fell into fragmentation and dispute when my father died suddenly of a heart attack in 1981.

THE MOURNING HAD barely ceased when the stitches that had held the land together for so long came undone. Like many heir holdings, there was no formal plan for what would happen when the land was no longer held under the watch of a faithful caretaker and steward. Amidst the family dissension, confusion, and greed, the two hundred acres, most of it a forest, were ravaged. The abundant and valuable sawtimber—tall and straight—was taken first. And so an essential part of the home place's character, the trees that fed the Ashley heater and so much more, went cheaply to unscrupulous profiteers who killed the goose to get at the precious golden egg. The priceless oaks, poplars, pines, and hickories—worth fortunes for generations if tended artfully, were cut down without care—a marginal but quick profit for folks desperate for cash. The trade of green canopies for green cash seemed immoral if not criminal.

Within a few years of Daddy's death, the landscape was reminiscent of something a tornado had torn through: largely barren, with cast-off limbs and misshapen timber like splintered corpses across eroded slopes. The logging interlopers cut everything down to the riverbanks and then pushed what they couldn't sell into the creek. Once rich forest was now bare land. Water once clear and free-flowing now ran muddy and sluggish. Soil once rich and productive was carried downstream to some faraway delta where it might grow marsh grass but no longer piedmont forests. Once it was cashed out, the land was divided up among my relatives who, bless them, cared little for the soil and the wild legacy that made this place a true treasure. Like so many that are uniformed, they didn't realize that they held deed to some of the richest bounty God ever created.

Of the original two hundred or so acres I once roamed so freely, I now own almost seven, a mere fiefdom of a former kingdom. My inheritance is now overtaken by anorexic loblolly pines, scraggly sweetgum, and winged elm that prospered like weeds after the timbering devastation of the 1980s. It's hardly enough tree cover for a decent walk. Meanwhile the languishing land's absentee heirs are comfortable in the suburban and urban sprawl of Metropolis, far removed from Edgefield and South Carolina.

On another family property in Greenwood, South Carolina, I am trying to reconnect and manage almost a hundred and fifty acres of forestland. It used to be more like three hundred, but a land sale to finance a business venture removed some of the most valuable mature hardwoods from our ownership. A decade or so later, the business venture has long since failed and the mature hardwoods are now dog hair pines. The struggle now is to keep a portion of the remaining land from being liquidated to pay for past mistakes. Again, the land sits on a razor's edge, ownership balanced between African American heritage and reality.

SADLY, LOSSES LIKE my family's are all too common among rural landowners and seemingly epidemic among those of African descent. African Americans are two percent of the agricultural landowners in the United States and hold roughly one percent of the acreage and an equally miniscule proportion of real estate value. In my native South Carolina, black folks comprise roughly one-third of the populous. They only own about five percent of the private forestland. Forty acres and a mule is history, and few seem to care.

Recent reports on the status of South Carolina's forests cite "legacy" as a primary motivating factor in the conservation of the state's family forests. The thousand-acre question is "who'll carry on that legacy?" The dominant demographic of the African-American farmer nationally, men at least sixty years old, offers little hope for maintaining or growing a legacy. As these caretakers die and subsequent generations leave the land, from whence will the love and connection grow? Maybe as we decry the loss of biodiversity—feathered, finned, and furred—across the Southeast, we should also bemoan the loss of our diverse land-ownership class and its irreplaceable tie to the soil, water, trees, and wildlife that once gave us sustenance.

For a people so deeply tied to the soil, the flight from and disassociation of black folks from their land is a tragic story that will bear consequences long into the future if it is not addressed. The sons and daughters of African descent now have some semblance of civic equality. They are indeed becoming "connected" but to what? The wealth and power that comes from owning land, an appreciating commodity that empowers families, generations and communities, continues to escape from our grip.

This disconnection, if not repaired, will have serious consequences for the future of our beloved South. A look at a map of the Southeast and the distribution and density of poor black folks is startling. In South Carolina, still a predominantly rural place, a map depicting where the poor people live shows one little red dot for every five hundred people living in poverty. Already denoted as a "red" state" politically, I would argue that this represents the true character of the state and much of the region—significant portions of the population that are both black and poor and living in rural areas. The little red dots cover not just the Palmetto state but also Mississippi and Alabama and significant portions of the Deep South. How much power—economic, social, political—do these people have? Not as much as they should have. When the land was under "minority" ownership, its value was low-balled. But then, when it comes under "majority" ownership, suddenly the roads are better, the water cleaner, new schools and opportunities arise. Why such metamorphoses do not occur where black folks retain ownership of the land is a curious conundrum but one whose answer is like the elephant in the room—undeniable and obvious.

So how in this new millennium in the supposedly New South do we find or reinvigorate an African American land ethic? Any new land ethic for the South must embrace the virtues of justice and equality. Perhaps a first step in this outreach is simply understanding the numbers and status of rural lands remaining under black ownership. Agriculture and farming, long an economic staple of the South, used to represent a significant proportion of the black land ownership across the region. However, state and federal governments have recognized for some time that the American farmer is spiraling towards extinction in a tornado fed by globalization and factory farming.

The conservation of wild things and wild places, the rivers and swamps, forests and fields that define so much of the South's character, must be a priority in the region. Just as our condition as human beings is closely allied with the condition of the other living beings with which we share the Earth, so are we tied to the birds and beasts, and the habitats on which they depend. But far too often conservation is presented as a "human-less" endeavor, nature without humans, nature as the province of the elite. Nature for those with enough disposable income and time to trek through the "wilderness" or watch endangered wildlife in some isolation far removed from the hand of man. This view of nature considers everything except the folks on the land, who all too often in the "backwards South" are black. But shouldn't the preservation of culture be just as critical as the bobwhite quail and painted buntings? The appreciation of nature is not just some elitist pursuit but an inalienable right. Just as black folks should not have to suffer in neighborhoods that are disproportionately close to unhealthy industrial sites, or have to drink or wash in filthy water, they should not have to suffer the indignities of being displaced by wildlife or an inhumane desire to "restore nature" to some human-free condition.

Humans, nature, and conservation are not mutually exclusive. My thoughts are borne out by stories of success in my native South Carolina. Sandy Island is a biologically diverse and culturally unique island that sits between the Waccamaw and Pee Dee rivers, just south of the burgeoning, engulfing amoeboid monster that is Myrtle Beach. Here federally endangered red-cockaded woodpeckers and a host of other wildlife species coexist with a community of African Americans whose Gullah roots lie in the rice culture of the antebellum period. An island of cultural and biological diversity, it was perhaps inevitable that it would come under pressure from developers who sought to bring it into the current day by building a bridge linking it to the outside world. The initial promise was that only the timber would leave. But the residents and people who really cared knew that the bridge would only have been the first step. As the forests and all of its biodiversity disappeared, exclusive coastal development would follow. The red-cockaded woodpecker and the unique culture of the small black community, Mt. Rena, would have both been pushed even closer to extinction. However, persistent efforts by the residents, conservation organizations and eventual compromise from the majority landowners "saved" both nature and ethnic culture, and the bridge that would have brought "progress" was never built.

Preserving the Southern and African American culture and environment are both critical missions. Sadly, success stories like Sandy Island are few and far between. On other fronts environmental protection veils the inequities that further drive a wedge between African Americans, nature and the land ethic.

But saving the land and all that it means is not simply an effort to be made by the majority community. Nature belongs to all and so it is an African American responsibility, too. We will love only what we understand, and an understanding that land is important for the ultimate survival of all living things depends upon our ability to reach those younglings living in a world of virtual reality. We must reconnect our children with the natural world outside of the digital realm. If black children, who have the freedom-loving genes of West Africans and resilient rural African Americans coursing through their bodies, can be reconnected to the long-lost memories of towering trees, flowing rivers, singing birds, and soul-sustaining soil, then we might stand a fighting chance.

I often travel to our family's home place in Edgefield in my mind. I imagine what things would have been like had my father survived or even if he had died with some directive as to how to keep the land and its legacy intact. But dreaming of what could have been does little to restore the failing legacy. My fear is that one day, I'll visit the property that used to be ours and there'll be gates and no trespassing signs. I'm afraid that some wealthy opportunist will take advantage of the situation and kidnap the legacy. Spirit it away to serve a very different master. A few dollars or negligence and ignorance exchanged for a legacy—again. History's propensity for repetition is well documented and I fear it may be targeting us. As my people strive to achieve, I hope that it is not at the cost of giving up one of the most precious commodities. Land is the ultimate investment. Living in the rural South without a connection to the land means limited power—economic, social, and political. Aldo Leopold said that "We shall never achieve harmony with land, any more than we shall achieve absolute justice or liberty for people. In these higher aspirations the important thing is not to achieve, but to strive." Maybe African American heirs will wake up. Maybe the government will devise programs that combine conservation of the land with conservation of the people. We have to try. I think the place to start is in the South—maybe in places like my home place, Edgefield, South Carolina. ⁊

THE TUPELO SOLUTION

A MEDIUM FOR THE COMMON GOOD

DANNY DUNCAN COLLUM

In the past five years, Americans have become painfully aware of the price we are paying for the monopolized and dumbed-down state of our mainstream news media. During those years, lax oversight by the Federal Communications Commission, combined with market forces, has resulted in a small number of very large multinational corporations owning the bulk of our information sources. Chain ownership of local media outlets has stilled independent voices in the heartland and disconnected many local broadcast and newspaper operations from the lives of the communities they serve. The Jeffersonian vision of a free and literate populace conducting an informed face-to-face debate has faded from memory. Instead we are becoming a nation of harried, distracted worker-consumers surrounded at all times by screens that tell us what to buy and what to think.

During the run-up to the Iraq war in 2002–2003, we saw what can happen to the nation when the free flow of information and ideas dries up. The corporate media institutions—the New York Times, the Washington Post and the television networks that follow their lead—abdicated the watchdog function and refused to ask critical questions as the nation was rushed to war. To its credit, a second-tier national newspaper chain, Knight-Ridder, did find facts that contradicted the official story. But because its papers were read in places like Philadelphia, Miami, and Akron—not

New York or Washington—the Knight-Ridder stories never got on the big screen.

That episode was a depressing example of a highly centralized, corporate-controlled news media at its worst. And by the way, the Knight-Ridder chain that got the story right no longer exists. It was sold off and broken up in 2005.

But down home in Mississippi, I have seen an equally vivid example of what a responsible, locally owned and community-oriented news media institution can do. It is impossible to overstate the importance of locally owned and locally engaged news media for the civic health of America. Consider the impact the *Northeast Mississippi Daily Journal* of Tupelo, Mississippi, has had on that community and the fifteen-county region around it.

Rather than pandering to the lowest common denominator, the *Daily Journal* has exercised leadership in its community, sometimes even getting a little bit ahead of its readership. And instead of pursuing an ever-growing profit margin at any cost, the *Daily Journal* has plowed its profits back into the community, with a special focus on public education.

In its seventy years of daily publication, the *Journal* has played the leading role in creating a healthy civic culture that has allowed people in the Tupelo area to find common ground and come together around common goals. In the 1930s, the *Daily Journal* supported workers' rights to organize. In the years after World War II, it led the Tupelo area to reject low-wage industries. Instead Tupelo invested in improving its work force through quality public education and waited for higher-paying industries to come. In 1954, when the White Citizens' Councils sprang up across Mississippi in response to the U.S. Supreme Court's *Brown* school desegregation decision, the *Daily Journal* editorialized against the Councils. Attempts to organize one in Tupelo failed. Soon after that controversy, a virulently segregationist daily paper was started in Tupelo to compete with the *Daily Journal*, but after a couple of years it failed, too.

This early stance bore fruit in the 1960s, when Tupelo became one of the only towns in the Deep South to voluntarily desegregate its schools, workforce, and public facilities.

Tupelo is still mainly known outside Mississippi as the birthplace of Elvis Presley. But largely as a result of the progressive civic culture nurtured by the leadership of its regional newspaper, northeast Mississippi has gone from being the poorest region in the nation's poorest state to become the most prosperous part of Mississippi, with incomes at or near the national average. The Tupelo public schools regularly receive national awards. The town has twice been named an "All-American City" by the National Civic League. There are more than two hundred furniture factories within an hour's drive of Tupelo (some are unionized), and the city's furniture market is the country's second largest.

In recent years Tupelo has become home to high-tech manufacturers, especially in auto parts. In 2009, a Toyota assembly plant will open near Tupelo and employ up to four thousand northeast Mississippians at a starting wage of twenty dollars per hour, almost double the current median per-capita wage for the state. The still-small town of thirty-six thousand population (with seventy-five thousand in surrounding Lee County) is an island of progressive, sustainable community development in a Southland still often mired in poverty and racial divisions. And it is a manufacturing center that is growing and adding better-paying jobs, even as the national U.S. manufacturing economy slides into deeper decline.

One important moving and guiding force behind Tupelo's community development process has been its local daily newspaper.

DANNY DUNCAN COLLUM, a native of Greenwood, Mississippi, is an assistant professor of English and journalism at Kentucky State University in Frankfort and a columnist and contributing editor for *Sojourners* magazine. He is also the author of three nonfiction books, most recently *Black and Catholic in the Jim Crow South* (Paulist 2006).

THE REMARKABLE STORY of the *Daily Journal* began in 1934 when a twenty-nine-year-old Winona, Mississippi, native named George McLean, as he later put it, "bought a bankrupt bi-weekly newspaper from a bankrupt bank in the middle of a depression." McLean had not intended to be a newspaper man. He'd grown up in a prosperous cotton-farming family and had set out to become a Presbyterian minister. He was a deeply religious young man—too religious, as it turned out. He read the Old Testament prophets and their cries against the oppression of the poor, and he read the parts of the New Testament that suggest our religion should be judged by the way we treat the hungry and the outcast, regardless of race. Worse, McLean took it all seriously. He soon decided that these "radical" views rendered him unfit for the Presbyterian ministry.

McLean turned to academia as a refuge of free thought. He did graduate work at Boston University, Stanford, and the University of Chicago and landed a job teaching philosophy and sociology at Adrian College, a small Methodist school in Michigan. Then he got the chance to come home to the Deep South and teach at Southwestern (now Rhodes) College in Memphis. Academia worked for McLean, as long as he confined his unconventional views to the classroom. But in Memphis he crossed that line, too, and got involved with the Christian socialists who were organizing the biracial Southern Tenant Farmers Union, just across the Mississippi River in the Arkansas cotton fields. McLean's activism led to confrontations with the Memphis political powers and got him fired from Southwestern.

Only then, when he had been driven from the respectable professions for which he was suited, did McLean turn to journalism. He went home to the Mississippi hills and took a job as a reporter at the local paper in Grenada, Mississippi. He enjoyed the work. And as he did it, he conceived the notion that a newspaper could provide both an independent platform for his progressive ideas and an economic institution with which to test them out. When he heard that the *Tupelo Journal* was for sale, he drew on some family money and made the purchase.

McLean turned out to have a knack for the newspaper business. In short order, he assembled a solid professional staff, made the biweekly paper a daily, and began making money. But in McLean's view, profit was never a goal for its own sake; profit was only valuable because it allowed him to accomplish a larger purpose.

As owner and publisher of the daily newspaper, McLean was a *de facto* community leader. He threw himself into this role. When northeast Mississippi business leaders wanted to diversify the region's agriculture, McLean volunteered to travel to the University of Wisconsin and became an expert on the dairy industry. The *Journal* supported the workers during a 1937 sit-down strike at the Tupelo Cotton Mill, and McLean was recognized by the socialist-leaning *Nation* magazine as its "man of the year." He was then an anathema to most of the Tupelo business community. But after World War II, by dint of his personality, vocal Christianity, and community enthusiasm, that earlier period seems to have been forgotten. McLean was appointed head of the Tupelo Chamber of Commerce. Within a couple of years he had changed the name of the organization to the Community Development Foundation and steered it away from a narrow focus on business interests and toward a broader, cooperative approach. One of his first projects was to organize Rural Community Development Councils, modeled on New England town meetings that organized people of the country around Tupelo, black and white alike, for service and development projects. The *Journal* reported on the activities of these Councils, and it began to develop a regional readership, beyond the confines of Tupelo. This set it on its way to becoming what it is today, the largest-circulation rural newspaper in America.

For the rest of his career, McLean served as the volunteer director of the Community Development Foundation, while continuing as publisher of the *Daily Journal*. Years later, McLean enumerated the principles by which he operated the *Journal* in a manifesto that is still found on the *Daily Journal* website (www.djournal. com). He wrote:

1. Human Resources are our most vital assets . . . Without good people you cannot build a good business or a good community.

2. The Journal is one of the important agencies in the development of this community . . . it has a vital role to play in cooperation with all other institutions in this area.

3. The Journal has the special responsibility of providing news and advertising messages as well as editorially expressing the honest convictions of its Editor and Publisher without fear or favor . . . The Daily Journal is an independent, locally owned newspaper . . . it does not believe that a newspaper's worth or influence is to be measured by being for or against a particular person or party.

4. . . . A newspaper must be financially strong if it hopes to survive during times of economic stress or withstand public or private pressure . . .

5. This Publisher believes that a local newspaper and other local business institutions must go far beyond written or oral support of worthwhile causes. This newspaper has a responsibility to freely give manpower and money to assist organizations that are seeking to make the Tupelo area a better place in which to live.

6. The Journal believes that informed, enlightened and active citizens constitute the only sure foundation of a democracy. Therefore, the Journal seeks to become one of the best newspapers in America in cities of comparable size.

7. Unless a newspaper is read by the people it cannot effectively serve its community. For that reason more emphasis is placed on an ever larger circulation than in any other small

city in America . . .

8. No city, no county is an island to itself alone. All of us go forward together or we tend to stagnate together . . . For this reason the Journal has for many years supported rural development and the development of human resources in every county or city in this region.

9. A basic obligation of any business institution is to provide for its own employees. Many years ago the Journal management started pension programs to help care for the needs of its retired employees. It also has a profit sharing, guaranteed annual wages, payroll insurance in case of sickness, as well as hospital and life insurance.

10. We are convinced both by the experience of this business institution and by careful study that the most basic foundation on which the life of an individual or of an institution can be erected is the one found in Luke 6:38 "Give, and it will be given to you; good measure, pressed down, shaken together, running over, will be put into your lap. For the measure you give will be the measure you get back." There is far more real truth in this than in anything that Adam Smith, the father of Capitalism, or Karl Marx, the father of Communism, ever said . . . We believe that the development throughout northeast Mississippi is due to this same unselfish, cooperative helpfulness that has characterized the majority of the people in this area . . . We pledge the best efforts of this newspaper and its staff to the promotion and realization of a better life for every person in every aspect of existence.

At the very beginning of his ownership, McLean gave the *Daily Journal* the slogan: "A locally owned newspaper dedicated to the service of God and Mankind" that still appears on its masthead. In 1973, McLean began preparing for his departure from the scene. At that time he and his wife started a charitable foundation, CRE-

ATE ("Christian Research, Educational and Technical Enterprises") and donated their controlling interest in the Journal Publishing Company to the foundation. Thus the dividends from the *Journal's* stock became a revenue stream for community development, and the local ownership of the newspaper was secured for all time. Of this decision McLean wrote:

> The owners of the Journal Publishing Company are so committed to local ownership and responsible service to all the people of this area that plans have been put into effect to enable the Northeast Mississippi Daily Journal to be perpetually owned and operated by local people . . . We feel that this service must include not only the contribution made through the printed word but also through the active involvement of members of its staff in every worthwhile civic undertaking . . .
>
> We regard the increasing concentration of ownership of newspapers, radio, and television stations in the hands of a few big chains as potentially very dangerous to freedom of information in this country. Another serious problem with increasing outside control of the media is that the . . . the desire for more and more profits, will take the place of service to readers, listeners or advertisers. We believe that the greatness of a newspaper should be judged not by its size of profitability, but by the quality of its news and advertising and particularly by the service it renders to all the people in the area it serves . . .
>
> Because we live here and love the people of this community we have sought to be a constructive force in this area . . . The Daily Journal is a responsible newspaper that does not believe every time a donkey brays it has to publicize the event. Since some people are seeking to set one group against another, we at the Journal believe our staff has the responsibility of deciding what is constructive and what is destructive . . . A newspaper or other news media should be judged as much by what it refuses

to print or broadcast as by what it does . . .

We firmly believe that it is more blessed to give than to receive; that the measure we give will be the measure we receive. This applies in a business. If any one of the following groups—management, labor, consumer—is out for all it can get, there will inevitably develop the feeling that others are "enemies or suckers" . . . Cooperation and unselfish service create a better company or community, whereas conflict and selfishness inevitably destroy a company, a community, or a nation.

In these statements, McLean's rhetoric echoes the speeches Frank Capra put into the mouths of his populist heroes in movies such as *Meet John Doe, Mr. Smith Goes to Washington* and *It's a Wonderful Life*. In fact, McLean's *Daily Journal* became in Tupelo what "George Bailey's" Building and Loan was in Bedford Falls, an institution through which people were both empowered to achieve their dreams and inspired to be their best selves.

McLean died in 1983. Twenty-five years later, Tupelo is a world center of upholstered furniture manufacturing and is poised to become a big player in the auto industry. McLean's newspaper no longer looms as large on the local landscape as it did forty years ago. But it is still a major force in the community, both in its pages (and, increasingly, on its website) and through the education and leadership development projects funded by its owner, CREATE. The Tupelo ethos of cooperation that McLean established through his newspaper is still very much evident in the political and economic culture of northeast Mississippi. It was widely cited as a reason for Tupelo's selection as a plant site by Toyota. And McLean's distinctive vision for community journalism is much evident in today's *Northeast Mississippi Daily Journal.*

GEORGE MCLEAN NEVER lost the commitment to social justice that led him to work with the Southern Tenant Farmers Union, or the fervent faith that had made him aspire to the ministry. He placed his social gospel brand of Christianity at the center of his vision for the *Daily Journal*, writing, unabashedly, in his statement of purpose:

> We believe that persons are of infinite importance on this planet and in the universe; that God is our Father and is not an abstract force; that God is a God whose mighty acts in history reveal his nature. He is a God of everlasting love "who practices kindness, justice, and righteousness in the earth," as Jeremiah said. This was supremely revealed in Jesus of Nazareth "who came not to be served but to serve and give his life for others." . . .

That might rub people the wrong way in New York. But it goes over well in northeast Mississippi, where the culture is almost monolithically Christian, Protestant, and evangelical. McLean's religious roots, and his willingness to expose them in his newspaper, contributed to his credibility and to the readers' sense of identification with the newspaper.

My own exposure to the *Daily Journal* began in the summer of 1997, my wife, Polly, and I were preparing to move to Ripley, a very small town in the hills of northeast Mississippi near Tupelo. Though Polly and I are both white and Catholic, we joke that we have a mixed marriage. She is from the landscaped eastern suburbs of Cleveland, Ohio, and I am from the herbicide-infused cotton fields of Greenwood, Mississippi. This move to the Magnolia State was a great adventure for each of us. She had never lived in Mississippi, and I was going back after nineteen years in mostly self-imposed exile.

On our first house-hunting trip to the area, we were staying in the better of Ripley's two motels when I went to the lobby early in the morning for a cup of coffee and a newspaper. Outside the lobby, I was confronted by two newspaper boxes—the omnipresent *U.S.A. Today* and the *Northeast Mississippi Daily Journal,* with McLean's "God and Mankind" banner slogan.

That didn't bode well. Only once before in my life had I seen a daily newspaper that touted God on the front page. That was a paper in Indianapolis that put out a Bible verse every day. And its contents would only have been considered centrist and mainstream if you belonged to the John Birch Society. I knew that the *Daily Journal* was published in nearby Tupelo, and I knew that Tupelo was the headquarters of the Reverend Donald Wildmon's American Family Association—a Christian Right outfit that specialized in calling boycotts of television programs.

Still, as I stood in the hot morning sun with my coffee in one hand and two quarters in the other, I figured that if we were going to live here we would have to get used to this sort of thing. So I dropped my coins in the *Daily Journal* slot and retreated to our room.

My reading of the *Daily Journal* that day did nothing to confirm my expectations. It turned out to be a thoroughly professional small-market daily paper. It was filled with news of the fifteen counties of Mississippi's hill country. To the urban reader, there appeared to be a shortage of crime stories. But if the paper betrayed any bias, it was one in favor of public education, economic development and racial harmony.

ONCE WE'D FOUND a house and moved in, we became subscribers to the *Daily Journal* and began to notice some its striking peculiarities. For instance, the paper employed a full-time religion reporter. At the time I was a daily reader, that reporter was John Armistead, a motorcycle-riding painter, novelist, and Baptist minister with a doctorate from the Graduate Theological Union in Berkeley, California. Armistead had been pastor of Harrisburg Baptist Church, the most prestigious Baptist congregation in town, until his first detective novel was published. Armistead was then pushed out of the pulpit by church ladies offended at his characters' profanity. At the *Daily Journal*, Armistead turned his Saturday religion page into a free-floating religious studies seminar in which discussions of Buddhism, Islam, or Judaism appeared alongside the usual reports of Vacation Bible Schools and revival meetings.

Today the editor of the *Daily Journal* is Lloyd Gray. Gray's grandfather, father and brother have all been Episcopal priests and bishops of Mississippi (all named Duncan Gray). In 1962, Lloyd Gray's father, the Episcopal chaplain at the University of Mississippi, heroically defended the right of James Meredith to become the first black student at Ole Miss.

Of his journalistic work, Gray told me, "Theologically I am drawn by the notion of community, and building community is the way the *Daily Journal* is in 'service of God and mankind.' It requires concern for the welfare of every individual, which in turn leads to the strengthening of the whole." Gray also notes, "We are probably one of the smallest daily papers . . . to have a full-time religion editor [and] we declare ourselves firmly in the Christian tradition each weekend with an editorial that reflects on the ramifications of faith in how we live our individual and corporate lives."

Those Sunday editorials are one of the *Journal's* most distinctive features. They might include reflections from Quaker Richard Foster or Catholic mystic Henri Nouwen; hardly what you'd expect in the Baptist-ruled Bible Belt. One piece on election-year religion consisted mostly of quotes from a book by progressive evangelical author Jim Wallis. Gray says the editorials "affirm the religiosity of our readership while offering, sometimes subtly and sometimes not, a different sort of theology than that of the dominant religious culture. I know of no chain-based newspaper that would believe 'faith-based' editorials to be appropriate. I may be wrong, but I believe this practice is virtually unique among secular daily newspapers."

The paper also provides its readers with a fair summary of national and world events, drawn from the wire services and national papers. I know that I felt less informed about the big world, and saw a lot less negative news about the then-new war in Iraq, when we moved outside the *Journal*'s home delivery area and started getting our daily news from a chain-owned paper in Memphis. The *Journal* also makes independent endorsements in state and national political races, pleasing almost no one in the process. For instance, in 2000 it endorsed Al Gore for president, and in 2003 it endorsed Republican lobbyist Haley Barbour for governor.

As the Tupelo region becomes more and more prosperous in decades ahead, we can bet that the *Daily Journal* will take on the role of holding new generations of business leaders to McLean's standards of "servant leadership" and echo his warning against becoming "materialistic-minded" people.

The history, and current practice, of the *Northeast Mississippi Daily Journal* proves, if we needed proof, that a local media outlet can change the way people see themselves and their community and inspire them to act in new ways. That is the possibility that is being extinguished with every media merger. As editorial page editor Joe Rutherford put it when I asked him what makes the *Journal* different from chain-owned newspapers, "We actually give a damn about place and people." ❧

Can a Third World Town Be Saved?

The Future of New Orleans

Jason Berry

In late July 2007, an engineer was murdered on a "quiet block" in the Carrollton neighborhood, seven blocks from the sunny, book-lined room where I write. Let me call his name, Anthony White, lest he sink into a forgotten roster of New Orleans murder victims since Hurricane Katrina. White was fifty-four, an engineer from the north Louisiana town of Pineville, a construction inspector working on two federal office buildings downtown, one of an army of specialists come to repair the flood-battered city. Just before 3 A.M., he returned to his home-away-from-home, a pool house behind a big house. You'd think that would be safe.

"Someone shot him once in the face at close range, then ran over him twice before fleeing in White's vehicle," the *Times-Picayune* reported. As of October there had been no arrest.

We are past the second anniversary of Hurricane Katrina and the epic flood that saturated 80 percent of the city. A tenth of New Orleans police officers bolted when Katrina hit on August 29, 2005, several taking Cadillacs from a dealership floor on their way out of town. Worse yet, NOPD lost its computerized records in the flood. A mounting tide of unsolved murders and botched prosecutions is one symptom of a criminal justice system in tatters. The DA's office has been in a free fall. District Attorney Eddie Jordan fired veteran white staffers and replaced them after his 2002 election with black supporters of his patron, Congressman Bill Jefferson. The sackees filed suit against Jordan, an African American, charging reverse discrimination. Jordan was humiliated by the $1.9 million verdict, which rose to $3.7 million as interest accumulated. With a year remaining in his term, Jordan resigned, leaving Mayor Ray Nagin and others to cobble together a payoff plan for the plaintiffs. Meanwhile, most homicides go unprosecuted.

In another season, the disasters of a backwater democracy might pass like a thundercloud with a yawn from jaded voters. But we have been to the apocalypse. The "recovery" transmogrified into an aching melodrama of corruption and incompetence: politics at every level—federal, state, local—is our waking nightmare. On top of that, New Orleans threatens to be remembered as the place where the civil rights movement went to die—a black-majority city that insisted on reelecting a disastrous mayor, C. Ray Nagin, simply because he was black. Nagin offered a cynical grin toward the gains of the civil rights movement, while the American city with the deepest African identity gasped on life support beneath his watch.

New Orleans in the early post-Katrina years is a schizophrenic city, with much of the historic beauty, many of its cultural attractions, and certain neighborhoods flourishing by virtue of being in areas away from the worst flooding. The failure of Nagin and other elected officials to rebuild the areas that did flood has turned New Orleans into a political psychodrama, dragged down by waste and decay we associate with urban nightmares of the Third World.

Most of its 455,000 residents evacuated when Katrina hit. The city was then 67 percent African-American. By the fall of 2007, 60 percent of the population had returned, with a 58 percent black

JASON BERRY is known for his investigations of the Catholic Church crisis, *Lead Us Not Into Temptation* and, with Gerald Renner, *Vows of Silence*, the subject of a forthcoming documentary film. His play *Earl Long in Purgatory* won a Big Easy award. His current book, *Last of the Red Hot Poppas*, is a comic novel about Louisiana politics.

majority. Hopes of "recovery" gave way to a succession of horror stories, amidst political blunders from Washington to Baton Rouge down to City Hall, while drug thugs turned the nightly TV news into a show on urban homicide.

The old persona of the good-times town, rocking to the rhythms of an ethnic crossroads, is undergoing an identity shift. Carnival parades use scalding satire as commentary on the pathologies that govern us; but deeper questions endure. Are we a victim city or a recovery city? Can the city transcend failed politics? Will it recede deeper into a Third World city, with prosperous areas ever-threatened by zones of poverty, abandoned by City Hall and riddled with crime . . . or will the best impulses of people seeking to rebuild the city find the means to make "reform" into a movement of critical mass?

The optimists ask a simpler question: how will the remade city look?

Politics and the Flood

Urban planners, architects, and an army of idealistic young people have put down stakes here, at least for the near term, believing that the best of what New Orleans used to be is worth preserving and building up. Those who came back made a statement of our own: we are here *by choice.* Many professionals, academics, medical personnel, attorneys and others moved away for perfectly understandable reasons: options for their children's schools, rising home insurance costs, better living environments, fear of crime, and aversion to the craven theatre hereabouts that we otherwise call politics.

New Orleans hovers at the top of America cities in per capita homicides, regaining a position it held a decade ago when a new police superintendent instituted reforms. That chief, Richard Pennington, had the misfortune to think that his success at reducing crime qualified him for higher office. He ran for mayor against

C. Ray Nagin in 2002 and went packing to Atlanta in the aftermath. Nagin might have waltzed through a second term, pushing tourism and ignoring the deplorable poverty in which roughly a third of the town was stuck. Instead Hurricane Katrina pounded New Orleans and Gulf Coast communities to the east. The city flooded, courtesy of a flawed levee system run by the U.S. Army Corps of Engineers.

Most of the population evacuated. Most of the people trapped in the flooding did not break laws; however the world watched looters wade through the streets, carting off DVD players, clothes, and shoes. The country that put men on the moon could not rescue people stranded in the Superdome. The police chief, Eddie Compass, had a nervous breakdown, though it was not fully apparent when he told a national TV audience that babies had been raped in the Dome—an urban myth to say the least. Realizing that Compass was damaged goods, Nagin replaced him with Warren Riley, an NOPD veteran who had been suspended three times in his rise through the ranks.

Mayor Nagin's TV performances since Katrina have been marked by spectacular verbal gaffes, as when he recently said of crime: "It's not good for us, but it also keeps the New Orleans brand out there"—oblivious to the sizzling impact his own utterances have on the branding.

As the Mississippi River flood of 1927 altered American politics, setting the stage for Huey Long, FDR, and the New Deal, so Hurricane Katrina hammered the George W. Bush presidency as the unpopular war in Iraq dragged on. Today a major political realignment seems at hand. Perhaps the 2008 election will see a philosophical sea change if the Democrats articulate a set of political values to heal a wounded land. (They could, alternatively, win back a decisive majority in Congress by default.)

New Orleans is the other side of the Iraq story, the domestic benchmark of a bad administration. Jim Amoss, the editor who guided the Pulitzer Prize-winning coverage of Katrina for the *Times-Picayune* writes: "The vast urban expanse that flooded—an area seven times the size of Manhattan that stayed for three weeks in five to twelve feet of saltwater—is still struggling back to life." When has the persona of a city been so altered so quickly, or a president been so damaged by a singular event? TV pictures across the globe showed people trapped on rooftops, bloated corpses and sunken cars, old folk in wheelchairs, women and babies, looters with grocery carts. Government took five days to evacuate hospitals. Most people fled to far-flung places, staying for weeks or months.

Ronald Reagan decried "big government" and dismantled the New Deal that lifted millions of people out of poverty. Twenty years later, George W. Bush slashed taxes and gave us obese government, spending trillions as America ran up a swollen debt to Chinese banks to finance his war in Iraq. Four years after the terrorist attacks of 9/11, Katrina's floodwaters exposed an inept emergency response system as more than one hundred thousand homes went underwater in southeast Louisiana. After telling his soon-to-be-sacked FEMA director, "Brownie, you're doing a heckuva job," Bush's popularity plunged, swamped by an image of detachment and incompetence.

Human error produced the flood: flawed Mississippi levee projects by the U.S. Army Corps of Engineers, and environmental wreckage by government and oil companies that caused eroision of the wetlands south and east of the city. Some ten thousand miles of finger canals carved by oil companies were central to the sinkage. The lost wetlands gave tidal waves an open alley to the city. But the dynamics of this failure are national in scope. Massive flooding has become a ten-second story in the flow of national television news—floods striking New England, the Midwest, Texas and New York, among other places, in the two years since Katrina. As the political system reacts to global climate change, communities along the Atlantic seaboard are at risk.

"The cost of a collapsing coast is one of fundamental survival," says Mark Davis, who as director of the Coalition to Restore Coastal Louisiana worked on the issue for years in Baton Rouge, before taking a position at Tulane University Law School. The flooding that followed Katrina "was the failure of a value system," he continues. "We assumed we had tamed the forces of nature. We need to understand that if we want there to be a New Orleans or a Miami or a New York five hundred years from now, we can't assume they'll be there. We have to *plan* for them to be there. That's why the rise in sea levels and freshwater management are so extraordinary."

The broad regional recovery that President Bush promised in a speech at Jackson Square in the week after Katrina has not materialized. In New Orleans, the first two years of recovery were meager at best, stillborn at worst.

Insurance companies stiff-armed many policy owners, particularly over water damage, telling them that the losses caused when roofs collapsed and rains poured into their homes were the result of flooding, not wind—and therefore, federally backed flood insurance policies should cover them. People without flood policies faced mammoth losses. Because the levee failure was produced by a federal agency, the Army Corps of Engineers, Congress allocated $7.5 billion to Louisiana for what became the Road Home program. Under this plan, tens of thousands of homeowners filed applications for grants to cover what insurance did not. Most of them waited . . . and waited . . . and waited for funds that were bottled up by ICF, a Virginia company which Gov. Kathleen Blanco—fearing Louisiana's reputation for political corruption—approved to process and disperse funds. The retarded pace at which ICF did its job wrecked Blanco's reelection prospects. ICF was itself a scandal; the CEO received a $1 million bonus for his work on the contract.

Keeping murders down is not much of a gauge on any town's progress; but in aging river city, so rich in culture, where the marshes south of us are being swallowed by the Gulf—leaving ten years to repair the wetlands lest the Gulf literally turns into our slurping back yard—homicides are a portent, a sign of greater collapse. Unless . . . unless.

Sell-out by GOP Social Darwinists

I wonder what readers a quarter-century hence will think of this book as they gaze back on the post-millennial South, a topography of beef-red electoral states where a white majority marched in Republican lockstep as the number of black males behind bars soared across the decades that followed the 1965 Voting Rights Act. Did those academics, writers, and intellectuals hatch a consensus in *American Crisis, Southern Solutions*? Or did they deliver an ironic echo of the Agrarians' pining for a lost world in *I'll Take My Stand*? The cultural conservatives and Fugitive poets associated with Vanderbilt University in the 1930s recoiled from the industrialization of the South, prophetically so. What they did not know about black people was gigantic; thus we fault their sentimental yearning for a paternalist order of neofeudalism. The sense of collective loss in the book you hold is more angry (and less eulogistic) in its regard for another type of lost order—the post-civil rights society in which, so many of us once hoped, the working class of black and white Southerners would find enlightened leadership to heal the wounds of division and chart a path toward prosperity and sustainable growth.

Some Southern governors did well—Reuben Askew and Lawton Chiles in Florida, Jimmy Carter in Georgia, Bill Clinton in Arkansas, William Winter in Mississippi, Terry Sanford in North Carolina, Doug Wilder and Mark Warner in Virginia, among others. But the region suffered from the heavy hand of religious zealots, and the big backlash from Republican presidents. Richard Nixon targeted fearful whites with the now-infamous "Southern strategy." Ronald Reagan appealed more blatantly to an Old South that would "rise again" as he launched his 1980 campaign in Philadelphia, Mississippi, where three civil rights workers were murdered sixteen years before. George W. Bush, who dodged his military duty in Vietnam, used the South Carolina primary in 2000 for a display of character assassination against Senator John McCain, who was tortured as a war prisoner in Hanoi, against a red-hot political backdrop of preserving the Rebel flag! What psychological projection Karl Rove wrought.

Genuine leadership, we have learned too painfully in the last seven years, really does matter; the people who win elections do make a difference, often a huge one in ordinary lives, as so many young soldiers returned from Iraq with missing limbs and battered minds, and their families, know only too well. The Southern Strategy of the GOP found a wonderful prize in the Evangelical Christian movement which, from its early outrage over abortion, managed to sell out the Book of Genesis's primordial emphasis on the purity of water and land. Christian conservatives marched like sheep behind demagogues like Rush Limbaugh as George W. Bush gutted environmental safeguards. Free-market cannibals devoured economies of scale across the small-town South, installing Wal-Mart as the New Jerusalem.

Can you hear the Agrarians groaning from the grave? They were, after all, environmentalists before the term was coined.

Police sirens wail as I type these lines.

It is tempting in the autumn of 2007 to speculate that the Republican South with basement ratings in literacy and child nutrition, with high marks in church attendance, sex crimes and gun ownership, will have a crock with the GOP values-fandango and turn toward the Democratic camp with a hand to the ear. Yet even if part of the South goes blue, in the current electoral jargon, we should be clear about what it means. Such a victory might not be a ringing endorsement for the Democrats' agenda, so much as a vote against the hypocrisy oozing out of a Republican Party, so entwined with Christian triumphalists and tarred by sex scandals.

There is also a simpler political law that has taken root with traditional party affiliations on the wane. People vote for personalities who make them feel comfortable and safe. They vote for people they think they like, based on their TV exposure. Political TV has simplified the American mind: feelings count more than issues. TV attack ads are designed to pump intestinal distress into the body politic so that fewer people vote and those who do will swallow *merde* to elect a candidate.

The social Darwinists who ran Congress for the twelve years before 2007 appealed to old-fashioned social values about childbearing and sexual orientation, harnessed to a putative agenda of conservative economics. The actual delivery system lagged some, starting with Newt Gingrich, who as House Speaker was cheating on his wife while he led the impeachment of Bill Clinton for cheating on his. That both men lied about their infidelities, at first, is truly an afterthought, though Clinton might have avoided being impeached if he had admitted so up front. Post-Gingrich, the GOP congressional majority became a penguin army behind Bush, approving his gigantic deficits, backing the war, betraying the essence of conservative governance with a parade of money-stuffing congressmen and lobbyists who ended up indicted or in the pen. Washington's version of the TV show *Law and Order* had begun unfolding as Katrina shattered New Orleans and the Mississippi coast.

When a city drowns on Monday morning television, sirens go off in the national brain. The congressional majority that kept its children out of Iraq, however, showed its pathological detachment when House Speaker Denny Hastert grumbled that New Orleans might be better off "bulldozed."

Whoa, now! Wha-bout that Gulf-a-Mexico oil, Mr. Speaker? Bulldoze dem Noo Awlins docks, too?

A government that ignores people in a flood, and then tries to screw them financially after a broken federal levee system, is a government most people don't want. That simple lesson of Katrina floated into the 2006 midterm elections alongside rising revulsion toward the Iraq war. Voters will inhale the small lies as a byproduct of democracy; they gag on floor shows of mendacity.

Rockin' Ray and the Civil Rights Sell-out Show

New Orleans faded from national media focus six months *before* the 2006 midterms because of Mayor Ray Nagin's reelection. As the media narrative moved from a disaster zone to recovery hopes, Nagin's loose-lipped remarks magnified the image of a city without a grip. His bizarre televised comments signaled a poverty of leadership, indeed a turn toward demagoguery by an African American who knew better. On Martin Luther King Jr. Day 2006, as the mayor's race accelerated, Nagin revealed that he'd had a conversation with God. Mind you, in these latitudes we are used to Protestant televangelists sharing with us details of their chats with the Almighty. (As a Catholic I marvel at these sound-bites of perspiring mysticism.) When a *politician* says he has heard from God, follow Jelly Roll Morton's lyrics: "Open up the window and let the bad air out."

Nagin announced that God disapproved of the Iraq War. It's not hard to believe that the Jesus who said "peacemakers will inherit the earth" is no fan of American policy in Iraq; but why would Our Savior tell . . . Ray Nagin?

And then, in the lines that would make him the butt of countless jokes on TV talk shows—and simultaneously secure his reelection—Nagin announced that New Orleans was "a chocolate city" and would always be one.

The comment jolted whites, who wondered where they fit in the mix, while African Americans—thousands of whom were displaced by the flood and livid at being politically stiff-armed—nodded. They saw Bush as a fraud and FEMA as an enemy. Nagin was standing up for them. That's how polarized this city had become. Indeed,

Nagin was on a strange odyssey of politics.

In the early weeks after Katrina, with barely a third of the population back, most of those who returned had homes and businesses in the "dry ridge" areas of higher ground that lay closest to the French Quarter and parts of Uptown. With mountains of debris lining streets across the city, one heard a mantra in the dry ridge: "Now we can get it *right*"—meaning a city rinsed of its underclass, wiped clean of a political past stigmatized by poverty and crime, and not meaning that regressive property taxes had short-sold city services and schools.

Nagin was an executive with Cox Cable when he ran as a reformer in 2002. "Nagin comes out of the business community and thinks the private sector has the keys to the kingdom and capacity for the solution," Dr. Rudy Lombard, an urban planner who got his start as a movement activist in Algiers, told me. "Nagin does not have an accurate perspective . . . The city's needs *overwhelm* the resources of government."

One saw early signs of Nagin's naïve faith in the marketplace soon after Katrina. Bush gave his speech at Jackson Square, promising the sky, and flew off to Washington. As Congress moved in no special hurry on desperately needed funds, Nagin never used his sudden fame to mount a bully pulpit, rallying the nation to support his city. Instead, he followed the advice of the biggest land developer in town, Joe Canizaro, one of Bush's biggest financial backers, and convened a seventeen-member Bring New Orleans Back Commission. The Commission relied heavily on the Urban Land Institute, a nonprofit think-tank in Washington, D.C., funded by real estate developers, for a strategy on how to design the new city. Canizaro, a former chairman of the U.L.I., was an instrumental figure in the process; though he ended up disappointed with Nagin.

Plans for a resurrected city called for upgrading the levee system to withstand Category 5 hurricanes, new buildings in neighborhoods that did not flood and a careful review of flooded areas with an eye for demolitions to create ponds and low-lying parks to absorb future flooding. All of this would turn on an idea embraced by editorial writers in lofty chambers of the *Chicago Tribune* and other papers: "A smaller urban footprint."

For Nagin, that meant a city without a large underclass. For many of the planners, it meant consolidating people in areas that were unlikely to flood; how would the city facilitate the return of marginalized black folks? Nagin's assumption that the underclass was gone would haunt him big time. As the city slowly resumed a semblance of normalcy, albeit with the majority of people gone, Nagin bragged about the sharp drop in violent crime. But as the trickle of people returning grew into streams, poor people were returning too, and Nagin realized he could not run for reelection as the man for a smaller footprint. He had won election the first time, in 2002, as the overwhelming choice of whites; now, faced with the reality that white candidates were going to run for mayor in a city where the racial demographics had changed—fewer blacks—he made his own shift, crabwalking away from the smaller footprint, telling neighborhood groups to work on plans for their areas, with help from consultants, and submit the results to the city. The subtle message was that New Orleans was no longer a city for working folk, who were finding conditions more desperate than before absent the safety net of Charity Hospital, walk-in health clinics, or adequate public transportation. Young men with guns and drugs returned to a shrunken geographic market space. The patchwork planning process emerged slowly, and painfully, without much guidance from City Hall.

"Blacks are caught up in the symbolism of having an African American occupy the mayor's office when the resources have eroded," continues Lombard, a partner in a small Chicago-based investment management company, though he comes home often. "[Blacks] believe that having a black mayor is absolutely essential. The circumstances in which the black community finds itself overwhelm the power available to them to control local issues. Urban mayors are less and less powerful because the funds are controlled by the state and federal government."

Nagin stood by passively as Bush's Housing and Urban Development department sought to demolish housing projects; several, solid brick medium-rises built in the 1940s, needed only modest repairs to welcome tenants back. HUD planned to raze them and hand tracts for the new city to land developers. This plan matched Nagin's "market-driven" solution for a city starved of affordable housing. Most people were disgusted with the projects as seedbeds for drug dealing, unwed young mothers and homicides; yet decent people who lived in those warrens had no other living options. As a matter of architecture and function in an urban grid, four of the complexes could have served tenants who had valid leases and wanted to return.

When the mayor's race began in the city of a shifting footprint, Nagin, who had raised most of his campaign money before Katrina, had several well-funded white opponents. But as the most telegenic candidate in the field, he managed the remarkable feat of figuratively winking at conservative whites, signaling that he wouldn't help poor blacks return, while casting himself to African American voters as standing up to the man. He sailed out of the primary into a runoff with Lieutenant Governor Mitch Landrieu (a son of former mayor Moon Landrieu and a brother of U.S. Senator Mary Landrieu) and won a final term as mayor.

Landrieu hurt himself by failing to attack Nagin for fear of losing the family's historic support of African Americans. His performance in the runoff was tepid. Six thousand blacks who voted for Landrieu in the primary jumped ship, voting for Nagin in the general election. In 2002 Nagin had won with 20 percent of the black vote; in 2006, with Al Sharpton and Jesse Jackson helping displaced voters travel home to vote, Nagin received 80 percent of the African American votes. Conservative whites, many of whom viewed the Landrieus as near-Communists for helping blacks, backed Nagin too.

Stranger coalitions have succeeded; yet within months, Nagin's inability to get the city moving left him alienated from both sides.

"When Nagin won," says Carl Cannon, the White House correspondent for *National Journal*, "a lot of people thought: You can't help these people—because they won't help themselves."

A *60 Minutes* interview before a trip to New York in which he called the Ground Zero site "a hole in the ground" made Nagin seem clowning and callous.

His suggestion to an African American journalists' convention that a white conspiracy was keeping blacks from returning to New Orleans was psychological projection and quite a stroke of demagoguery. The reelected Nagin stood next to Jesse Jackson at a local news event for the Right to Return and Reconstruction conference, and proclaimed, "My citizens are frustrated"—posturing himself as an advocate of the displaced poor.

Nagin unveiled a $1.1 billion neighborhood revival plan with zones for rebuilding. But the money was coming down at a snail's pace. With scant clout in Washington, Nagin had a poor relationship with Governor Blanco, having crossed party lines to endorse her Republican opponent, Bobby Jindal, in 2003. Nagin subsequently blamed Blanco for not getting help to the city soon enough in the chaos after Katrina hit. Whatever else poisoned the well between them, the enmity was widely known. As personality types, they clashed. A former school teacher, Blanco is sunny and somewhat modest. Nagin is a media ham. With charm and charisma to burn, he waltzed across the public stage, tossing verbal hand grenades like some Comedy Channel wannabe, alienating the city council with an aloofness bordering on disdain, cutting distance from people who tried to help him. He is among the strangest politicians that Louisiana, a strange outback of democracy, has ever seen.

"What went wrong is that we started electing personalities," intones Don Hubbard, an African American businessman and political powerhouse who got his start as a 1960s' community organizer. For Hubbard, Nagin signals "the first generation of black leaders with no history of a civil rights background. We wound up with style and no substance."

Hubbard Mansion, a brick Greek Revival house with a long veranda on St. Charles Avenue, is the home he built as a combined bed-and-breakfast with Rose, his wife of many years. She died in February 2007. The wintry bachelor grew up in the 1940s a few blocks back of St. Charles with its dreamy oak-shaded streetcar tracks in a working-class central city neighborhood of shotgun houses. He graduated from Walter L. Cohen High School, married and moved to Old Gentilly (what is now eastern New Orleans) and began organizing on neighborhood issues. Eschewing public office for himself, Hubbard became a political consultant, prizefight promoter, and real estate investor.

Seated in the dining room of his urban plantation home, Hubbard cuts an ironic picture of success, a black man in architectural trappings of the Old South. He was an early ally of Moon Landrieu, who was elected mayor in 1969 with 90 percent of the newly enfranchised black vote—a constituency Landrieu cultivated for years. As a young state legislator in the early 1960s, Landrieu stood virtually alone against a rash of segregationist bills. In the 1970s, as mayor, he ushered blacks into city government and jobs, while the city hummed to a booming economy. Landrieu was a major force behind the building of the Louisiana Superdome and the line of corporate towers that arose on Poydras Street. Hubbard has supported every politician since then who was elected mayor. When Nagin, before he ever ran for mayor, was pondering a way to get himself named superintendent of the public schools, Hubbard counseled him. "I told him the job was a garbage disposal. He'd go down and never come up in enough pieces to run for anything."

Nagin waited and ran for mayor in 2002, with Hubbard's support. In the 2006 mayoralty runoff, Hubbard backed Mitch Landrieu. By Hubbard's lights, Nagin's pivotal mistake came right after Katrina hit. "My recommendation was to get the recovery going by contacting Colin Powell. Make him the head of an intervention team. '*Hey, man, you led us into this Iraq mess. Bush owes you. You know where the bones are buried in Washington.*' That would have been my first choice. Second, I would have called Jimmy Carter. Third, I would have called Andrew Young. You get national figures who know Washington, D.C., and what it took to get New York reorganized after 9/11. Nagin didn't know how to do that. Blanco didn't know. We needed someone on our team *immediately* who could get a phone call returned."

The moment that many consider Nagin's best hour—his angry interview on WWL Radio with newsman Garland Robinette during the flood, excoriating federal and state failures to rescue the city—was "good show business," stewed Hubbard. "I call it style and no substance: How does that get someone to write you a check?" Hubbard paused. "We had such great hopes for this guy. But he refused to hire people with strong experience in state government." He rattles off the names of the mayors since Landrieu—Dutch Morial, Sidney Bartholmey, Marc Morial (Dutch's son). "*They had friends in Baton Rouge.* Nagin depended on people who didn't have friends in Baton Rouge to carry water for him [with the Legislature] . . . Marc made sure the ministers had little programs to keep the kids off the street. Ray cut that."

Sunlight bathes the room as Hubbard makes a gesture toward the outside world. "I remember the 'Colored Only' signs in buses. I remember not being able to eat at the lunch counter in Krauss. Those of us whom God has blessed have a responsibility to give something back." He pauses. "You've got to spend time in the trenches."

What the Market Gave the Mayor

"One undeniable fact is that the official poverty level did decline in the United States" in the early 1970s, according to historian Kent Germany in *New Orleans After the Promises* on the lost legacy of LBJ. Poverty dropped "from 19 percent in 1968 to a low of 11.4 percent in 1978." The New Orleans poverty rate among blacks fell from "almost 50 percent in 1960 to near 30 percent in 2000."

When George W. Bush took office, the national poverty rate was 12.6 percent. In six years, it has risen by a third. Nagin, who contributed $1000 to Bush in 2000, was oblivious toward history's counter-punch. When Nagin took office in 2002, New Orleans had suffered a long recession caused by the plunge in international oil prices, which saw white-collar jobs head for the suburbs or out of state. After a generation of federal cutbacks, the city had fewer than six thousand workers—half the number Moon Landrieu supervised. Katrina shattered the city's revenue collection, forcing Nagin to cut city employees by half again, to three thousand.

As Moon Landrieu was a beneficiary of the domestic policies of Nixon and LBJ, Nagin was a victim of Reagan's and Bush's. As the city's economy went south in the 1980s, the safety valve of federal programs went with it. With the Reagan Administration routing funds for highways and mortgages, bolstering the suburbs, the city grew poorer. As an ever-spiraling number of young black males went to prison or dropped out of schools, out-of-wedlock births surged, too. Not all of this can be faulted on the gutting of antipoverty programs; welfare bred its own set of dependencies. But as Kent Germany and others have pointed out, poverty decreased after LBJ's Great Society initiatives. Nothing like it has been tried since. In 1989 crack cocaine came down on the city like a scriptural plague; the drug market cut bloody furrows through Dutch Morial's childhood neighborhood in the Seventh Ward, sending a river of homicides deep into the Ninth Ward.

If the Bush years have produced a single lesson about market-driven approaches to poverty, it is that poor people have little chance to escape traumatized living spaces without the programs to help them build better lives. The alternative is to build more prisons.

Post-Katrina, the crisis that began when "poverty won" has become acute. Congress did begin a funding stream to Louisiana for rebuilding; however Mississippi, which had far less damage, received substantially more. Governor Haley Barbour was a close Bush ally. Mississippi's Republican Senator Thad Cochran chaired the Appropriations Committee. The main allocation of $7.5 billion to Louisiana for assistance to people who lacked sufficient insurance to rebuild after the flood was $3 billion less than needed.

By September of 2007, at the two-year mark after Katrina, parts of the city seemed tranquil on the surface. The campuses at Tulane and Loyola across from Audubon Park were bustling. Xavier University in MidCity made a miraculous recovery from some of the deepest flooding under the visionary leadership of its president, Dr. Norman Francis. Dr. Marvalene Hughes, the president of Dillard University—in the deeply flooded Gentilly area—led a comeback that was also a testament to the power of African-American leaders and educators on the national level. With the French Quarter and Uptown comparatively at peace, Central City became a war zone leaching homicides into other parts of town. Farther downtown, the Gentilly and Lakeview areas still showed houses with waterlines, amidst other houses where people had returned or were in the process of repairing—raggedy streets with dead houses and high weeds. Out in New Orleans East, where the flooding was heaviest, sawtooth residential patterns in many streets are common. The *Times-Picayune*'s August 2007 issue on debutantes in the Living Section ran a large story beneath the fold by Chris Bynum on a hard-working Hispanic who was murdered while repairing his New Orleans East house. Shot in the head, he left behind a pregnant wife.

Politics: A Buffoons' Carnival

As candidates for president scrambled for news time in the run-up to the '08 election, a new Congress under Democratic House Speaker Nancy Pelosi seemed intent on funding a larger scope of recovery needs. With the stars moving toward a favorable realignment, New Orleans politicians kept blowing it.

In 2005 the FBI raided the Washington home of Congressman William Jefferson, who represents New Orleans, and found $90,000 in his freezer—money given by a would-be investor (who helpfully wore a hidden mike) as an alleged bribe to a Nigerian official in hatching an internet deal in Africa.

Being caught by the feds with ninety grand in your freezer would sound a dirge for most candidates; yet Jefferson won his ninth term in November 2006 in a manner akin to that of Nagin (who had relied on Jefferson's support in his reelection, and returned the favor, further tarnishing the mayor's reform credentials). Jefferson stumped hard for votes from his base in the majority-black district, where many sympathized with him as a target of the federal government—a far cry from the 1960s when federal courts were considered an ally of the movement. Dollar Bill, as the late mayor, Dutch Morial, dubbed him, would profit from an ironic boost by suburban whites in that part of the district that lies in Jefferson Parish, where many voters revered Sheriff Harry Lee. The story is almost too convoluted to tell, but it's worth hearing. The sheriff was angry with Jefferson's opponent, State Representative Karen Carter, for her comments in Spike Lee's documentary about Katrina, *When the Levees Broke*. In the film, Carter criticizes Gretna Police and Jefferson Parish deputies for blocking the Crescent City Connection—the bridge that leads from downtown New Orleans to suburbs across the Mississippi—on the burning afternoon when Katrina refugees tried to escape the flood and looting. The lawmen forced people (most of whom who were black and on foot) seeking safety back across the bridge at gunpoint, back into the hellish city. Carter called their actions "inhumane and unacceptable." For that, Harry Lee sent flyers to twenty-five thousand people attacking her candidacy. Better a guy with ninety grand in the freezer than a woman uppity on civil liberties.

Jefferson went back to Washington and was hit with a sixteen-count federal indictment for misusing his office; the government charges that he bilked a former partner in a deal to provide high-speed internet access to Africa, forcing the guy to pay certain family members and cronies in the scheme. The man who paid the money pleaded guilty and went to prison, prepared to testify against Jefferson; a former staffer of the congressman took a plea and was poised to testify as the book went to press. Jefferson has insisted he is innocent, and was digging in for trial.

In contrast, the most popular member of the city council, Oliver Thomas, struck a tone of contrition when he resigned in August 2007, after being caught by federal authorities in a different bribery scheme. "I stand before you today humbled, disappointed in myself, and seeking your forgiveness for what I am about to say," he told U.S. District Judge Sarah Vance at his hearing.

Thomas admitted taking slightly more than $19,000 from Stan "Pampy" Barré, an ex-cop-turned-insider friendly with former mayor Marc Morial. Pampy wanted to insure that he kept a concession on downtown parking lots after Nagin succeeded Morial. Thomas took money to help him do that. This was three years *before* the populist councilman lost his brother in the 2005 flood. During Katrina, I was out in a tree-trapped house in Covington, on the far side of Lake Pontchartrain, glued to WWL Radio like a life support when Oliver Thomas came on, telling listeners "we are all *one place now*"—a quavering plea for unity, pulling together, a voice directed at Jefferson Parish: the city is underwater, poor folk trapped on rooftops, we (the black city) need help from you (the white-majority suburb).

Many years before, Thomas knocked on my front door in his

first campaign for city council. I invited him in, we chatted. As he left I thought, *What a great guy . . . he might be mayor one day.* With his large frame shambling across the stage of Anthony Bean's theatre in one of the August Wilson plays, I liked Oliver even more. How many politicians appreciate "the arts" enough to actually perform in a world-class drama? (Wilson won two Pulitzers; Bean staged the plays beautifully.)

In another season, so much dirt might count little; but for a city with dead spaces in the grid—you can see chest-high grass three blocks from the empty Ninth Ward mansion of music star Fats Domino—the pathology of politics is glaring.

"I'm not going to condone machine politics," Massachusetts-bred FBI Special Agent James Bernazanni of New Orleans said as Thomas went down. "In Boston we elected a mayor from prison [James Michael Curley]. Machine politics in the North will skim the cream. Here in Louisiana, they skim the cream, they steal the milk, hijack the bottles and look for the cow."

Anti-homosexual Senator Tarnished by Hookers!

It is not just African Americans like Nagin, Jefferson, Thomas, Barré, and several former members of Morial's inner circle (including his uncle) who have starred in this dismal drama of greed and gross incompetence.

Senator David Vitter (Harvard '83) derided his 2004 campaign opponents as "Massachusetts liberals," which was laughable considering that one opponent graduated from Vanderbilt and the other, a hapless Cajun, was hammered by the Humane Society for having called cockfighting "family type culture." Vitter won in a walk. His Senate website omits reference to Harvard. He seems bent on airbrushing his academic pedigree, presumably to avoid bad impressions with his more rock-ribbed constituents. As a Catholic from New Orleans (which many voters in the pentecostal woodlands consider a Babylonian city), Vitter wooed the Christian right by casting himself as a moral absolutist on abortion and other issues of the human body. He sneered at John Kerry "as a perfect candidate—for president of France" and wondrously announced that America's greatest crisis was—gay marriage. There seems not an ounce of shame in his oxygen supply.

"His moral stand was so rigid that it almost made you question it," remarks the New Orleans correspondent for the *New York Times*, Adam Nossiter, who graduated from Harvard a year ahead of Vitter and covered the 2004 election for the Associated Press. "There were the rumors about Vitter's past but there was also the extremeness of his positions, the unyielding aspect to it." The "rumors" in 2004 that he had visited a since-shuttered local bordello were largely ignored by reporters after Vitter denied them. His wife was an accomplished attorney; they had four young children.

Jump cut to July 2007. An investigator for pornographer Larry Flynt finds Vitter's phone number on billing records of the "D.C. Madam," Deborah Jean Palfrey, who is accused by federal prosecutors of racketeering, mail fraud and a $300-an-hour call girl operation. Vitter issues a terse written apology for a "very serious sin" caused by unspecified "actions in my past." The senator has "received forgiveness from God" and his family. Then, in a huge miscalculation, Vitter disappears for a week, missing a Senate debate over Iraq, ducking questions from the media, notably his hometown daily. A *Times-Picayune* story quotes the New Orleans madam, saying Vitter *was* a customer back in the day, and a second woman comes forth, saying that she slept with him for pay in the 1990s when he was a state representative, but they broke up when Vitter learned that the woman and his wife had the same first name.

Vitter's base followers were enraged; but GOP leaders stood by him—a damaged senator being preferable to none at all. Had he quit, Governor Blanco, though a lame duck, would choose his replacement; you could bet your car that the senator installed would have been a Democrat. The scandal erupted a week after

Vitter had endorsed presidential candidate Rudy Giuliani, feeding speculation of his potential as a running mate. Now Vitter was being gored for hypocrisy by columnists, talk radio hosts and late night comedians.

The Aftermath

Nagin, Dollar Bill Jefferson, Oliver Thomas, Vitter—these are grownups. Men who went to college, men who know how to speak with bankers, men who have traveled on airplanes. *Where did we get this buffoons' carnival? Why do people like this happen here?*

Standing out in high relief from the debacle of New Orleans politics is the economic boom in the suburbs of Jefferson and St. Tammany parishes, thanks to transplants from St. Bernard and Orleans. That is the future of this metropolitan region as things stand now: prosperous suburbs and a decaying city where cops can't keep up with the pace of homicides, the DA can't put the killers away, and politicians have no idea, nor much stated interest, in a coordinated strategy to reverse the poverty.

The vacuum in leadership is staggering.

"Traditionally, in Louisiana, using political office or political favors to enrich oneself and one's friends has not been swept under the rug; it has been openly advertised," wrote William J. "Big Bad Bill" Dodd, a former lieutenant governor, in a 1991 memoir, *Peapatch Politics.* "For as long as I can remember, a big-time state politician who failed to get rich and make his friends and relatives rich has been considered stupid."

The difference between our time and the era Dodd writes about, the decades before and after World War II, is that city political machines have been shrinking as the suburbs have grown. In New Orleans there is not much left to steal from the public fisc.

There is a pathology in the black community, of folk who will vote for a greed addict like Dollar Bill or a lackadaisical egotist like Nagin *because he's one of us.* Instead of judging people, as Dr. King said, "by the content of our character," black voters embrace con-spiracy theories that turn crooks into victims. White voters recoil, aghast. But it was Catholics in suburban Metairie who as swing votes delivered a state house seat to ex-Klansman David Duke in 1989. Duke ran for the U.S. Senate the following year and for governor the year after that, making a spectacle of Louisiana as revelations of his neo-Nazi activities leached out in the media. Nevertheless, he carried a majority of the white vote in both elections, while losing both times.

Since the flood many Mexicans and Latinos from Central America have moved into the city as laborers. "The health care, manufacturing, construction and hospitality industries expect that in the next five years the [metropolitan] region will need at least another fifty thousand workers to fill new jobs—not including the workers who will have to be replaced because of retirement or other reasons," Pam Radtke Russell of the *Times-Picayune* reports. "Others predict shortages of more than one hundred thousand."

This may be one of the most important lessons post-Katrina—that jobs await those who want to work in a city that is trying to put itself back to work. As Las Vegas with its booming market in housing became a magnet for people in the late 1990s, New Orleans and the surrounding metropolitan area could well see an economic surge, provided the next mayor does not drive people off.

As Road Home stalled, Nagin had little in the way of other sources to kick-start the city's recovery. His best move was hiring Ed Blakely, a politically adroit urban planner from California who worked on the 9/11 recovery and left a professor's job in Australia to become the city's recovery director. Blakely organized seventeen target areas to spur commercial development with federal funds and bond revenues, and is managing the complex financial ma-chinery to make it happen. Blakely envisions a cosmopolitan city with medium-rises clustered in downtown commercial areas that missed the flooding. Half of New Orleans is above sea level: that's where the smart money seems destined to be spent, at whatever pace it arrives.

When the pieces of the recovery jigsaw puzzle finally fall into place, Ed Blakely's vision of a city with apartments in downtown and warehouse-district neighborhoods should add a more cosmopolitan layer to the Caribbean feel in the many streets with shotgun houses. Whether people who have returned to homes in the hardest-hit areas, living on streets with dead houses and jungular swatches of floribunda, will find their way to stronger neighborhoods on higher ground is one of the next mayor's core challenges (Nagin isn't up to it)—convincing people to sell their flood-prone property, move and resettle in the dry ridge areas. We need politicians willing to deliver hard news.

If the jobs requiring an educated work force can be filled in tandem with artisans and semiskilled laborers on building projects, the economic drive could pull us through the bloody nightmare of Nagin's final years. Finding a first-rate chief of police to rebuild NOPD is a fundamental responsibility of being mayor. Repairing streets, staffing city departments with people capable of streamlining permits to those ready to build, attracting new business, collaborating with (rather than avoiding) people elected to the city council, the congressional and state legislative delegations to improve the infrastructure and deliver services to the citizenry—these tasks are fundamental to the skills-set we should expect of any mayor. If they are present in Nagin's successor, the city stands a chance at achieving some kind of rebirth.

Hurricanes are recurrent forces in our history. The Army Corps of Engineers is working on a massive levee restoration project with guardian gates strategically positioned outside Lake Pontchartrain. Without an oversight mechanism like the Government Accountability Office, no one knows whether the Corps can reinvent itself sufficient to the task. It will take a huge investment of state and federal funds to restore the wetlands outside the city as buffers against future storm surges from the Gulf in the age of rising sea waters and global climate change. Rebuilding the coast is perhaps the most important job of the next governor, requiring solid ties with the congressional delegation and the next president. Negotiation and compromise, classic political virtues discarded by our current lot of politicians, will be critical.

These things can happen if the political leadership is pressed to make them happen. For now, New Orleans is living on borrowed time. The breakdown of the criminal justice system—mirrored in the larcenous, ham-fisted behavior of officials and side-dealers aforementioned—is as an extreme sign of the failed politics before the flood, made magnified today.

Through its history New Orleans has been a crossroads of humanity, a Creole city that fuses strands of varied ethnic traditions into a common vernacular with a premium placed on good living. Jazz began as dance music for a new century—functional music for people of all colors; African polyrhythms and black churchsong reimagined European instrumentation and melody, creating a new American art form. Jazz mirrored the society of New Orleans as the idiom sang of a human comedy, transcending the violent repression of Jim Crow. These traits have carried down the years in the music and other expressions of culture; the city as a way of life has long set it apart from the rest of the South as an island of American dreams. That essential character of the town may be our best shot at redemption—finding the joystreams in daily life; but it takes hard work to bridge the bitter racial chasm. It takes politicians genuinely willing to strike the chords of unity, and put aside the tired riffs of identity politics and victim-posturing.

The task of uniting people in a community so polarized is one that harks back to the civil rights era. Social protest movements succeed when they strike empathy with the middle class. Martin Luther King, Jr., Fred Shuttlesworth, Ralph David Abernathy, Andrew Young, and A. L. Davis of New Orleans were ministers who became activists in the civil rights era; they resisted militant strategies, banking on the hope that as the national media reported the movement as a religious quest for justice, the white South would eventually submit to the federal courts.

The violence ripping through many American cities, in the poorest neighborhoods with the darkest peoples, is a crisis that begs for black leadership of the kind that the South saw in the 1950s and sixties, and the political wisdom we saw in a bipartisan Congress during those years.

New Orleans post-Katrina has become a graveyard of the civil rights movement. The corruption or incompetence of leading African-American politicians should not be seen as a racial trait—indeed, they have acted like any number of corrupt, bumbling or hypocritical white politicians (viz., Vitter). Perhaps the anguish of a leaderless city will reach a point where people will come together across the racial divide, and close ranks behind someone genuinely capable of leading. Though betrayed by the likes of Jefferson, Nagin and Thomas, that was the promise of the movement.

Signs of Hope

Standing out like a bas-relief from such torpid politics, the cultural ferment that has enriched the city with musicians, writers, artists and chefs has shown a striking resilience. The Jazz and Heritage Festival rebounded and remains an economic magnet each spring. Hundreds of musicians are struggling to join the others who have returned since the flood. Art galleries outnumber music clubs. "The literary infrastructure has certainly come back," says Susan Larson, the prolific book review editor of the *Times-Picayune*.

"Many elements contribute to a literary culture in addition to the presence of writers—libraries, bookstores, festivals, creative writing programs, book wholesalers, established and independent publishers—as well as a dedicated core of individuals who make things happen, all the things that writers need and readers want.

Before the storm, New Orleans had them all. After the storm, residents rejoiced in the opening of each bookstore, the return of each festival. Before long, poets were showing up at the Maple Leaf Bar on Sunday afternoons, just as they have for decades. Is there a feeling of literary community now? There is indeed. And while our literary infrastructure is a rambling affair, with twenty-year-old festivals and brand-new bookstores, creative writing programs and libraries, it is bound together by good will and a hope for the future. No one's in charge, but each person who plays a part is pressing on with a renewed sense of passion."

The failed school system has been supplanted by a combination of charter schools, a state-run Recovery School District and a skeletal version of the old Orleans Parish Public Schools, which was financially pillaged by selected employees, vendors, and a now plea-copped former president of the school board. (Is the list of shamed politicians too long for you, gentle reader?)

Apres le deluge, New Orleans has become a laboratory for educational rebuilding that has attracted young college graduates from many states for stints at teaching. This is one of the most encouraging developments of all, the response of those who felt a call akin to that of Peace Corps volunteers, or Freedom Riders in the civil rights buses, young Americans wanting to contribute to the rebuilding of a city the devastation of which they watched on television. New Orleans is thus renewed as a city of the young. Another lesson for America is found in post-Katrina New Orleans: learn to tap the tremendous idealism and willingness to work of the young generation.

The great man theory of history, long discredited in contemporary academia, holds that societies are shaped by individuals who achieve power and use it forcefully, for good or ill, molding institutions and policies that affect large numbers of people. The collapse of effective governing in New Orleans can be read as what happens when small men fail to meet the challenge at a time of epic crisis. It may not take a "great" individual, male or female, to repair this broken city, but the competence and vision by which cities grow and prosper begs for someone with the smarts and will to deliver the goods.

People will move to an area teeming with jobs and put down roots if the environment is welcoming—if it is not a Third World town of politicos with greasy palms who yawn at the poverty and violence. Poverty is the octopus at the lawn party here; if we do not challenge it with progressive remedies, the tentacles will squeeze the city's life force and tattoo the streets with blood. Politics succeeds when genuine leaders call the better angels of our nature to a fair, intelligent management of society. Such is the promise of democracy which this traumatized, resilient, nay, indomitable city at the bottom of America still awaits. ❧

Hospitality or Exile?

Race, Sexual Orientation, and Sophocles

Susan Ford Wiltshire

*The eastbound and westbound buses came together for the first
and only time to pose the question to Bethany Lutheran: "Will
you choose hospitality or rejection?"* — Report of the 2007
Soulforce Equality Rides, East Ride

*Who would reject his friendship? Is he not One who would
have, in any case, an ally's right to our hospitality?* — Theseus,
king of Athens, in Sophocles, Oedipus at Colonus[1]

In the spring of 2006 thirty-three young adult leaders of Soulforce set out on their first bus ride across America to challenge
the policies of Christian and military colleges and universities
hostile to lesbian, gay, bisexual, and transgender persons. Their
precedent was explicit—they were consciously re-enacting a dramatic civil rights confrontation in the American South. In 1961
the young adult leaders of the Nashville Student Movement set out
for Birmingham and Montgomery to ensure the continuity of the
Freedom Rides challenging Jim Crow segregation in the South.
They in turn were following the example of Gandhi's heroic campaign of nonviolence in India in the 1940s, which also influenced
a 1947 Freedom Ride into the South by Bayard Rustin and others,
sponsored by the Fellowship of Reconciliation.

But the story is older still, so old it seems timeless. In 406 BCE, the Athenian playwright Sophocles at age ninety wrote about it in his last play *Oedipus at Colonus*. Old and gray, blind and disfigured, an outcast from his own city of Thebes where his two sons are quarreling over control of the city, Oedipus is guided by his daughter Antigone into the holy grove of Colonus near Athens. Oedipus seeks a place to rest and die after the troubles prophesied for him that he had tried valiantly to avoid. Initially he is anathema at Colonus, reviled by the local inhabitants as one whose very presence pollutes their holy place. But Theseus, king of nearby Athens, arrives, identifies with the sufferings of Oedipus, and says that having been an exile himself, he will never turn a fellow sufferer away from his land. In this gift of hospitality Oedipus finds comfort and acceptance. He reciprocates by conferring great blessings on Colonus.

Sophocles's play invites comparison with the freedom and equality rides only in its theme of hostility or hospitality to strangers. In other ways the stories are quite different. The infant Oedipus was left on a mountain to die because of prophesies that he would kill his father and marry his mother. Adopted into the royal family of Corinth, he heard mutterings about his status and set out to consult the truth at the oracle of Delphi. In a moment of road rage (by no means nonviolent!), he killed a stranger, in time revealed to be his father. Then he answered the riddle of the Sphinx and thereby won the kingship of Thebes with the widowed Jocasta as queen, learning only much later she was also his mother.

The Freedom Riders and Equality Riders, in contrast, knew their truths already. The purpose of their journeys was not only to discover more truth about themselves but also to live out their truths in conscious and caring confrontation with those who would reject them.

The stories of Sophocles, the Freedom Rides of 1947 and 1961, and the Equality Rides demonstrate the power of leaving one's place of exile, even if familiar, to confront rejection at its source. When one puts one's life on the line by going physically to the source, always in a spirit of nonviolence, the process of healing long-established wrongs has a chance to begin. Staying in comfort zones is death to dreams.

For me, two journeys to Birmingham within a three-month period in 2007 brought all these stories together. The first was participating in a traveling seminar recalling the history of the 1961 Freedom Rides from Nashville. The other was joining for two days the East bus of the 2007 Equality Rides during its visit to Samford University, a Baptist institution in Birmingham.

Soulforce was founded in 1998 by Mel White, an ordained minister, filmmaker, and former ghostwriter for Jerry Falwell, Pat Robertson, and others. After Reverend White came out as a gay man, he eventually despaired of attempts to engage his former employers and the nation's churches concerning their hostility to LGBT persons and issues. When he circulated a message to that effect to his wide array of friends, his many responses included one from the King Center in Atlanta telling him he was violating one of the key tenets of soulforce: One must never give up on one's adversaries. For White and his partner Gary Nixon, everything changed from that moment. White began extensive study of both Gandhi's and King's principles and practices, spent time in India, then turned his extraordinary abilities to establishing a nationwide organization to confront anti-LGBT policies of the religious establishments. Today Soulforce is the modern movement most spiritually akin to the civil rights movement of the King era.

On January 28-29, 2007, forty-six years after the Nashville

Susan Ford Wiltshire is Professor of Classics Emerita at Vanderbilt University. She is author of *Public and Private in Vergil's Aeneid*; *Greece, Rome, and the Bill of Rights*; *Seasons of Grief and Grace*; *Athena's Disguises*; and *Windmills and Bridges: Poems Near and Far*. She serves on the editorial board of the Progressive Book Club and lives with her husband on their farm in rural Middle Tennessee.

Student Movement leaders went to Alabama after the bus-burning at Anniston, I joined four busloads of students, staff, and administrators from American Baptist College, Fisk University, Tennessee State University, and Vanderbilt University to commemorate their courage by retracing their journey from Nashville to Birmingham and Montgomery. Accompanying the Ride were original planners, journalists, and participants, including James Lawson, John Lewis, C. T. Vivian, Diane Nash, James Zwerg (in 1961, a white exchange student at Fisk), Bernard Lafayette, and John Siegenthaler. Raymond Arsenault, author of the definitive *Freedom Riders: 1961 and the Struggle for Racial Justice*, also accompanied the group.

In Birmingham, the Rev. C. T. Vivian told of the decision of the Nashville students to continue the Freedom Ride after the earlier violence in Alabama:

> This was life and death—and we knew it. We all went outside. I remember how starry the sky was. Everyone was very solemn. There were tears in our eyes. It was a "feelable silence." It was like church. Then we came back in ready to go, and the ten students left the next morning. The students gave Diane Nash sealed letters to be sent to their loved ones in event of their death.

Nash, chair of the Nashville Student Movement at the time, spoke of the power of the workshops in relentless Gandhian nonviolence led by Reverend Lawson:

> Jim Lawson's workshops were life-changing. Few people understand nonviolence. It's not just "turning the other cheek." It's a powerful tool for change." [Then she summarized:] There were three factors in our success. The first was Jim Lawson's weekly workshops. We had an excellent education in nonviolence. The second was the Student Central Committee itself, comprised of about thirty students. We operated on consensus—Quaker

style. I have looked back and marveled at what we were able to do. No one ever failed to complete an assigned task. We all had to be committed and efficient, because we knew we were going to be in harm's way. Our lives depended on it. Our 'litmus test' may sound corny now, but always we would ask ourselves: "Is this the loving thing to do?" Third, by the time of the Freedom Ride we had already had a victory: desegregating the Nashville lunch counters. We had demonstrated that it could be done, using nonviolence. We were shocked at our own power—that we didn't know we had until we started using it.

Lawson observed:

The Nashville Movement had cohesion—morally, spiritually, intellectually. I agreed with their decision completely. I told Diane to call Martin Luther King and Robert Kennedy to tell them that Nashville was picking up the Freedom Rides. (You notice, I didn't offer to call them myself.)

Then Rev. Lawson recalls the reaction of Rev. Fred Shuttlesworth in Birmingham, on hearing Diane tell him they were coming. She was "as cool as a butcher cutting meat." She simply said: "The Nashville Movement is coming."

Raymond Arsenault concluded: "This was the first unambiguous victory in the Deep South. In six months all the Interstate Commerce Commission facilities were desegregated. *And* this was done in Alabama and Mississippi. The mystique of Jim Crow was broken."

One of the most poignant moments of Freedom Ride 2007 occurred at the Birmingham Civil Rights Institute. A repeating video clip there shows an interview with the young Jim Zwerg in an Alabama hospital bed, badly beaten. On the video he says: "We will take hitting, we'll take beatings. We're willing to accept death. But we are going to keep coming until we can ride from anywhere in the South to any place else in the South, as Americans, without anyone making any comment." A crowd of students gathered around Zwerg as he watched the video, standing with him in reverent silence.

More important even than the history revisited during Freedom Ride 2007 was the clarion challenge for the future. Lewis insisted: "We have to continue to build pockets of the beloved community. Even if it's only a half step forward. Do not violently resist the violent. The American people are too quiet. We must speak with our feet. We have to do it. Allow yourself to be *used*. Just get in the way. Just do it. We must all become maladjusted." (At this point Barnard Lafayette, Lewis's one-time roommate at American Baptist, interjected: "Go ye into all the world and be maladjusted!"] Lewis concluded: "We are living in a world house. Don't stay in just one room. Sometimes the route to getting home is through the wilderness."

AFTER SHARING IN the January journey from Nashville to Alabama, I drove the same route two months later at the end of March to meet up with the Equality Ride 2007 East Bus during its visit to Samford University. Jacob Reitan, active in Soulforce since high school, originated the idea for the Equality Rides, which he modeled explicitly on the Freedom Rides. His investigation of the original Freedom Rides led him to Dr. Rodney Powell, one of the leading members of the Nashville Student Movement. Now a retired physician in Hawaii, Powell energetically offered advice and support and serves as a continuing mentor for the project. On a speaking engagement at the University of Richmond, Reitan met a gentle student from Texas, Haven Herrin, who soon knew she would be involved in the Equality Rides. The project would require her organizing skills, she thought, but also she had much to learn. "I have never considered it a job," she said later. "It is my life."

When the idea of the Ride was presented to Mel White, chair of the Board of Soulforce, White proposed that they make a trial run from Soulforce headquarters in Lynchburg, Virginia, to nearby Liberty University. They did, and they were convinced it would work. Soulforce Q (the young adult section of Soulforce; Q for queer or questing) started raising its own funds and soon was ready to begin. On the eve of their departure the first year in 2006, the Equality Riders met with Congressman Lewis for a blessing and a send-off. Lewis's life, Reitan and Haven report, provided for them three important lessons:

- The need for an expansive youth movement for social change
- The need of the gay rights movement for more direct activism
- The imperative that the goal of youth activism must be always be reconciliation

Soulforce Q staffer Alexey Bulokhov wrote of his participation in the 2006 Equality Ride:

> To be a part of the tidal wave of dialogue and change sweeping Christian America has been a transformational experience which brought me closer to my family, my friends, God, and myself. I have had the privilege of comforting closeted gay students, empowering allies amongst faculty and staff, and worshipping alongside brothers and sisters in the deep spirit of love. Moreover, Soulforce Q Equality Ride has emboldened me to believe in the possibility of positive change for LGBT people in my homeland, Russia, and elsewhere. Nonviolence as a philosophy of loving resistance is the only way to change the world: one person, one campus, one community, one nation at a time.

Numbers from the 2006 Equality Ride help tell the story:
- Number of schools visited: 19

- Number of miles traveled: 11,178
- Number of schools that worked with us to create programming: 8
- Number of schools that arrested us: 6
- Total number of arrests: 99
- Number of school presidents who dined with us: 7
- Number of school presidents who met with us: 10
- Total number of school policies changed: 3
- Total number of gay-straight alliances formed: 3
- Total number of conversations on LGBT issues: well over 10,000

The cost for the first Equality Ride in 2006 was $288,516. The Riders themselves raised $294,107, much of it from on-line donations. (Internet and cell phones, they say, offer a huge advantage in organizing.) The cost for the two East and West Equality Rides in 2007 was $354,537, also raised by the Riders.

A typical campus visit of an Equality Ride is preceded by a letter from the Soulforce Q organizers to the college or university president explaining the purpose of their journey and the hope that occasions for dialogue with students would be opened by the institution. In every case the Equality Riders carefully studied in advance the official school policies toward LGBT people, which often include expulsion. The language of the student handbook at Samford is somewhat less draconian than most, stating that sexual misconduct, including "rape and homosexual acts," will receive a minimum sanction of probation and a $75 fine. (I understand that Samford changed its policy for the better after the visit by the Equality Riders.) At Samford, Riders were invited to attend a class and to present a panel in a large auditorium practically filled with Samford students. The university chaplain who hosted the panel observed that he himself as a student would never have had the nerve to attend such a presentation.

No arrests took place that day. The stories were different elsewhere. Altogether in the 2007 Rides there were eighty-three arrests, nine people spent the night in jail, and three people did six days of community service. Altogether in the East Bus and the West Bus, fifty individuals participated in the rides lasting two months. Among them were straight allies as well as LGBT young people. At institutions where no contact with students was permitted, the Riders were resourceful in creating opportunities for communication. Sometimes they would write their cell phone numbers on placards visible from across the street. Usually they would announce a later time for informal conversation with students at a safer site off-campus, often a food court in a local mall.

AFTER THE 2007 Equality Rides, I traveled to Minneapolis to interview the young adult leadership at their Soulforce Q headquarters. This group consists of co-directors Haven Herrin and Jake Reitan; Katie Higgins, director of operations; Jarrett Lucas, director of outreach; and Alexey Bulokhov, director of international outreach.

When asked their most important qualities as leaders of a movement, they replied that in their interactions with each other, they always try to emulate Gandhi's avoidance of "violence of thought, word, or fist." Their examples, as well as their thorough training in the principles and practices of nonviolence, set the tone for the movement. On the night I spent with the East Bus group in Birmingham, at a near-rancorous gathering after a particularly difficult day, I observed co-leaders Katie Higgins and Jarrett Lucas conduct themselves and the meeting with the quiet poise of individuals who know who they are, what they are about, and why they are about it with the methods they use.

These young people are setting out to change the culture of this country by challenging through their personal presence the misuse of random religious texts against LGBT people and the tragic consequences this foments. And they are relentless in their non-violent approach to social change. In the summer of 2007 Soulforce Q young adults and volunteers drove in four vans throughout each of four sections of New York State for a two-week period, calling on State senators, assembly members, and their constituents to lobby on behalf of Governor Eliot Spitzer's marriage equality legislation.

The two compelling political outcomes of the 1961 Freedom Rides were, first, that young people, well-enough trained and organized, could bring about enormous social change. This was new in America. It had not happened before. Second, through these efforts, the movement for civil rights became national. Discrimination was no longer conceived as only a Southern problem.

Congressman Lewis pointed out that Nashville was among the first sites where successful civil rights demonstrations were planned and directed without adult leadership. Later, as the movement grew regionally, Ella Baker of the Southern Christian Leadership Conference urged Nash and others against becoming a branch of the SCLC or any other organization, but to keep autonomy. Howard Zinn wrote at the time: "[F]or the first time in our history, a major social movement, shaking the nation to its bone, is being led by youngsters." In 2006 Arsenault observed: "By demonstrating the power of personal commitment and sacrifice in a new and dramatic way, the Freedom Riders countered traditional assumptions of institutional authority and top-down politics."

Scholars soon realized also that it was the Freedom Riders who transformed race and civil rights into a national problem. Sociologist James Laue observed as early as 1962: "The national mobilization of conscience which had begun in Montgomery and grown in 1960 reached full bloom with the Freedom Rides." From this point forward, he said, few would see Jim Crow as only a local matter in Southern communities.

The legacy of Gandhi engendered both of these movements. As early as the 1940s in the civil rights struggles of the Fellowship of Reconciliation and the Congress on Racial Equality, Gandhi's principles had profound influence. Rev. James Lawson, who had lived in India and studied Gandhi's principles and practices of militant nonviolence, taught the workshops that were the solid rock from which the Nashville students walked downtown to integrate the city and then boarded buses as Freedom Riders to change the world.

Gandhi's lifework itself began with transportation. On June 7, 1893, having been in South Africa from India for only a week, Gandhi was thrown out of a first-class compartment of a train heading from Durban to Johannesburg because of his race. On a now mostly desolate railroad platform in Pietermaritzburg, KwaZulu-Natal, South Africa, stands a modest marble monument with this inscription:

> In the vicinity of this statue M. K. Gandhi was evicted from a first class compartment on the night of June 7, 1893. This incident changed the course of his life. He took up the fight against racial oppression. His active nonviolence started from that date.

The first reference I have seen to nonviolence as a method for the gay rights movement occurred in the mid-1960s when fiery trailblazer Frank Kameny "like an Old Testament prophet" delivered to the Mattachine-New York Society the message that "the homophile movement should be modeled on the black civil rights movement as formulated by nonviolent militant leaders such as Rev. Martin Luther King, Jr."[2]

INSPIRED BY GANDHI, two modern prophets merit central attention in this account of movements for racial and sexual justice. Both are gay black men. Both are brilliant and creative. Both have an extraordinary sense of history and where we are in it. Both, by coincidence, came from Pennsylvania. Their part in these contemporary stories casts them as Theseus in Sophocles's old story because both are able to recognize the validity and urgency of more than one kind of suffering. The world is their stage and hospitality is their script. Their names are Bayard Rustin (1912–1987) and Rodney N. Powell, M.D.

Rustin was raised in West Chester, Pennsylvania, by his grandmother Julia Rustin, a Quaker who named her grandson after a Quaker leader of the nineteenth century. Rustin attended an integrated high school and was a leader in his every endeavor. After turns at Wilberforce and City College, he eventually became a field secretary for the Rev. A. J. Muste's Fellowship of Reconciliation. Rustin was not closeted as a gay man, and in time his sexual orientation became an issue for some civil rights leaders in the fifties and sixties. Nevertheless, it was he who tutored Dr. King on essentials of Gandhian nonviolence when he noticed early in the Montgomery bus boycott that King kept armed guards on his porch and guns in his home (the Dexter Avenue Baptist Church parsonage). Andrew Young calls Rustin an "older brother" to King, who was only twenty-five at the time. Rustin's largest public triumph was the 1963 March on Washington, for which he helped to organize 250,000 people—on three-by-five index cards.

In his later years Rustin began writing and speaking on gay issues. Toward the end of his life he was asked in an interview if, knowing what he knew now and living his life over again, he would want to be gay. He answers in the negative for one reason only—because he might have been more effective as straight than gay in campaigning for the rights of LGBT people. His response provides a measure of the range and depth of his imagination:

> I think, if I had a choice, I would probably elect not to be gay. Because I think that I might be able to do more to fight against the prejudice to gays if I weren't gay, because some people say I'm simply trying to defend myself. But that's the

only reason. I want to get rid of all kinds of prejudices . . . That brings me to a very important point—people who do not fight against all kinds of prejudice are doing three terrible things. They are, first of all, perpetuating harm to others. Secondly, they are denying their own selves because every heterosexual is a part of homosexuality and every homosexual is part of this so-called straight world. And, finally, every indifference to prejudice is suicide because, if I don't fight all bigotry, bigotry itself will be strengthened and, sooner or later, it will turn on me . . . I think one of the things we have to be very careful of in the gay and lesbian community is that we do not under any circumstances permit ourselves to hold onto any indifference to the suffering of any other human being.[3]

Not all the original participants in the Freedom Rides supported the Equality Rides. During the 2007 Freedom Ride revisit to Alabama, the only original rider to mention LGBT issues at all during three days was John Lewis. Resistance to the gay rights movement lodges in the traditional black churches, as it does in the traditional white churches: Homosexuality is a sin because the Bible tells us so.

RODNEY POWELL WAS centrally involved in the Nashville Student Movement while a student at Meharry Medical College. One of the eight leaders profiled in David Halberstam's *The Children* (1998), Powell was the most senior member of the group and the only one to be fully involved in both struggles for justice. His leadership was—and is—notable for what the Romans called "gravitas," a combination of inner authority and outward calm. Powell chose not to join the Freedom Rides because the dean of Meharry told him he would never graduate from medical school if he did. First as a Peace Corps physician in Africa, then with a lifelong commitment to international public health medicine, Powell now lives with his long-time partner Bob Eddinger in active retirement in Hawaii, where he was a leader in the state's right to marry campaign.

In 1998 a launch event was held in the Fisk University Chapel for Halberstam's *The Children.* Halberstam as well as all eight individuals profiled in the book were present. As the occasion seemed to end, Powell rose and said: "I want to add one more thing. I predict that someday the churches will have to apologize for their treatment of gays as they are now beginning to apologize about slavery."

Powell said later he had not planned in advance to say this, but the comment soon led to his active involvement in Soulforce. He has been mentor to the young adults of Soulforce Q for the Equality Rides and in other ways supports their work. Powell wrote to Herrin and Reitan:

> The Equality Rides offer the opportunity to stigmatize homophobia and American society's acceptance of conservative Christian homophobia based on the Bible. We must vigorously embrace the redemptive power of love and nonviolence used by Gandhi and King. We must follow the guidelines and strategies used by the African American Civil Rights Movement to sustain massive nonviolent resistance and social protest throughout the nation until justice is achieved. We must inspire our fellow Americans who believe in equality and justice to join us and work together to expedite political and social change.
>
> Soulforce teaches and applies the nonviolent principles of Mahatma Gandhi and Martin Luther King, Jr., to the liberation of sexual minorities. The legacies of Mahatma Gandhi and Martin Luther King, Jr., are so powerful that they have provided principles and guidelines that have taught and inspired oppressed people worldwide to understand and seek liberation from oppression through the redemptive power of love and nonviolent resistance strategies. Soulforce has created the most comprehensive understanding, codification and presentation of the

principles and strategies of nonviolence that exists. [Here Powell refers to Soulforce principles and strategies that are available as a web-based resource: http//www.Soulforce.org.]

Then Powell, as did Rustin, brings the two justice movements together. He refers to the riots at the Stonewall Inn in New York starting on June 28, 1969, that marked the launch of the gay rights movement.

> I believe without a doubt that if Dr. King had lived to experience Stonewall he would have transformed the Stonewall activists with his visions of the power of nonviolence when disciplined by love and redemptive suffering. I believe that Dr. King would have opposed the bigotry of many Black preachers and welcomed homosexuals to the table as part of his "beloved community." I think he would have inspired and motivated the LGBT community to organize and fully utilize the forceful revolutionary social protests he first applied in the Montgomery Bus Boycott and later in the Civil Rights Movement. I believe, under Dr. King's inspiration and leadership, powerful nonviolent strategies and sustained nonviolent confrontations would have permeated the many judicial and legislative activities by LGBT organizations and groups inspired by Stonewall. The assassination fourteen months earlier silenced his voice, but not the legacy of his bold, radical strategies of nonviolent resistance for social justice and transformation of American society.
>
> In the spirit of love and nonviolence,
>
> Rodney N. Powell, M.D.

MANY YEARS AFTER growing up in Texas as a child formed and informed by Methodist pietism, I am beginning to sense from these stories something about the meaning of "redemptive suffering." Our redemption results from our perceiving as genuine, at long last, sufferings different from our own. In his first speech of Sophocles's play, Oedipus declares that "sufferings and vast time" have been his teachers. Now he wants to bestow grace on others. The saving grace for Oedipus when Theseus welcomes him is that his awful sufferings are finally recognized and affirmed as true. To know someone requires that we know what that person has suffered. That is the knowledge that redeems us from our own narrowness and bigotry. That is redemptive suffering—and we are the ones redeemed.

Traditions about Theseus include his having to grow up in a city far from Athens, having to wrest victories from at least six monsters, and then, in the version of Bacchylides, as a young man being sent to the labyrinth in Crete as a human sacrifice to the Minotaur. Theseus knows suffering. This knowledge enables him to recognize as compelling the sufferings of Oedipus.

Theseus addresses Oedipus in the grove of Colonus:

> I am sorry for you,
> And I should like to know what favor here
> You hope for from the city and from me:
> Both you and your unfortunate companion.
> Tell me. It would be something dire indeed
> To make me leave you comfortless; for I
> Too was an exile. I grew up abroad,
> And in strange lands I fought as few men have
> With danger and with death.
> Therefore, no wanderer shall come, as you do,
> And be denied my audience or aid.[4]

Later Theseus adds words that confirm his welcome:

> Moreover he has asked grace of our deities,
> And offers no small favor in return.

As I value that favor, I shall not refuse
This man's desire; I declare him a citizen.
And if it should please our friend to remain here,
I direct you to take care of him;
Or else he may come with me.
Whatever you choose,
Oedipus, we shall be happy to accord.
You know your own needs best; I accede to them.[5]

"You know your own needs best." This is the final redemption required of the ones who would offer hospitality instead of rejection: Never to presume to dictate responses to the needs of those who have suffered. The gift of the sufferers is to suggest solutions. Ours is to listen, embrace, and respond.

Those who have gone before, in both literature and life, give us courage and hope. They demonstrate that we can change things and that we must never give up. We are lifted up by a cloud of witnesses—the witness of all our brothers, all our sisters, then and now, near and far, who lean with us toward life, toward redemption, toward the beloved community. ❧

Labor's Failure in the South

The Key to the Puzzle

Wade Rathke

One of the great organizing arguments dating back fifty or more years, when organized labor was still on the move, was whether the setbacks and final abandonment by the Congress of Industrial Organization (CIO) of its Operation Dixie in 1953 were inevitable—because the South can't be organized—or circumstantial, the result of bad timing, the lack of coordination, or . . . The question is certainly relevant still, but more pressing is labor's collective inability since that date to create a different result for both the South and its own future. The overarching concern looking both backward and forward is that the continued inability to master this Southern organizing problem is the key to the puzzle of labor's overall national demise.

The tremendous population growth in the South in the last five decades has led the nation, but meanwhile the South's political climate has pulled industries from other regions of the country industries that are looking for cheaper labor, lower transportation costs, favorable subsidies, and reduced taxes. Not being able to hold its own in the South has meant that organized labor has lost its footing across the nation.

Union leadership has not been unconcerned or naïve about the risks of a giant, unorganized South, and there have been many serious and sophisticated efforts at building pockets of mass unionization. Lane Kirkland's AFL-CIO created and supported the seminal Houston Organizing Project (HOP) in the late 1970s to mid-1980s. John Sweeney's "outsider" campaign to win a convention-floor election contest to take over the AFL-CIO in the mid-1990s carried with it a call to organize the South and several important initiatives to do so, including the HOTROC campaign in New Orleans and the Gulf Coast Mariners' Campaign. Other major campaigns have focused on specific sectors. The UAW has been particularly active—and unsuccessful—among the foreign automakers who have built plants in a corridor of jobs and investment running across Tennessee, Mississippi, and Alabama. The Service Employees have run a number of important campaigns among janitors, public employees, and health workers in various markets in the South, especially southern Florida, Houston, Atlanta, and New Orleans. Other unions have had moments in the South that are worth exploring, but "moments" have not created "movements" to organize the unorganized—despite all of the rhetoric and expenditure.

In looking at the record and its implications, we hope to find the lessons offered from that history, but also understand where we are now and how an unorganized South is pulling down the entire labor movement. Regardless of labor's noble history, the twenty-first century finds the South with "membership density" that is less than two digits in every state of the South (see table).

The high-water mark is now Kentucky at 9.8 percent, and the low water level finds both of the Carolinas at only 3.3 percent union membership. In the past thirty years we have gone nationally from a situation where almost one of every three workers was a union

WADE RATHKE is chief organizer of Local 100, Service Employees International Union, as well as chief organizer and founder of ACORN, both headquartered in New Orleans. He was chief organizer of the HOTROC, AFL-CIO project and secretary-treasurer of the Greater New Orleans AFL-CIO during the growth surge in labor in New Orleans.

UNION MEMBERSHIP, COVERAGE, DENSITY AND EMPLOYMENT BY STATE, 2006

State	Employment	Members	Covered	% Members	% Covered	%Total US Employment
AL	1,930,249	170,113	193,988	8.8	10.0	1.51
AR	1,130,108	58,127	67,488	5.1	6.0	0.88
FL	7,675,747	396,958	497,350	5.2	6.5	5.99
GA	3,973,751	175,802	229,688	4.4	5.8	3.10
KY	1,752,214	172,106	196,338	9.8	11.2	1.37
LA	1,676,436	107,008	121,163	6.4	7.2	1.31
MS	1,064,772	60,044	77,593	5.6	7.3	0.83
NC	3,809,761	125,627	155,114	3.3	4.1	2.97
SC	1,775,394	58,655	74,288	3.3	4.2	1.38
TN	2,549,584	152,962	174,002	6.0	6.8	1.99
TX	9,750,865	476,209	575,809	4.9	5.9	7.60
VA	3,445,961	139,498	179,326	4.0	5.2	2.69
Total	40,534,842	2,093,109	2,542,147	5.2	6.3	31.61

*Data Sources: Current Population Survey (CPS) Outgoing Rotation Group (ORG) Earnings Files, 2006. Sample includes employed wage and salary workers, ages 16 and over. Variable definitions are: Employment=wage and salary employment, Members=employed workers who are union members, Covered=workers covered by a collective bargaining agreement, %Members=percent of employed workers who are union members, and %Covered=percent of employed workers who are covered by a collective bargaining agreement. © 2002 by Barry T. Hirsch and David A. Macpherson. The use of data requires citation.[1]

member and in four Southern states at that time (Tennessee, Kentucky, Alabama, and Louisiana) almost one of every five workers was union, to today when roughly one of every eight workers is in a union and, in the South, one of about every twenty workers.

Given the lack of large-scale or consistent current organizing efforts there is no reason to believe that these figures will not continue to fall in the South and nationally. Can this situation still be changed?

Operation Dixie (1946-1953)

The leadership and organizing staff of the CIO had the right analysis when they launched Operation Dixie. In the aftermath of WWII they could see the impact of increasing industrialization in the South. Soldiers were returning, there had been a huge upsurge of African Americans in the workforce, and the CIO had every reason to believe It could be successful. One of its affiliates, the Food, Tobacco, Agricultural and Allied Workers of America (FTA, CIO) had launched sixty-two organizing drives prior to Operation Dixie, winning fifty-two and gaining 12,500 workers, largely in North Carolina of all places.

Historians have not been kind to Operation Dixie.[2] The failure to organize the South has been attributed to everything from the CIO's lack of clarity on race; subterfuge and opposition from the AFL-CIO; use of non-Southern organizers; a strategy that assumed tactics could be easily transplanted from the prior CIO success to the more hostile environment of the South; the advent of the Cold War, which included the expulsion of the leftist unions (seeing a drop in CIO membership from 5.2 million members during the war to 3.7 by 1950); passage of Taft-Hartley (1947) and its anti-labor provisions (which propelled the expulsions); as well as the difficult relationships with the Dixiecrats as part of the "governing" Roosevelt coalition nationally.

All these factors may have contributed, but from an organizer's perspective, the campaign's reports from that time seem not so different from reports one could read today. Organizing was hard work. The managers at union headquarters didn't get it. Money and resources were too thin. Staff was insufficient. You don't need to put these letters in a time capsule to get a sense of the late 1940s and early 1950s or to believe that the life of an organizer on the road in the hills and hollers of the South was as tough then as it is now. Reading the campaign reports is depressing because so many of the messages and tactics of management in these anti-union drives are almost identical to what an organizer faces in a campaign today. Technology may be modernizing the world, but a lot of the head butting of labor and management is totally "old school," as if neither party has learned anything over the years.

The reports Barbara Griffiths cited in the best history of Operation Dixie indicate that the organizers were for the most part strangers in a strange land. They were confronting their own biases as much as they were hearing from workers in the mills, especially in the Kannapolis area in the drives for the great Cannon Mills: workers "can and do read," they owned cars and knew there was a world outside of the mill and the town, yet they still did not grab the cards from the organizers. Organizers kept trying to put a finger on the "fear" but that was largely just a headline for whatever the more complex story might have been from the perspective of the workers.[3]

The hard thing to understand more than fifty years later is that Operation Dixie does not seem a disaster in pure organizing terms. Elections were being won more often than not. Workers were being organized. The work of the CIO was being mirrored, even in the South, by AFL organizers as well. The problem was more one of will, resources, and circumstance than a simple story of unions being handed their asses on a platter by a bunch of yahoos in small, red-dirt towns.

The problem was the way the unions perceived the obstacles. The primary target was the Carolinas-based textile industry where labor was the weakest. Missing was the blending of the community/union strengths which had been the CIO's most successful models in auto and steel. The comparison between community hostility and recent memories of a genuine movement of workers in the North made the slogging work of organizing in the South seem so much worse by comparison.

From an organizer's perspective, it seems as though simple persistence would have meant increased progress throughout the South.

Lessons were being learned and strategies were being reshaped, and had the commitment continued over time, there is every reason to believe that labor would have prevailed more often than not.

Why then the loss of focus and will to organize the South? I believe the last straw for the campaign managers at union headquarters was the inability to believe that the work could be sustainable in the wake of Taft-Hartley. In short order, one state after another locked the door on the union shop and killed the prospects for an effective union dues structure. Tennessee, Virginia, North Carolina (where the textile drives were at their apex!), Arkansas, Texas, and Georgia passed "right-to-work" statutes immediately with the passage of the Taft-Hartley Act in 1947. By the chronological end of Operation Dixie, all the Southern states except Louisiana had passed or implemented some effective version of "right-to-work." The writing was more than on the wall, it was in the law. Labor could see it was going to be very difficult to "make organizing pay," especially if it were going to be a long, drawn-out battle from city to city, county to county, and state to state across the South, all of which of course it was proving to be.

Priorities and problems were building elsewhere in the nation and the sense of crusade for the South had dissipated before 1953 when the project finally collapsed. The golden age of labor organizing in the United States had passed and reaction was setting as hard as concrete. By 1956 the AFL and CIO had already recognized the political and organizational climate shift and merged, and effectively ceded the responsibility of organizing to the affiliates rather than directly coordinating and mediating organizing institutions. It would take a long while for that to change, and the South paid the price along with the rest of the nation's workers.

The Houston Organizing Project (1979–1984)

Twenty-five years passed before there was another concerted effort to create an organizing initiative with scale and substance in the South. Lane Kirkland stepped into the shoes of George Meany in 1979, and not long afterward—to his credit and perhaps as a surprise to many—there was a commitment of more than $1 million per year (real money then!) to create the Houston Organizing Project (HOP). The idea was to prove in the "new Detroit," as some called Houston, that labor could find a place and make its way in the Deep South.

> Under Mr. Kirkland's direction, the federation also is involved in an organization drive called the Houston project, in which 40 unions are pooling money and organizers to launch what the federation hopes will be a major organizational drive in that city, where workers and management often resist unions and where unions represent a fraction of the work force. The federation believes there are more than 700,000 potential union members in the Houston area. — William Serrin, *New York Times*, November 15, 1981

The results of HOP were less than stellar, though the "fraction" that Serrin denigrated would look good to many cities in the South (and elsewhere) at this point, since they were up to 10 percent density at the end of the project. [Union density is calculated as the percentage of union members compared to the total number of non-agricultural workers in the economy of the specific jurisdiction.] That is almost double the density in Southern cities today, twenty-five years later.

There were successes.[4] The increase in members of the Houston teachers union and the city workers units at the time were the bright lights of the project.[5] The Service Employees International Union had a nursing home campaign with Beverly Enterprises, the largest such U.S. company at the time, and election results from Houston to Marshall, in the northern part of the state, all padded the totals for a project desperate for results.

Nonetheless, the disappointments of the Houston Organizing Project were legion. In fairness part of the dysfunction of the project had to do with the very nature of the AFL-CIO, a federation composed of unions that were fundamentally independent and autonomous bodies with firm beliefs about their own entitlements. They did not see themselves as embarking on an organizing mission for the common good. Nowhere was this more obvious than around issues of jurisdiction. The CIO efforts of the fifties were radically centralized, compared to the loose coordinated cooperative campaign run by the affiliates. This was a classic example of "neither fish nor fowl" organizing. The AFL-CIO contributed general services, assigned and dispatched some staff and coordinators (like Robert Comeaux), husbanded the money and pitched in some of their own, and then tried to herd the cats to organize their own sectors.

Much of the "organizing" work implemented under the auspices of the AFL-CIO consisted of "cooperative" projects and a complex "clearing" process around organizing targets, that became quite controversial and counterproductive. Any union that was part of the "cooperative" campaign had the right to "clear" future organizing targets on the eminently reasonable grounds that resources were scarce and that unnecessary competition between unions needed to be avoided. A union would indicate in these regular meetings—and during the heyday of the HOP they were occurring almost weekly— the organizing targets their international union was pursuing; but this system of self-certification in too many cases was employed to obstruct organizing by other unions (seen as competitors). Once a target was declared, a union essentially froze that target for a year, and this process of "reservation" could be extended if there was any activity—or if no one cared one way or another. For many unions that understood protecting jurisdiction more clearly than they did organizing new workers, the process worked fine, but it impeded rather than stimulated more recruitment.[6]

Furthermore, the program never really tested its theory that Houston was a developing new industrial center, replacing unionized labor from the Midwest and East, and that "Big Labor" could follow the jobs. The problem was that the big industrial unions did not fully subscribe to the organizing campaign. The Steelworkers in the mid to late 1970s, under Regional Director Eddie Ball (later secretary-treasurer of the national) had been the labor powerhouse in the Houston area, with more than twenty thousand members at its heyday. The Steelworkers' influence, numbers, and resources, along with their political and racial liberalism during that period, made Houston one of the shining progressive lights of the South. But the Steelworkers were not there for the Houston Organizing Project, because unfortunately the advent of HOP coincided with the massive hemorrhaging and downsizing in basic steel all over the country, which decimated the Steelworkers in Houston as well.

Campaign leadership was also a problem, particularly given the chaotic structure (or anarchy?) of the project. Robert Comeaux, HOP organizing director, was not an organizing director from any of the participating unions, nor was he a major organizing figure in Houston or the South at the time. A union representative with UFCW (United Food and Commercial Workers) based in San Antonio, he neither had particular specialized knowledge nor information about Houston and its organizing problems or potential, nor on the other side did he have sufficient relationships with the top levels and leadership of the national unions to assure commitments and investment. Nor did he even have particular experience running large organizing programs and staff. He had been on the UFCW national staff and had run or participated in some campaigns largely in the West and Midwest. He was essentially dispatched over to the position as a compromise candidate on the assumption that he would not create problems for the partners or the federation.

By the time HOP took its last jump in the middle of complaints, recriminations, firings, and financial commitments exhausted and undelivered, the project had never really gained traction with workers. Oil prices had declined and the economy in Houston was no longer booming, which led to weakness in real estate and other local markets. There was no new social contract with labor waiting to be negotiated in the city. For some, this proved that the AFL-CIO was inept at organizing, but in the larger context of plummeting membership that lesson was swept away in the pursuit of survival.

Sweeney Organizing Initiatives (1998–2001)

The next big push for the South came twenty years later as part of John Sweeney's clarion call to organize after he won the first contested presidential election in AFL-CIO history. Consistent with Sweeney's mission to jump-start growth was an often expressed commitment to organize the South.[7] Interestingly much of that work ended up concentrated in the New Orleans area around three campaigns from 1998 through 2001: "Justice at Avondale," "HOTROC," and the "Gulf Coast Mariners."

These projects were all multi-union partnerships, which were the easiest program for the federation to support politically. With more than one union involved there was no question of preferential treatment or favoritism in spending and allocating resources. In other ways all of the campaigns were fundamentally different.

Justice at Avondale is the easiest to describe. For many years the Avondale Shipyards were the largest shipbuilding facility in the country and one of the only non-union ship fabrication sites. Avondale was the largest employer in the New Orleans area with more than five thousand hourly workers. There had been many failed organizing efforts at the yards over the years by different unions and the employer was virulently anti-union. Many workers in the late 1960s remember vividly the shadow of the water tower over the yard and the last vote count (and union defeat) painted in huge relief on the tower. Every so often Avondale workers, battling the constant turnover and unsafe conditions, would show up at various union halls all over New Orleans begging for assistance in organizing. Finally, the Metal Trades Council, AFL-CIO, composed of a coalition of mostly trades-based unions, responded and despite a contentious and litigious campaign lasting years finally prevailed and was certified at around the time of Sweeney's election. Support by the AFL-CIO consisted largely of assistance in running a contract campaign rather than a new organizing effort, but there is little doubt that this campaign was important in finally bring this work to harvest. The AFL-CIO contributed resources and staff with the right experience to force the unions that were part of the Metal Trades Council to maintain their focus during this lengthy struggle. A change in ownership to a less antagonistic employer finally provided the breakpoint to settle the campaign successfully. Disappointingly, this contract victory was not converted into increased new organizing in other unorganized Gulf Coast shipyards. The Operating Engineers organized one location on their own, but the Metal Trades Council did not continue as an effective organizing or coordinating formation, and the opportunity faded away.

Simultaneously, a significant private-sector organizing effort targeted the largest employment sector in New Orleans: the hospitality industries, with twenty thousand to fifty thousand workers.[8] The HOTROC campaign (Hospitality, Hotels, and Restaurants Organizing Council, AFL-CIO) was initiated by the Service Employees International Union (SEIU) under Local 100 in New Orleans and partnered with the Hotel Employees and Restaurant Employees International Union (HERE) and the International Union of Operating Engineers (IUOE) through its New Orleans local.[9] The AFL-CIO provided resources and staffing and used the project as part of their training programs for lead organizers. This effort began in 1998 and ended in the wake of 9/11, which eliminated tourist air travel and made the organizing strategy largely moot. The campaign strategy dictated by the partnership attempted to use both direct organizing and other tools to create leverage to organize the hotels, primarily by creating "labor peace" or "neutrality agreements" in areas where we had private-public partnerships.[10] Extensive time and effort was spent integrating the local political realities with the project organizing work, so that Mayor Marc Morial and the majority of the New Orleans City Council became pivotal to the success of the campaign. HOTROC prevailed in a direct NLRB election with a unit of more than 350 workers employed by ARAMARK at the New Orleans Convention Center. In July 1998, HOTROC organized the largest pro-labor march in New Orleans history with 7,500 to 10,000 people demonstrating community support for a worker-centered set of municipal policies. And the campaign created the labor peace agreement with the Piazza d'Italia project that led to the wall-to-wall unionization of the Loew's Hotel on Poydras Street. But other labor peace agreements then in process, including at an airport hotel and at a World Trade Center hotel conversion, were swept away in the industry downturn in the aftermath of 9/11.

Other events at the time contributed to both the potential and the positive performance of labor in New Orleans. The victory of an electoral initiative by ACORN (the Association of Community Organizations for Reform Now) and SEIU Local 100 to raise the minimum wage by one dollar in the City of New Orleans was phenomenally popular with the base. This electoral strength helped create a majority coalition in the City Council in support of progressive community and labor programs and built an increasingly productive working relationship with Mayor Morial. Local 100 parlayed this into a long-sought prize by negotiating an agreement allowing city workers to finally vote on the question of unionization, then successfully winning elections and bargaining the contract to represent 1,500 municipal workers after decades of illusive and futile efforts.

Nonetheless, despite these advances the work did not continue meaningfully after 9/11 in the hospitality and hotels sector, because of problems which almost seem inherent to multi-union partnerships. The Hotel union had little appetite for the New Orleans hotel market, as it turned out, being much more interested in Mississippi casinos, which their huge base in Las Vegas made lower-hanging fruit. So, rather than retool organizing strategies as the investment and expansion of the market changed nationally and in New Orleans in the wake of 9/11, the partners left the AFL-CIO holding the bag and finally shut the project down.

The Gulf Coast Mariners campaign was a joint project of the maritime unions seeking to organize sailors on the Gulf Coast, the only remaining unorganized jurisdiction in the U.S. The campaign was spearheaded by the Seafarers International Union (SIU) and managed largely by their organizing director, Jessica Smith, with heavy staffing and research from the AFL-CIO. The campaign began with an important community organizing component designed to create a mariners association, particularly in the south Louisiana parishes of Lafourche, Terrebone, and Plaquemines. Additional campaign elements sought to create leverage from Texas to Florida engaging the industry and owners. The companies responded in virulent fashion by organizing a divisive grassroots anti-union campaign founded on the deeply connected families of managers and supervisors. The anti-union campaign was run like a political campaign with yard signs speckled everywhere, including public right of ways, saying "There is NO You in Union," all of which was reminiscent of the anti-union efforts in the rural textile towns that confronted Operation Dixie. The companies implemented their resistance before the unions could build sufficient local political support to sustain the local mariner organizing; thus much of the energy of the campaign became directed at saving what local labor already had, including a supportive state senator. ACORN, Project Vote, and the Mariners mounted a huge voter registration

campaign that created a sufficient base from the previously disen-
franchised (the Houma Indian Nation even added voter registration to their constitution) for the senator's reelection. But against
the long onslaught, the worker organizing never gained sufficient
ground. There was no long-term commitment by labor, so the
effort petered out.

Other Efforts

The story of other efforts to organize the South over the last
generation is also episodic. On the industrial side the real story is
deindustrialization, rather than new organizing. Setbacks in oil,
chemical, and paper manufacturing have all led to mergers of these
unions (some largely based in the South) with the Steelworkers to
survive. The United Automobile Workers (UAW) has supported
huge drives among "transplants" (domestic plants of foreign manufacturers) as the auto industry has grown in the corridor across Mississippi, Alabama, and Georgia. To date, except for the bargained
accretion at the Tennessee Saturn plants, the UAW has been unable
to organize any transplants.

Service sector organizing has generally trailed the phenomenal
growth of these jobs throughout the South. Hotels are not organized
in any significant number, though recent work around Mississippi
casinos has shown promise. Disney workers, through various multi-
union councils in the Orlando area, have some strength. The Service
Employees, famed for their innovative efforts among janitors in the
last twenty years, have recently made inroads on a city-wide basis
among property service workers in Houston and Miami, where a
campaign seems to be building. Nursing home workers found their
way with Retail Workers Distribution Workers (RWDSU) (now
a part of the UFCW) in Alabama, and health care workers have
some increasing density with SEIU in South Florida. But in the
main success has been spotty.

Public sector success has also been hard to achieve. Teachers have probably fared best because they have sustained an organizing model for decades in both the American Federation of Teachers (AFT) and the National Education Association (NEA) that did not depend on collective bargaining for sustainability or on local bargaining laws and procedures for success. A collective bargaining law in Florida has led to extensive certifications for many unions, including AFSCME, SEIU, Teamsters, and of course the teachers who have the largest merged union in the South with more than 130,000 members in the state [but another 250,000 workers under their agreements are not members]. But the ability to create a sustainable membership model and a servicing model in a right-to-work environment has prevented the building of real power by Florida workers in many of these units.

Poultry and catfish workers in the rural South were targeted in the 1990s by three unions (UFCW, LIUNA, and RWDSU) at different times. The textile workers in the 1980s and early 1990s were very active in manufacturing locations all over the South through the ILGWU, ACTWU, and other unions that became UNITE, but there is little evidence that the work survived in many areas. The Mineworkers led some heroic struggles and strikes, but entered the twenty-first century a shadow of their former glory, having never cracked a new organizing methodology in the Southern underground.

The giant shipyards at Pascagoula spurred some organizing success in the Gulf Coast areas between Mobile, Alabama, and Gulfport, Mississippi. The areas around Birmingham, where steel held sway back to the great drives of the 1930s, were pockets of residual strength. The failure of big employers to pass right-to-work legislation in Kentucky helped unions maintain density in that state over most of the twentieth century. Yet in looking at the organizing successes in the South over the period since Operation Dixie, we only find little islands of organization in the vast unorganized sea of workers.

Slipping and Sliding: The New Orleans Exception

The last available figures indicate that the highest union membership density in a Southern city in 2004 is—importantly and perhaps not surprisingly—in New Orleans with 8.5 percent, leading all of the other cities by almost two full percentage points. Again, the only city with more than 10 percent coverage was also New Orleans, with 10.2 percent of workers covered by unions. The next largest coverage in 2004 was the Tampa/St. Petersburg area with 9 percent. Other cities, including Birmingham and Memphis, leaders of twenty years prior, had dropped by more than half of their membership and even more precipitously in their coverage. True, New Orleans had fallen during the period, but only by 20 percent in both membership and coverage. Clearly the New Orleans organizing initiatives had overcome the dominant trends in the South.

Tragically, in 2005 Hurricane Katrina devastated everything and everybody in New Orleans, leading to an unprecedented assault on organized labor. UTNO (United Teachers of New Orleans), the largest union before the storm with more than five thousand members was totally decimated, and three years later has hardly two hundred members. Other public sector unions also were hammered with layoffs and permanent displacements. Several of the construction trades were amalgamated with Baton Rouge unions (Sheet Metal and Laborers, for example).

Why It All Matters

The original strategists in the CIO could not have been more clairvoyant. The South matters, and in fact is central. The country increasingly tilts towards the sun. In 1950, in the midst of Operation Dixie. the South had 26.21 percent of the nation's population. By 2002, the South had risen to almost one-third at 31.63 percent.

The original analysis that propelled Operation Dixie—that labor could not survive by allowing a vast unorganized pool of workers in the South—is truer today than then, but unfortunately the capacity to change conditions is dramatically lessened. The legal environment under the National Labor Relations Act has deteriorated to the point that the AFL-CIO has declared that changes in the labor law are its top priority. The lack of resources that forced the CIO pullback in 1953 has become even greater now as organizing, and new-member acquisition costs have steadily risen for most unions to more than $1,000 per member. Unions are generally weaker now than in almost a hundred years, so it is clearly unlikely—using contemporary organizing methodology—that they could find the money, manpower, and material along with the necessary will to tackle a mass organizing problem that numbers in the millions and millions of unorganized workers.

THE SOUTH'S PROBLEMS are classically *colonial.* The CIO, the partners within HOP, and the AFL-CIO repeatedly pulled the plug on important organizing efforts in the South *because they could.* This was not home to them. It was not at their front porch in Washington or New York or Chicago or even really in their backyard. It was to them alien soil, out of sight and out of mind, a long car, bus, train, or plane trip away, and therefore easy to avoid and ignore. These Southern workers were invisible to institutional labor in a way that it would have been impossible to imagine in another context. Now, the South is perhaps harder to ignore when cities like Houston, Dallas, and San Antonio are all in the top ten largest in the country and the labor giants of the past in New York, Chicago, and Philadelphia are increasingly unable to carry all of the weight of the remnants of labor power. But labor unions are fiercely political institutions, whose strength is now failing, and labor leaders are consumed with trying to hold the line for their existing members who are mainly outside the South. Organizational reality, however, dictates that you are either growing or you are dying, and labor has been dying for a long time.[11]

Ironically, it seems clear that this is not how it had to be, that a different strategy, methodology, and, frankly, commitment to organizing could have produced a much different history—and, if finally adopted, might still create a different future.

Lessons and Steps Forward

To imagine the South moving in a more progressive direction, we also have to imagine citizens having full social, economic, civic, and political participation in the various dimensions of their lives, including their work. It is impossible to imagine any of this without vibrant, robust and powerful community and workplace-based organizations that serve as vehicles for such participation and give voice and strength to people, their demands, and their dreams. Unions or some similar worker-based associations must be part of that future. Change in the South is essential, or else the South drags the nation down. To achieve any of this we finally have to learn some lessons and move forward.

Stick to the Cities: The people, the jobs, and the political leverage (along with any imaginable resources) are in the cities, not the countryside. That's where our success has been and where we can use whatever resources we still have in a concentrated and efficient manner. I learned this lesson early as an organizer when still in Arkansas in conversations with the great organizer, H. L. Mitchell. "Mitch" was one of the founders and the chief organizer of the Southern Tenant Farmers Union in the eastern Arkansas delta country in the 1930s where STFU organized sharecroppers with some modest success amid a world of opposition. Mitch spent much of his career trying to organize rural workers, from fishermen to sugarcane workers. As he told me more than once, "Wade, it just don't pay."

Ground First, Job Sectors Second: A lesson of organizing workers in the South that is often overlooked is the fact that "space" not "sector" trumps everything. Concentrating resources and organizing across many sectors (private and public) makes a difference and multiplies the impact more than any results isolated in any separate sector. The Sweeny AFL-CIO concentrated on metropolitan New Orleans through various broad-based efforts, and within the short span of several years it managed to hold and maintain (and in some cases increase) density in New Orleans more than in any other major city in the South. The New Orleans model, involving community-wide issues and political efforts, has been overlooked and needs to be replicated in city after city.

Leveraging Markets and Firms: The lesson the Service Employees learned in failing to organize janitors in Atlanta was that they needed to combine a market-based strategy with an analysis of firms where they have relationships and leverage in the market, and this led to the eventual victory in organizing janitors in Houston.

Leverage Remaining Strength To Organize the South: The secondary lesson here is part of the anti-colonial organizing reality: to organize the South, existing unions will have to be willing to lend some of what strength they have left through leverage in specific markets and with individual firms to create organizing rights and concessions in the South to even the playing field. Unwillingness to broker these relationships aggressively is an established formula for failure. This has certainly been the story in the Service Employee success in Houston where they targeted the city *solely* based on the concentration of their existing contractors working non-union there. They also leveraged the HCA and Tenet Hospital nationally to win organizing rights in hospitals in the south Florida market around Miami.

It's a Marathon, Not a Sprint: Organizing the South means a long-term and permanent commitment to building organizational density in fixed locations over decades to achieve results. This is also a lesson from the New Orleans experience. The groundwork undergirding the successful initiatives had been laid by years of constant organizing, building political relationships, and deepening community organizing and social-movement strength not just around jobs and income, but other issues as well. SEIU Local 100 made its first recognition demand for a public sector city workers unit under Mayor Ernest "Dutch" Morial in 1985, and it took almost twenty years of constant pressure and organizing to create the "opportunity" to organize the 1,500 municipal workers under Mayor Marc Morial, Dutch's son. Organizing success has to be based on building long-term settlements and not colonial outposts and trading stations. This is a challenge for institutional labor because these are political institutions with limited resources that are primarily focused on short-term results, rather than long-term projects, but no success will be achieved without a long-term commitment.[12]

Organization First and Foremost, the Rest Whenever: Organizing models being used by most unions are inadequate to organize anywhere, much less the hardscrabble South. In an era where the law is inaccessible, dilatory, and expensive, organizing methodology needs to escape the collective bargaining regime and concentrate on worker-driven rather than employer-dependent strategies for realizing organization first, and outcomes in terms of improved working and economic conditions down the line. The organizing rule has to be: build power first among workers by any means necessary on our own terms and in a sustainable way, with dues-paying members at whatever level, and the issues of wages, hours, term and conditions of employment will fall into place later.[13] The success of public sector associations and unions in the South has been largely independent of collective bargaining laws or election and recognition procedures, and the same model is applicable in the private sector as well.[14]

Summary

The challenges faced just living in the South rest heavily on the shoulders of low- and moderate-income working families. Relief from our economic and social challenges will come from organizations which give voice and create power through participation in the workplaces and communities of this region. One hand holding up this part of the sky should be organized and institutional labor. But without a change of vision and methodology, without long term commitment, and without deeply rooted leaders and organizers able to take the stand and weather the storm, it is unlikely that labor's Southern initiatives will be more than repeated disappointments in pursuit of an unrealized and delayed dream. In the meantime the South is a huge magnet pulling people and jobs from throughout the country into our cities and growing towns. With vanishing unionized participation and experience, a new and terrible social contract is being forged *de facto* in the South. It depends not on justice and fair wages on the job, but on submission or flight. The weak must submit to bad working conditions, and the strong may flee when possible to other jobs. As this cancerous experience spreads, national and multinational employers have no reason to do anything other than make casual accommodation to the last vestiges of unionized strength, and the Southern business model epitomized by Arkansas-based Wal-Mart, the world's largest company, will become the American standard.

It is a shame, since actual organizing has proven, time and time again, that success is possible, even perhaps inevitable, with consistent and continuous work. However, if we are ever to live in a more equitable America, we must radically change course in the South. We have to lead the way, on the ground, throughout our cities, to create a fair and progressive workplace model, as Southern as spitting and grits, that can be transported around the country—just like Wal-Mart. ❧

On Human Rights & Immigration

The South Moves Ahead

Doug Davis

Surrounded by soldiers, a huge green tank, gun turret pointed at the horizon, looms in view at the main intersection of my hometown. It is 1956, and I am a wide-eyed six-year-old riding in the backseat of our family car through Clinton, the seat of Anderson County, Tennessee. The "soldiers" are actually National Guardsmen called into town by Tennessee's governor to maintain order in a community enduring the struggle to end public school segregation. Although I do not understand it at the time, what I am witnessing is a small segment of the monumental changes that are underway in the South. Like a sweeping flood across the earth, dramatic alterations are being made to the Southern psyche, and those transformations will continue in the coming decades.

I watch as Alejandro Barada works. A small, lithe man, he is respectfully chided by co-workers for his ability to stay clean while doing dirty work. A few years ago I showed him what little I knew about the use of stone in landscaping. Now his craft far exceeds my abilities. The joints in his work describe artistry and understanding reminiscent of the Incas. His comprehension of leveling lines and geometry are self-taught. Had he been born in America, he would have been among the professional or artistic elite. But here he labors for my business, adding personal touches to his creations that always garner admiration from our clients and me.

As do many Latinos, he reminds me of a simple formula that

not enough Americans still appreciate. The more one works, the more money one makes.

Thirty months ago, the INS raided one of our job sites and caught Alejandro as an undocumented worker. The papers he had given us appeared legitimate. He then spent three months in prison before being deported to the Mexican border. After another six months or so, he returned to our employ as Jorge Vasqueles. As an employer, we conform to the law by making sure that all employees have the required proof of identity. So far, it is not up to the employer to ascertain the validity of such papers. When one of my managers inquired how we could figure out if documentation was valid, the government official said, "We don't want you to know that." I am at a loss to explain his rationale.

As a result of owning and operating a landscape business in the South for the past thirty years, I am particularly sensitive to the issues and concerns facing immigrants and undocumented workers. I continually witness prejudices and hatred against Latinos that are reminiscent of the way blacks were treated and thought of in the years of my Tennessee boyhood.

From our first Latino hire in 1986, that segment of our employee population has now grown to most of our seventy-person work force. Our "discrimination" as an employer is limited to our evaluation of the employee's knowledge, attitude, skills, and habits; in other words, we willingly conform to EEOC guidelines and we want people who want to work outdoors on a year-round basis. I do not know many American mothers whose aspirations for their children include manual labor, nor do I see American fathers who value a thickly calloused palm as much as a diploma from the right school. What I do believe is that there are lessons learned in the decades-ago Clinton, Tennessee, experience that have a significant bearing on how we should act today on the immigration issue.

Prior to the National Guard arriving to protect the streets in 1956, Clinton considered itself the model small Southern town:

quiet, friendly, and *segregated*. But the seeds of revolution were sprouting through the hard-packed soil of the racist Southern conscience. In 1950, the year after I was born, five black families backed by the NAACP sued the Anderson County School Board so that their children might attend the all-white Clinton High. Initially, the federal judge, Robert L. Taylor, threw out their case because Anderson County was in compliance with the law by providing "separate but equal facilities." The families appealed, and this time the same judge withheld his ruling pending the outcome of *Brown vs. Board of Education*, which was then before the United States Supreme Court.

After the Supreme Court made its historic decision in 1954, Judge Taylor made his. Reluctantly following the new law, Taylor ordered the desegregation of Clinton High. The school would become the first testing ground for the gradual crumbling of the segregated public educational system in the Jim Crow South.

However, a large part of the county accepted the order to de-segregate, and Clinton High took a progressive stance and made preparations by holding forums and having papers on the topic distributed among the student body. The local newspaper, the *Clinton Courier,* printed ample notices. Despite underlying resent-ment, most of the white community expressed willingness to abide by the law and to comply with the new court ruling. Many people had seen desegregation coming, and there was a sense of resignation that integration was here to stay. In the fall of 1956 twelve black students made history as they nervously walked through the hallways and into the classrooms of Clinton High. The next spring, one of

---

Doug Davis is a native of east Tennessee. Witnessing the prejudices and racism of the Jim Crow era imbued Davis with a lifelong interest in fair treatment of all peoples. Working hard to apply principles of equality, he has owned and operated a landscape contracting business for the past thirty years in the South.

these, Bobby Cain, made national news as the first black graduate of a desegregated public high school in the South.

However, that brief description is a tremendous oversimplification of events of that era. A few days before the fall term began in 1956, John Kasper of Washington, D.C., an ardent segregationist, worshiper of Ezra Pound, and leader of his national White Citizens' Council, came to Clinton. In addition to racism, abolition of rock'n'roll was part of this group's agenda. His vitriolic message gained attention and over the next few months Kasper was arrested several times and played a pivotal role in fomenting dissension in my formerly quiet hometown. Soon, Asa Carter of the Birmingham White Citizens' Council joined Kasper and his cronies. In addition to espousing race hatred, the White Citizen's Council proposed a candidate for mayor in Clinton's upcoming elections who swore to restore segregation.

In the classroom, taunting by white students and outside protestors made school life miserable for the ground-breaking black scholars. Vilified from several arenas, few teachers would return for the academic year in the fall of 1957. Principal David J. Brittain would also resign in the spring of 1957 after he and his wife were faced with almost constant harassment both in and out of school.

Yet the difficult environment in the classrooms of Clinton High was tame compared to events unfolding outside. Civil unrest quickly got out of hand and overwhelmed Clinton's two-man police department. Mayor W. E. Lewallen deputized a volunteer force to supplement the outmatched police department. A key football game on a Friday night with Lake City High School added to the tension as rumors circulated through town that the segregationists would burn a cross on the field at halftime. That didn't happen, but word went out for segregation forces to congregate near the courthouse the next night. In a moment captured by an infamous photo, an angry crowd confronted the deputized citizens downtown. Shots were fired. Forced to retreat, the home guard sought haven inside the courthouse. The picture of that tumultuous evening made the front pages of newspapers across the country.

The beleaguered volunteers behind the courthouse doors made a call to Tennessee Governor Frank Clement who ordered the Highway Patrol into Clinton that same evening to dispel the crowd. Six-foot-eight Greg O'Rear, head of the patrol, led a procession of cars into town, stepped out of his vehicle with a double-barreled shotgun slung over his shoulder and proclaimed, "All right boys, it's all over." And for a while it was. The next day the National Guard replaced the Highway Patrol. Its tank made an indelible stamp on my memory, and the Guard maintained order in Clinton for the next several weeks.

Local citizenry made a positive contribution. Among others, the Reverend Paul Turner, pastor of the First Baptist Church of Clinton, escorted some of the black students to class daily to help ensure their safety. One morning a group of White Citizens' Council members severely beat Turner. The intended result of this and other contemptible actions by this racist group was to coerce the citizenry of Clinton into supporting their agenda and candidate. However, their strong-arm methods soon backfired. The community spirit and conscience of my small town were beginning to stir.

At the school where Reverend Turner's wife was a home economics teacher, a student intervened to save her from injury when outsiders entered the building. The football team, captained by Jerry Shattuck, stationed themselves at key positions in the hallways to prevent harassment of the black students by the recently formed Junior White Citizens' Council that had been organized by Kasper and his followers. Other volunteers provided security at the homes of the high school's faculty and principal Brittain's homes. Many of Clinton's citizens were fed up with the outside protestors, their rancor, and their bludgeoning of east Tennessee's proud image of fair-mindedness.

What happened next in Clinton is that the "silent majority" stood up to be counted. Disgusted with the disruption of peace and decorum, voters soundly defeated the segregationist slate in the December elections. Many local whites may not have liked the changes, but their distaste for the inhumanity and unfairness inflicted upon their community and its reputation was even stronger.

But two years later, a blast from an estimated one hundred sticks of dynamite effectively destroyed Clinton High and the town's hard-won peace. No one was injured as the explosion occurred in the early morning hours of Sunday, October 5, 1958. A lengthy federal investigation failed to find anyone responsible for this atrocity.

Once again neighboring areas of east Tennessee united to rebuild. Oak Ridge, Clinton's better-known sister city in the county, loaned the use of Linden Elementary. Within three days, Clinton High students began attending the replacement facility. Although it took two years and sacrifices on the part of many, the community completed rebuilding of the new high school in 1960.

CLINTON CHANGED, AND conflicts in Little Rock, Birmingham, Selma, and other Southern cities displaced these first struggles in Clinton from the national memory. But the lesson for me was that nothing changes unless unjust written law, in this case the law of segregation, is forced to give way. If any law favors one group's prejudices and fears of another group who are different by racial characteristics or language, then it should be reconsidered. And when it is used to deny legitimate status for the millions of undocumented inhabitants who reside and work in this country, it should be changed.

Some Americans have forgotten that laws were once used to segregate an important segment of our citizenry simply due to their skin color. Those laws, grown from hatred and prejudice, manifested themselves in the Jim Crow South in numerous despicable ways: the illogic of poll taxes, being forced to sit at the back of the bus, and the sufferings borne by those who experienced the absurd imbalance of "separate but equal." Just as it was true for blacks from the days of Reconstruction through the twentieth century, many of the immigrants to our country are tacitly valued for their low-cost contributions in jobs that most Americans don't want. But as with the American craving for illicit drugs, the finger is pointed at the countries that are sources for these "commodities." The real issue is our own appetite.

Where would Clinton and Anderson County be if they had remained obstinate and had stuck to outdated views? No doubt there must be laws that govern our society and give guidance to our conduct as citizens. Yet few laws are above reproach, and what may have been acceptable and reasonable in one era can become obsolete in the next.

Those worried about the influx of undocumented immigrants may find the following quote from *The Writings of Benjamin Franklin, Volume 1* . . . instructive:

> For I remember when they modestly declined intermeddling in our elections, but now they come in droves, and carry all before them, except in one or two Counties; Few of their children in the Country learn English; they import many books from Germany; and of the six printing houses in the Province, two are entirely German, two half German half English, and but two entirely English; They have one German News-paper, and one half German. Advertisements intended to be general are now printed in Dutch and English; the Signs in our Streets have inscriptions in both languages, and in some places only German: They begin of late to make all of their Bonds and other legal Writings in their own Language, which (though I think it ought not to be) are allowed good in our Courts, where the German Business so increases that there is the continual need of Interpreters; and I suppose in a few years they will be also necessary in the Assem-

bly, to tell one half of our Legislators what the other half say;
In short unless the stream of their importation could be turned
from this to other colonies, as you very judiciously propose, they
will soon outnumber us, that all the advantages we have will not
in My Opinion be able to preserve our language, and even our
Government will become precarious.

Franklin's fears for the Colonies' cultural identity and the "threat"
posed by German immigrants proved unfounded. Just as would
future nineteenth- and twentieth-century waves of immigrants,
the feared Germans of Franklin's era assimilated and adopted the
language, educational, and artistic mores of their new land. Too
many American citizens have forgotten that all of us stand on the
shoulders of our own ancestors, with roots in foreign lands.

Distanced from the time when our own relatives' feet first
touched our shores, many of us have forgotten that it takes tremendous courage to leave one's motherland, culture, and family and
risk everything to make one's way in an unfamiliar realm. We are
getting the best of other citizenry when those who are so motivated,
daring, and inspired make their way to our country. We need to
remember that that kind of boldness forms our foundation.

Jesus Quintero, one of the men who works with me, spent ten
years, hundreds of hours, and thousands of dollars to become a
U.S. citizen. In October 2006 he finally reached his long-awaited
goal. Describing his happiness that day as "ecstasy" would be an
understatement. Yet now he can only hope to get his wife and
children here to live with him. How many of today's Americans
would exhibit such sacrifice, joy, and patience over a status they
obtained by birth and without any effort on their part?

I once saw a Latino man cut himself badly while painting a house.
Although bleeding profusely, he refused my suggestion that he go
to the hospital for care because he feared discovery of his status by
the INS and then deportation. People who are here illegally tend

to take all kinds of personal risks, often don't report crimes against themselves, and are averse to contact with any authority for the simple reason that they don't want to be found out. Routine commerce for undocumented workers is substantially impeded by the impossibility of obtaining driver's licenses, borrowing money, and having equal protection under U.S. law. The ability to become full-fledged citizens with the right to "pursue life, liberty, and happiness" is just as huge a barrier to today's immigrant workers as it was for people of color decades ago because there are no legitimate options in place for those who contribute so mightily to our standard of living to become legal equals to the rest of us.

Every legitimate business I know of files the required I-9 documentation for every employee, and also taxes the wages of every worker. For those who have never owned and operated a business with employees, it is important to understand that there are enough risks in trying to make a profit without taking unnecessary chances and breaking the law. But it is an obvious fact that the government is coming out ahead monetarily. Our social security system would be much closer to collapse without the taxes of millions of undocumented immigrants who will never claim a penny back.

Words also do much damage. Consider the phrase "illegal alien." Perhaps I read too much science fiction in my youth, but the term "alien" conjures up images of multi-limbed, warty, nefarious creatures certain to do harm to us humans. The labeling of human beings as "illegal aliens" dehumanizes them into an epithet. Brutal, racist labels facilitate the short jump from nasty words to violence. Vigilantes have shot people with brown skin in the Arizona desert in recent months, and the victims were not questioned as to their citizenry.

In the 1980s, our nation was involved in a debate about whether or not we should return possession of the Panama Canal to the Panamanians. Then-U.S. Senator S. I. Hayakawa, from California, remarked, "Why should we; we stole it from them fair and square,

didn't we?" Our presence on this soil we call the United States is no
less tenuous as a result of the means and methods used to cobble
our nation from disparate pieces. Yet some Americans still advocate
that we seal our borders, pull up the drawbridges, and make the
oceans impassable moats that guard our coasts. It is way too late
for such absurd isolationism in an interdependent world.

Lessons learned in my small hometown of Clinton are highly
applicable today. It is up to us who remember the wholesale unfairness of the Jim Crow South to recognize that the same indignities
are being imposed on people who currently sweat and labor at the
bottom of our economic feet. It makes a lot more sense for us to
extend a hand and steady the ladder of upward mobility for those
who are climbing the same steps as our ancestors.

The South's silent majority of decent people who are well-
acquainted with racist rhetoric need to stand up for common
sense and the continued vitality of the American experience. Most
of our citizenry are decent, caring, hard-working people like the
Tennesseans of that difficult period decades ago. We must be wary
of that minority who would fill our prisons and graveyards with
people who have no blame other than their skin color and their
ambition to be a full-fledged U.S. citizen. We need to remember
that the man roofing our house in the hot sun is an upwardly mobile
immigrant who should have the same chance as yesterday's black
youngster who wanted to go to Clinton High, and he should not
be disparaged as an "illegal alien" as today's incendiary John Kaspers
would have us believe. Just as the intrepid citizens of Clinton realized fifty years ago, intolerance and emotion need to be displaced
by empathy and the remembrance that America is truly a melting
pot . . . with the steel that flows from that pot creating the lasting
strength of our nation. ❧

Reducing Environmental Burdens

A Southern Agenda

Ellen G. Spears

When I first began reporting on the environmental justice movement for *Southern Changes* at the Southern Regional Council in 1992, the unexpectedly large turnout of local activists at a conference at Xavier University in New Orleans revealed a widespread, locally based new phase of the civil rights movement in the South. Following close on the First National People of Color Environmental Leadership Summit held in Washington, D.C., in 1991, the New Orleans conference, organized by the Southern Organizing Committee for Social and Economic Justice, brought together an amazing range of organizations from across the South and around the nation. For example, attendees included members of Jesus People Against Pollution, a local organization in Columbia, Mississippi, where a chemical factory explosion in March 1977 had left a toxic legacy in a black neighborhood; African American residents of Homer, Louisiana, who opposed the siting of a uranium enrichment plant near their homes; and Native American activists seeking to close General Atomics's Sequoyah Fuels nuclear facility in Gore, Oklahoma.

The upsurge in activism was prompted in part by a 1987 report on environmental racism, *Toxic Wastes and Race*, issued by the Commission for Racial Justice of the United Church of Christ, which had found that neighborhoods near toxic waste dumps had two to three times the minority population as neighborhoods without such facilities. Socioeconomic variables mattered, too, but race was more significant.

Now, twenty years after the *Toxic Wastes and Race* report, new data suggest that the problem may be worse than we previously understood. During this period, Congress has passed no significant legislation to address the uneven distribution of pollution. Still, Southern activists are winning victories and proposing solutions that would benefit scarred neighborhoods across the country. Their proposals deserve attention.

Emerging Movement Yields Federal Action

In 1992, the emerging Southern environmental movement spurred the introduction of the Environmental Justice Act, co-sponsored by Georgia Congressman John Lewis and Tennessee Senator Al Gore. That legislative proposal, which would have required federal agencies to assess environmental health hazards and restrict toxic chemicals in highly impacted geographical areas, was buried in Congress. But the initiative led to a policy breakthrough two years later, in the form of an Executive Order from the Clinton White House which called for all federal agencies, not just the Environmental Protection Agency (EPA), to identify "disproportionately high and adverse human health or environmental effects on minority populations and low-income populations."

The Clinton measure proved crucial in helping the Homer residents, members of Citizens Against Nuclear Trash, to stop Louisiana Energy Services from opening a uranium enrichment plant in their town. In 1997, the Nuclear Regulatory Commission, though not technically covered by the Clinton order, rejected Louisiana Energy Services' bid on grounds, in part, that the facility would have a "racially disparate impact" on two Claiborne Parish communities. The parish (or county) was 46 percent black with an average annual income of $5,800, about half of the national average. (Louisiana Energy Services moved on—to Lea County, New Mexico, nearly

40 percent Hispanic.) But the Clinton order did not give private individuals or groups the right to sue to enforce the order, nor did it authorize withholding funding if an agency failed to comply.

Environmental justice advocates had hoped that Title VI of the Civil Rights Act of 1964—which prohibits discrimination on the basis of race, color, or national origin in all federally supported programs—could be used to redress environmental harm upon minority communities. However, in 2001, the Rehnquist Supreme Court, overturning more than thirty-five years of legal practice, ruled in an unrelated Alabama case, *Alexander v. Sandoval*, that challengers under Title VI must prove that agency decision-makers *intended* to discriminate, not simply that their decisions had the effect of doing so. The Court also ruled that private parties could not use Title VI to sue against regulatory actions that yielded racially discriminatory results.

Despite regression at the national level, local people have nevertheless managed to stop some discriminatory environmental decisions. They have relied on vigorous organizing, broad environmental laws, and civil damages lawsuits. In 1996, Citizens Against Toxic Exposure in Pensacola, Florida, scored a landmark win when the EPA granted their demand to be moved from away from "Mt. Dioxin," a mountain of waste in their neighborhood. Situated near a wood-processing facility and a now-closed Agrico Chemical plant, the community was exposed to high levels of dioxin, which can suppress the immune system and cause cancer. The Pensacola contamination prompted the third largest environmentally driven

ELLEN GRIFFITH SPEARS teaches environmental studies at Emory University in Atlanta. She served as managing editor of the Southern Regional Council's quarterly journal *Southern Changes* for more than a decade. Her book, *The Newtown Story: One Community's Fight for Environmental Justice*, is a concise journalistic account of the civil rights and environmental work of the Newtown Florist Club in Gainesville, Georgia.

permanent relocation in the U.S., just behind Times Beach, Missouri, and Love Canal, New York. By 2007, 358 of 400 families had been moved, the first and largest relocation of African Americans by the Environmental Protection Agency.

However, on June 2, 2007, the EPA announced its plan to *rebury* more than 560,000 cubic tons of dioxin-contaminated soil in a single-lined landfill at this same site, despite the objections of the remaining residents. Francine Ishmael grew up a quarter-mile from what from one blogger called "the purple mountains majesty of Mt. Dioxin." Ishmael and other Pensacolans fear that EPA is taking the cheap route, failing to neutralize and detoxify the dioxin wastes, leaving a hazard in place that could harm future generations. A day care center still operates near the site.

Ishmael's mother, Margaret Williams, who led the local fight for relocation in the 1990s, was critical of the EPA's plan. "I don't feel like it is a safe one," said Williams, "and I guess they are operating the least expensively like they always do." Ishmael sees further legal challenge unlikely. "It is disheartening," said Ishmael, "I think [the EPA's plan] is pretty much set in stone at this point."

Civil actions seeking damages from corporate polluters have been especially significant in some locales. For example, settlements with Monsanto and its corporate partners for causing PCB contamination in Anniston, Alabama, by members of Community Against Pollution and the Sweet Valley/Cobb Town Task Force for Environmental Justice together totaled a record $740 million. PCBs (polychlorinated biphenyls) are classified by the EPA as probable human carcinogens. Substantial sums were set aside for cleanup (or containment) operations. The Anniston settlements even included partial support for a health clinic. At the end of the day, however, negative news is often hidden within the local victories. Payments in the 2003 Anniston settlements averaged $7,725, hardly enough to cover relocation and medical bills. In many such cases, the environmental assaults are so varied, appear so technically complex, and regulators are so slow to act that people have a hard time feeling safe about their health. And sometimes the victories do not help the people who need help most. In 2006, Glynn County and selected residents in Brunswick, Georgia, obtained $50 million compensation from Allied Chemical/LCP for mercury and PCB contamination. But low-income African American residents of what's known as the "ARCO community" were not included in the settlement, and their struggle continues.

Still missing is a legal framework that would provide an opportunity to weigh conflicting environmental injustice claims. The historic, broad, environmental laws such as the Clean Air Act or the Clean Water Act make no provision for combating unequal enforcement. And, high dollar settlements, however much needed, do not address long-standing patterns of segregated housing that leave people of color and low-income residents living too close to toxic facilities. Four years after the record-setting agreements, Anniston residents are fighting an EPA decision to allow Monsanto's spin-off, Solutia, to place low level PCB-contaminated soil dug up from residents' yards into an EPA-approved landfill in the very heart of the old neighborhood.

HAZARDOUS SOUTHERN POLITICS

Two decades after the publication of *Toxic Wastes and Race,* a group of scholars revisited the subject. Robert Bullard and his colleagues found in 2007 that "racial disparities in the distribution of hazardous wastes are greater than previously reported." Using an updated method based on calculating the distance from hazardous waste facilities, *Toxic Wastes and Race at Twenty* researchers Paul Mohai and Robin Saba found both greater concentrations of people of color living near the nation's hazardous waste facilities (46 percent of people living within a 1.8 mile radius were people of color) and a greater difference in minority population (a gap of 20 percent) between areas with and without hazardous waste sites.

While environmental injustice is a national problem, and the industrial northeast as a region still has a higher concentrations of such "hazards," of the top ten states with disproportionately high percentages of people of color living within 1.8 miles of hazardous waste facilities, four—Alabama, Kentucky, Tennessee, and Arkansas—are in the South.

Why? Obviously, the legacies of racism and state-sponsored segregation have permeated Southern life. The ecological hazards of the South's great enterprises—agriculture and extractive timber, turpentine harvesting, and coal mining—are legendary. As the region's fledgling 1930s chemical factories and other industries took root in the post-World War II era, environmental assaults intensified in new ways, and the South also became a favored dumping ground for the hazardous leavings from other states.

By the late 1970s, Southern governors had found there was money to be made on waste. Hazardous waste facilities became a growth industry, often sited in black neighborhoods. In 1978, Chemical Waste Management expanded a small dump at Emelle in Sumter County, Alabama, into the nation's largest hazardous waste site (where Monsanto later shipped thousands of barrels of toxic PCB byproducts from its Anniston, Alabama, plant). Sumter County, in the Alabama Black Belt near the Mississippi line, was 69 percent black in 1980 and is nearly 75 percent black today. The mammoth Emelle landfill and others like it in Alabama have virtually endless supplies of new hazardous materials and very low labor costs. They produce huge profits for their owners, some of whom are highly placed in state government. For example, as the *Anniston Star* reported in January 1997, tax returns released by former Alabama Governor Fob James show that the Escambia County (not a majority-minority county) landfill he developed paid him $428,343 in 1995, about five times his salary as governor that year.

During the 1980s, in a renewed effort to recruit industry, several Southern states instituted "one-stop shopping," offering polluting industries a rapid permitting process for building new facilities. EPA reports that toxic emissions of certain chemicals the agency began tracking nationally in 1987 had declined by 2005. Yet, a 2007 U.S. Public Interest Research Group analysis of the EPA data shows that concentrations of toxic emissions increased in the U.S. South after 1987. Eight of the top ten counties releasing carcinogens in 2004 were in the South.

The national movement to address environmental discrimination is diverse, multiracial, and rooted in the South. It is intertwined with the black freedom struggle, which has always been broader than civil and political rights, and has long addressed environmental concerns. Contests over land ownership, road paving, municipal health and sanitary services, and access to recreation facilities challenged environmental neglect. African American writings, from the slave narratives of Henry Bibb and Harriet Jacobs to the books and essays of W. E. B. Du Bois and literary figures from Jean Toomer to Toni Morrison, remind us that African American intellectuals have long thought and taught about nature and the physical landscape.

We are still engaged in a long-term battle for hearts and minds on racial fairness, but today's Southern movement also has a specific environmental justice agenda.

REINFORCE TITLE VI OF THE CIVIL RIGHTS ACT OF 1964

Stronger legal remedies are necessary to meet the deeply ingrained discriminatory patterns the nation faces in the post-*de jure* segregation era. These patterns reproduce themselves even absent discriminatory intent. Title VI of the Civil Rights Act should have offered redress, but it has not.

The first Title VI environmental injustice administrative complaint was filed with the EPA in 1992. Seventy percent of the nearly two hundred Title VI complaints filed with the EPA since then have been rejected or dismissed. And the EPA's foot-dragging has been encouraged by Congress. Not until 1998 did the EPA even issue an "Interim Guide for Investigating Title VI Civil Rights Complaints," and from 1998 to 2001 Republicans in Congress routinely blocked implementation of these "interim" regulations in riders attached to the agency's budget. Supreme Court decisions in unrelated cases further buttressed EPA reluctance to press environmental claims.

The current shift in the balance of power in Congress offers an opportunity to strengthen Title VI enforcement.

VOTING RIGHTS LAW: A MODEL

Voting rights law provides an excellent model for bolstering Title VI. Arguably the most successful of all civil rights laws, the Voting Rights Act of 1965 has been so effective in part because Congress anticipated the ingenuity with which Southern legislators would attempt to undermine it. The law made provisions for executive branch enforcement and required federal court or U.S. Justice Department approval of election changes in covered jurisdictions. The Act also provided for registration examiners and election observers and authorized not only the attorney general but also private parties to bring suit. Similar teeth should be added to strengthen and clarify the application of the Civil Rights Act to environmental claims.

The Voting Rights Act also faced—and overcame—a challenge over whether discriminatory intent or discriminatory effects would determine case outcomes. The Supreme Court had ruled in a 1980 Mobile, Alabama, voting discrimination case that to win judicial relief black voters must demonstrate that decision-makers *intended* to reduce black citizens' right to participate in the electoral process. In 1982, at the depths of the Reagan counterrevolution, a skillful coalition effort managed to strengthen the Voting Rights Act, directly targeting the standard imposed by the Supreme Court. Under a hostile administration, Congress not only renewed the Act, but clarified its legislative mandate, amending the Act to prohibit any practice "which results" in voting discrimination and prohibiting voting changes in covered jurisdictions which have the "purpose" or "effect" of discrimination.

Under the two Bush administrations, federal enforcement of voting rights, just like environmental enforcement, has suffered severely. Private enforcement actions have been crucial to the Voting Rights Act's continued effectiveness. We need "unambiguous" congressional action to address the problems created by the Supreme Court decisions in *Sandoval* and since, to guarantee an effects standard and allow private parties the right to sue.

The Voting Rights Act also forms an especially good model since it is based on an understanding of citizenship, that the right to vote is preservative of all other rights. In this era in which our physical environment is so threatened, we must expand our notion of the environmental rights of citizens, and begin to think of laws protecting our health as preservative of all other rights as well.

International institutions already recognize environmental rights as a component of human rights. Other countries are far ahead of the United States in defining a clean environment as a right of citizenship.

A PRECAUTIONARY APPROACH

Repair of civil rights laws would be an important step, but U.S. law long operated on an "after-the-event" approach, under which industrial processes are unimpeded and industries are essentially allowed to pollute. Often, cleanup is enforced only after damage has been done. Instead we should take a "precautionary approach" to avoid environmental harms.

Dissenting voices in U.S. legal history have long supported a precautionary view. In one of the worst chemical disasters in U.S.

history, a deadly 1947 fertilizer explosion in the hold of a U.S. government ordnance ship destroyed the vessel and nearly leveled a chemical plant in Texas City, Texas, killing 567 people. A subsequent civil action brought by a woman whose husband was killed sought damages from the U.S. government, which were awarded by a lower court. The Supreme Court reversed, denying the claim. Dissenting from the Supreme Court's majority opinion, Justice Robert H. Jackson, joined by Felix Frankfurter and Alabamian Hugo Black, made a case for a precautionary approach:

> We who would hold the Government liable here cannot avoid consideration of the basic criteria by which courts determine liability in the conditions of modern life. This is a day of synthetic living, when to an ever-increasing extent our population is dependent upon mass producers for its food and drink, its cures and complexions, its apparel and gadgets. These no longer are natural or simple products but complex ones whose composition and qualities are often secret. Such a dependent society must exact greater care than in more simple days and must require from manufacturers or producers increased integrity and caution as the only protection of its safety and well-being.

Justice Jackson continued:

> Where experiment or research is necessary to determine the presence or the degree of danger, the product must not be tried out on the public, nor must the public be expected to possess the facilities or the technical knowledge to learn for itself of inherent but latent dangers. The claim that a hazard was not foreseen is not available to one who did not use foresight appropriate to his enterprise.

The judges in the Texas City case anticipated by five decades the Wingspread Statement of 1998, which spelled out the precautionary principle:

> When an activity raises threats of harm to human health or the environment, precautionary measures should be taken even if some cause-and-effect relationships are not established scientifically.

It is beneficial that the European Union has already adopted a precautionary approach in REACH (Registration, Evaluation, Authorization, and Restriction of Chemicals), despite active interference from the Bush Administration. REACH is the EU protocol which requires further investigation into the potential harms associated with new chemicals before they are marketed, rather than after they are used. In April 2003, the Bush administration had Secretary of State Colin Powell cable U.S. diplomats in Europe to oppose the REACH standards on behalf of U.S. industry. Still, the REACH protocol went into effect in December 2006, and the U.S. chemical industry is feeling the pressure to improve safety standards. As *Fortune* magazine reported in April 2007, Linda Fisher, who served as a senior official at the EPA and is now DuPont's chief sustainability officer, said that if the European Union forces the company to phase out certain chemicals, "it's going to be hard to explain to our markets and our public in the U.S. or in Asia why the Europeans don't think it's safe for them, but we're going to continue to expose you."

With a war now underway to maintain America's access to oil, and the strain gas-guzzling places on our economy and national security, environmental concerns are finally getting noticed again. Many priorities will face the next administration, but the growing toll on the environment caused by increasing energy production, voracious energy consumption, and our chemical economy needs to be high on the list. As long as environmental problems can be shifted onto minority and poor citizens, at home or overseas, not only will they suffer disproportionately, but drastically needed improvements in our overall environmental quality will come too slowly to help us. Without a remedy targeting discrimination, unequal sharing of environmental burdens will continue to be the American rule.

In a new administration, as the nation recovers from disastrous years of environmental neglect, strengthening the nation's civil rights laws should be high priority. Passing the Environmental Justice Act would mark an important first step. Congress should look South to see what made the Voting Rights Act work, and provide similar rights and remedies for environmental claims. Congress and the new administration should recognize environmental human rights and adopt the precautionary principle as fundamental policy. And people in neighborhoods everywhere, wondering what to do about the waste dump next door, might draw on the organizing experiences of residents of Pensacola, Anniston, and Brunswick. They can help. ❧

DIXIE REACHES THE BOILING POINT

AND REPUBLICANS TURN GREEN

JANISSE RAY

In the summer of 2007, after six months in office, Florida's Republican governor, Charlie Crist, signed a proclamation that earned him the astounding moniker "Crist Almighty."

That was the summer a heat wave lingered over the South for eleven straight days, killing more than fifty people. Somewhere, almost every day, an old weather record was trumped—there were hundreds of new record highs. In August, Nashville, Tennessee, registered fifteen days above one hundred degrees, the most recorded for any month; on August 22 the thermometer peaked at one hundred and two blistering degrees, a new daily record. The South had never been hotter. Alabama's Browns Ferry nuclear plant shut down one of its reactors when the Tennessee River became too hot to cool the plant, the first time such a thing had happened in the United States.

Nine of the ten warmest years on record had occurred since 1990, and as 2007 drew to a close it looked to be the hottest ever. No longer was there any doubt about the reason: global climate disruption, caused mostly by fossil fuel emissions and by deforestation.

Charlie Crist decided to do something about it.

Not only are temperature records being set left and right, but polar ice caps, glaciers, and the permafrost are melting. Arctic sea ice is thawing, and not only in summer; it has begun to melt even in winter. This extra water is causing seas worldwide to rise, a phenomenon that parallels the escalation of ocean temperatures. That, in turn, affects ocean circulation. Overall, global temperatures have increased by more than one degree Fahrenheit, bringing shifts in drought and rainfall; broad weather changes on a large scale, including longer, more extreme hurricanes and droughts; as well as an increase in smaller events, like thunderstorms. Epochs-old migration patterns of insects and animals are changing.

This transformation is occurring because greenhouse gases are piling up like blankets in our atmosphere, where they ensnare the sun's heat, much like glass traps a day's heat in a greenhouse. The most common of the gases is carbon dioxide, which accounts for over 80 percent. Methane, nitrous and nitric oxide, black soot, and refrigerants occur in lesser amounts.[1]

What was causing all this change? Humans, mostly through the burning of fossil fuels.

Yes, climate has always fluctuated, and wild species along with it, but as Jim Hansen, director of the NASA Goddard Institute for Space Studies, puts it, "climate change driven by human activity is reaching a level that dwarfs natural rates of change."[2]

As London's *Guardian Weekly*[3] reported, if we humans take no action to cut greenhouse gases, the planet will get another four to six degrees warmer within fifty years. Mounting temperatures will transform the physical geography of the planet and the way we live: floods, disease, storms and water shortages will become more frequent. A quarter of terrestrial species are at risk of extinction.

"Without radical measures to reduce carbon emissions within the next ten to fifteen years," British Prime Minister Tony Blair said, "there is compelling evidence to suggest we might lose the chance to control temperature rises."

On July 13 of that hot summer of 2007, Governor Crist signed an executive order that required of Florida's government *immediate action to reduce greenhouse gas emissions*. That was the title of his decree.

It made sense that Florida would take action, since models of
the impending disaster portend that the state stands to lose more
than any other. Nearly 1,350 miles of coast borders the peninsula,
and a majority of Florida's eighteen million citizens live near that
coast. All of Florida's coastal cities and an astounding portion of
its coastal plain will be flooded if sea levels rise twenty inches over
the next century as predicted.

One afternoon six or seven years ago I was hiking with my friend
Jeff Chanton, a Florida State University oceanographer and global
warming scientist, at St. Marks Wildlife Refuge on the Big Bend
coast of Florida. Fifty yards inland we came upon a cabbage palm
that was dying, its fronds already brown and brittle.

"Here's a victim of global warming," Jeff said.

"You mean the rising ocean has killed this tree?"

"Cabbage palms can take a certain salinity but when their roots
are inundated they perish," he said.

"I thought this wasn't supposed to happen for decades."

"It's already happening. I've seen cabbage palms dying all around
Florida."

That scared me. Suddenly a scientific phenomenon was real.
Seas were rising, and I could see the effects.

Crist's bill required a 10 percent reduction of emissions from
current levels by 2012, a 25 percent cutback by 2017, and 40 percent by 2025. Government agencies were instructed immediately
to assess their energy usage and form plans of action.

For the vehicle fleet, any maintenance that would increase mile-
age (tune-ups, tires at correct air pressure) was to be performed

JANISSE RAY is a writer, naturalist, and activist. She is the author of
three books of creative nonfiction, *Ecology of a Cracker Childhood, Wild
Card Quilt: Taking a Chance on Home,* and *Pinhook: Finding Wholeness
in a Fragmented Land.* In addition to personal narratives, the books are
commentary on social and ecological life and calls to action.

immediately. New vehicles were required to have the greatest fuel efficiency in their class, and unbelievably, Crist mandated that state agencies use ethanol and biofuel when locally available. Any new building had to be LEED certified.[4] (For non-engineers, that's the "Leadership in Energy and Environmental Design" standard.) Leased buildings had to meet the Environmental Protection Agency's Energy Star requirements. Conference space had to meet "Green Lodging" certification.

Earlier that year, global warming had caused me, too, to do something crazy. At the time, for family reasons, I was living in Brattleboro, Vermont.

All during the fall of 2006 snow did not fall in southern Vermont. That was a place where snow, even if only a few flurries, normally flies by Halloween.

"We used to get snow in November and keep it until April," my letter carrier, Homer, a native Vermonter, told me. "When I was a kid we had a four-string barbed wire fence around the pasture at the farm, and in the middle of winter I always skied and slid over the top of it."

In November the *Wall Street Journal* [5] published an editorial that pooh-poohed climate disruption as human error. "The Earth is warmer now than it was in the recent past," it said, starting out promisingly but then delivering a poison arrow, "and this may be partly attributable to human behavior." *May be partly.* Then the editors proceeded to point out positive aspects of climate change—"a longer growing season in Siberia or Canada is at least one possible benefit of warming." The editorial affirmed that more urgent, less speculative problems need solving, including communicable diseases, sanitation, water, hunger, and education. "Socialism was supposed to have died with the Soviet Union," it warned, "but it is making a comeback under the guise of coping with global warming."

By December in Vermont there was still not even a snow-cloud in the sky; nor had the West River, which joins the Connecticut River just north of Brattleboro, frozen over. Climate change, it seemed, was catching up with extravagant Americans far more quickly than we had thought. That December, New York City had no snow for the first time in two hundred years. Duluth, Minnesota, registered its first completely brown Christmas since 1875. When no blizzard had arrived in Vermont by January, and the weather news worldwide was increasingly bad, we knew we had to act.

On the morning of January 6, 2007, with temperatures in the balmy fifties, wearing wetsuits, four of us "snow" activists set out on inner tubes from Dummerston, on the West River, toward Brattleboro. The "we" included my husband and two friends, one of whom had thought up the idea. We hung a banner from the Dummerston covered bridge that read, *Where's Winter?* and carried pictures of snowflakes, along with placards that read *I'd Rather Be Snowshoeing*—I would rather have been water-skiing, actually, but I was making a point—and *Stop Neglecting Our World.*

At the covered bridge we emerged dripping from forty-one-degree water to talk to reporters.

"There's usually one to two feet of ice on this river this time of year," said Jonathan Crowell. "It's ludicrous that we are able to tube it in January."

We said that some people are in denial about climate change. They want to blame El Nino, or anything. We said that Vermont will suffer hard. Rising global temperatures will affect maple syrup production, fall foliage tourism, trout fishing, and the ski industry.[6] We said that we're in a crisis.

THAT SPRING OF 2007, the Southern Environmental Law Center published some startling information.[7] It pointed out the major role that the South plays in climate change. Turns out, the South is one of the largest producers of greenhouse gases on the planet. "If the southeastern United States were viewed as a country, it would

rank seventh in the world for its contribution to global warming."
And six Southeastern states rank in the top fifteen worst polluted
states in the nation for carbon dioxide.

Nearly half the carbon dioxide rising into the region's skies
comes from coal-burning power plants,[8] which supply more than
61 percent of the South's electricity. (In most states, zero percent of
electricity comes from renewable sources, such as wind, solar, landfill
methane, and certain types of biomass.) Many plants still operate
with dirty, decades-old coal technology, which belches hundreds
of millions of tons of greenhouse gases. Many utility companies,
including Southern Company, are building and proposing to build
new coal plants, despite the science on climate change that is now
almost universally accepted and despite the fact that approximately
twenty million Americans have asthma. According to the Southern
Alliance for Clean Energy, southeastern power plants contribute
more than 763 million tons of carbon dioxide annually, more than
any other region in the nation!

Southerners are responsible for the highest per capita use of
electric power. In addition, Southerners have become overdependent
on their vehicles. They drive more miles per than any other Americans. Alabamians (I'm from Georgia!) ramble around especially
much, 28 percent more than the national average.[9] One-third of
the South's greenhouse emissions come from cars and trucks. One
gallon of gasoline turns into nineteen pounds of carbon dioxide
in the atmosphere.

Unchecked urban and suburban sprawl, made possible by cheap
fossil fuel, has partly driven this increase. We all know that "sprawl"
gobbles up open space, destroys wildlife habitat, contributes to obe-
sity and other human health problems, and leads to social isolation.
Sixteen of the most sprawling big metros are east of the Mississippi.
Four of the top five, you guessed it, are in the Southeast: Nashville;
Charlotte; Greensboro, N.C.; and Atlanta.[10]

To make matters worse, rampant clearcutting in the South is

destroying the forests that process and sequester carbon dioxide. Dogwood Alliance, a forest watchdog group based in Asheville, reports that the South produces approximately 77 percent of the nation's pulpwood, although it contains only 40 percent of the nation's forests. Based on U.S. Forest Service data, five million acres are cut per year on both public and private land in the region. Removal of pines (and in some areas, hardwoods) far exceeds growth.[11]

THAT SOUTHERNERS WOULD be among the first Americans to take action on climate change makes a lot of sense for a number of reasons. Not only are we the biggest contributors of greenhouse gases to the atmosphere, but scientists predict that our region will be especially hard-hit. Already the target of most hurricanes, the South will see an increase in hurricane intensity and duration, and perhaps in their frequency as well. And in a warmer, moister world, inland storms will also increase in intensity and frequency.[12]

Probably the South is already taking the biggest blow. Freak tornadoes in February 2007 ripped through central Florida, killing twenty people. A March tornado struck the high school in Enterprise, Alabama, and eight students died. On the same day, more than thirty tornadoes killed at least twenty people across the Midwest and Southeast. Severe drought over much of the region, but centered in Alabama, severely damaged crop yields.

We know that in the throes of climate change, the poorest regions in the world will suffer earliest and most. This too, bodes ill for my homeland: the South lags in average income.

The use of coal is destroying our Appalachian region by strip-mining and mountaintop removal. This unspeakable atrocity, a beheading of the oldest mountains in the world, has sparked tremendous outrage among Southerners, who point out that our sub-tropical region is a perfect place to develop solar power as an alternative source of energy. We are feeding the rest of the country cheap coal while neglecting our own ability to support ourselves.

Climate disruption seems like a vast, unmanageable problem to which there are no easy answers. But there are solutions. State and local governments are getting on board with action to end climate change, following the lead of Florida's Governor Crist and California's Governor Arnold Schwarzenegger—the Republican Greens—with "Climate Action Plans." And many nonprofit groups have put this crisis as the top of their action agendas.

The first group I heard about that called for immediate and direct action by people was Heart of the Earth, based in Tallahassee, Florida, which signed up hundreds of residents in the "Red Hills bioregion" to pledge personal lifestyle changes in an effort to reduce their carbon footprints by 30 percent in three years. People replaced appliances with more efficient ones. They insulated their houses. They switched light bulbs.

"Initially, my husband and I decided we could carpool with each other at least once or twice a week," said Lucyann Fraser, a member of the board. "We set a goal of reducing our driving by another fifty miles per week by planning and combining trips and getting bicycle baskets for occasional bike trips to the grocery store. (Our fifteen-year-old is scandalized at the thought of her mother riding a bike to the supermarket, but she'll live.) The combined benefits include $434 a year in savings on gasoline costs and a reduction of 3.1 tons per year in our total carbon dioxide emissions."

At about the same time, the city of Asheville began to promote local food. Maybe its original purpose was to advance local agriculture, but the benefits to the climate couldn't be missed—most of our food travels an extraordinary average of fifteen hundred miles to reach our plates. Billing itself as America's Tuscany, western North Carolina established tailgate markets and published a local-food guide, creating one of the most extensive and effective local-eating movements in the country. Their motto is "Thousands of Miles Fresher!"

Even more cities began to push for bicycle and pedestrian travel.

Knoxville, for example, hired Kelley Segars as a transportation planner in charge of its bicycle program. She has implemented Bike to Work Week, cycling workshops, and social rides, and has published a map of bike routes throughout the city.

Change is in the air, and on Southern campuses the pitch is more fevered. A school in Chapel Hill has a ninety-thousand-gallon underground cistern that collects rainwater to flush toilets and irrigate grounds. The University of Louisville is building a certified green lab. The Social Sciences building at the University of North Florida in Jacksonville is the city's first green-certified building. Florida State University has broken ground for their first LEED-certified building. Florida Gulf Coast University, which requires all its first-year students to enroll in a basic environmental class, has begun a Center for Environmental and Sustainability Education. Warren Wilson College in North Carolina is a leader among sustainable campuses, offsetting 100 percent of its emissions with renewable energy credits.[13]

Across the South there are untold examples of citizens acting to stop climatic disruption. At their 2006 conference, the Environmental Educators of North Carolina distributed compact florescent bulbs (donated) to offset some of the carbon generated by travel. At their eco-picnic, held in a longleaf pine grove on Fort Bragg, picnic lunches were served in reusable cooler bags, napkins were cotton washcloths, and most of the lunch was local and organic. A Covington, Georgia, Montessori school is aiming for zero waste. I attended a reception the school sponsored in which the hors d'oeuvres were bowls of cherry tomatoes and carrot sticks, grown by local gardeners—no brownies from a box, no cheese sticks. With porcelain plates and cloth napkins, the group met its goal of zero waste and saved countless transportation miles.

Two events of 2007 galvanized the public around the issue of climate change, and one was facilitated by a Southerner. Our own Al Gore released his powerful film, *An Inconvenient Truth*, viewed by millions and changing the landscape of public discourse on the issue permanently. Then on April 14, Bill McKibben and a group of students at Middlebury College organized Step It Up!, a national day of protests ranging from rallies to letter-writing parties to showings of Gore's documentary.

Some Southerners have taken to an art form the necessity of living lightly, for the sake of the climate and nature in general. They are traveling by bicycle; replacing incandescent light bulbs and high-use shower heads; shopping at farmers' markets; starting gardens and farms; buying Priuses and Insights; making biodiesel; and protesting polluting industries.

Susana Lein is one. Lein runs Salamander Springs Farm near Berea, Kentucky. She spent the better part of the 1980s as a landscape architect in the Boston area, then seven years living in her husband's native Guatemala, learning to live simply, making do. When her marriage ended, she returned to the United States, bought ninety-eight acres with friends, and began to live on the land. She farms six acres without tillage or chemicals of any kind. As a designer and alternative builder, and a person determined to live within her means and the earth's means, she's built a rough house by raiding dumpsters for building supplies and trading labor with friends. She uses a composting toilet, a spring for water, solar energy.

I heard Lein speak at a Northeast Organic Farming Association conference. What attracted me to her talk was its title: "Creating a Farm and Homestead on Marginal Land (While Penniless.)" Humble and unassuming, private and down-to-earth, Susana Lein was the most inspiring person I'd seen in a long time. Without a doubt she's doing her part to end global warming, and has improved her quality of life in the process.

We now know for sure that the future of civilization depends on our quick response to climate disruption. I firmly believe that the South can lead the world in solving this crisis. In addition to making personal changes, Southern states must implement policy changes, not just to benefit the entire planet but to save ourselves.

We must set a regional target for reducing greenhouse-gas emissions (first carbon dioxide, then methane, then other gases) based on the latest science, and then use that target to set an annual carbon cap. It follows that there must be personal and industrial carbon rations, limiting what can be spent on gas and electricity, and train and plane tickets, or alternately, we must tax our carbon emissions. We could, for example, institute a fee on utility bills (the more you use, the higher the fee) to pay for research in alternative energy generation and distribution.

We have to set building regulations that impose energy-efficiency requirements on refurbishments and new dwellings, set minimum standards for efficiency for appliances and lighting, and ban the sale of wasteful and unnecessary technologies such as incandescent light bulbs, patio heaters, and garden floodlights.

It would also help to abandon all road-building and road-widening projects, and spend the money instead on reversing climate change, to freeze new airport construction (setting a quota for landing spots), and to pass legislation prohibiting out-of-town superstores. And we could follow California's lead and tighten emissions standards on our beloved SUVs and pick-up trucks.

We could outlaw mountaintop removal, and ban the construction of new coal-fired plants. We could teach our students how to conserve.

While we're at it, we could send leaders to Congress and the White House who would "redeploy" the money earmarked for new nuclear missiles towards a massive investment in low-carbon and high-efficiency technologies and who would invest in our rail system. They would get the United States to sign the Kyoto Protocol. (The U.S. emits nearly 25 percent of the world's greenhouse gases, yet refuses to do anything about global warming.) They would pass a bold national renewable electricity standard, a minimum percentage of electricity to come from renewable sources. They would bring manufacturing back to the United States, so that we can quit using fossil fuels to transport to and from manufacturing nations like China, and so that we can again be self-reliant.

Sound like big government?

How about high tide in Richmond? ❧

"Ballot Security"

Racial and Partisan Bias Masquerading as "Good Government" Reform

Laughlin McDonald

During and after Reconstruction, it was Democrats in the South who led the way with restrictions on access to the ballot, such as literacy tests, poll taxes, onerous registration requirements, and the white primary. Although these measures were adopted for partisan and racially discriminatory purposes—to take the ballot out of the hands of newly enfranchised blacks— they frequently masqueraded as "good government" reform and high-minded attacks on election fraud. As one historian has put it, "legalized restrictions on Negro voting . . . reflected a movement for purifying the electoral process in Southern states."[1] Today, it is Republicans who are leading the charge to suppress the minority— and largely Democratic—vote in the name of good government.

A notorious ballot security initiative was implemented in the 1981 New Jersey gubernatorial election. The Republican National Committee formed a National Ballot Security Force (NBSF) which mailed letters to registered Democrats in predominantly black or Hispanic areas, ostensibly to insure that only actual residents were allowed to vote. The returned letters were then used to challenge voters to have them removed from the voter lists.

On election day, the NBSF dispatched off-duty police officers with weapons and wearing official-looking armbands to the heavily black Democratic precincts in Newark, Camden, and Trenton. The

Republicans also posted signs warning that the polls were being patrolled by security force members and offering a thousand-dollar reward for information leading to the arrest and conviction of election law violators. A toll-free number was listed to report possible voter fraud.

A ten-million-dollar damage suit filed by the Democratic National Committee against the New Jersey and national Republican parties was eventually settled by consent of the parties. The defendants agreed not to post security forces at polling places or to allow other election tactics that targeted minorities or deterred them from voting.[2]

Despite the consent agreement in the New Jersey case, Republicans resorted to "ballot integrity" tactics in Louisiana in the 1986 senatorial campaign between Democrat John Breaux and Republican Henson Moore. Moore backers sent letters marked "Do Not Forward" to voters in predominantly black precincts, and used the returned letters to request local registrars to purge approximately thirty thousand names from the voter rolls. In a subsequent lawsuit brought by local voters, the judge invalidated the ballot security program which he said "was an insidious scheme by the Republican Party to remove blacks from the voting rolls . . . The only reasonable conclusion is that they initiated this purge with the specific intent of disfranchising these blacks of their right to vote."[3]

Republicans launched another comprehensive "ballot security" program in North Carolina in 1990 during the heated U.S. Senate contest involving Republican Jesse Helms and Democrat Harvey Gantt, an African American. The state board of elections had released figures showing a significant increase in black voter registration throughout the state, while a *Charlotte Observer* poll showed that Gantt had an eight percentage point advantage over Helms. To counter Gantt's lead, Republican party operatives targeted eighty-six precincts for mailing some eighty-one thousand postcards to households with at least one registered Democrat. Black voters were nearly 94 percent of the registered voters within the selected precincts. The cards were marked "address correction requested," and advised voters—falsely—that to vote they must have resided in the precinct for the previous thirty days. State law in fact made various provisions for voting by those who moved from one precinct to another prior to election day. The card further warned that it was a federal crime punishable by up to five years in prison to give false information about residence to election officials. A week later, a second mailing of forty-four thousand similar postcards was sent exclusively to black voters in the state. The Republican Party planned to use cards that were returned to challenge voters on election day.

After Helms won the election, the U.S. Department of Justice sued the North Carolina Republican Party and the Helms for Senate Committee over their "ballot security" program. The defendants, without admitting wrongdoing, entered into a consent decree in which they agreed not to undertake similar projects targeting minority voters without the express approval of the court.[4]

REPUBLICANS NOW HAVE a name for the mail/challenge practice, which by many accounts is ongoing. It is called "caging."[5]

In a voting rights lawsuit in South Carolina, a string of witnesses testified about a "Ballot Security Group" organized by Republicans in Charleston County, whose purpose was to target black Democratic voters and deny them assistance at the polls. Despite the fact that a state court judge had previously enjoined election

---

LAUGHLIN MCDONALD is the director of the Voting Rights Project of the American Civil Liberties Union. He has represented minorities in numerous voting and other cases, testified frequently before Congress, and has written extensively on constitutional and civil liberties issues. His most recent book is a *A Voting Rights Odyssey: Black Enfranchisement in Georgia*.

officials from failing to provide assistance to voters who needed it,[6] the selective targeting of voters continued. Maurice Washington, a black candidate for mayor of Charleston in 1999, said on election day his campaign received "complaints all day long, coming from those predominantly black precincts where many of the black voters complained about wanting to vote . . . but for some reason their voting status was questioned."[7] Truett Nettles, a member of the county election commission, testified that "every time, every election we would have controversies in African American precincts about voter assistance, or just the way voters are treated."[8] Similar treatment was never reported at the predominantly white precincts, he said.

Prior to the 2002 elections, there was a nationwide flurry of new allegations of discriminatory ballot security initiatives. Democrats in Arkansas accused Republican poll watchers in Pine Bluff of using bullying tactics to keep early voters away from the polls in predominantly black precincts by demanding identification and taking photos of voters.[9] Democrats in Michigan charged that a plan by Republicans to station hundreds of "spotters" at heavily Democratic precincts was an effort to intimidate black voters and suppress Democratic turnout.[10] In Beaufort County, South Carolina, a class action lawsuit was filed the day before the election alleging that local officials had adopted a new and unauthorized policy of challenging voters solely on the basis that their registration address was a rural route or box number.[11] According to the complaint, a disproportionate number of those affected by the new rule were African American voters who lived in the rural areas of the county.

Given the history of "ballot security" measures, the announcement by the U.S. Department of Justice before the 2002 general election that it had formed a Voting Integrity Initiative to deal with voter fraud raised concerns among civil rights groups that it might be used for partisan purposes or that it would unfairly target minority voters. Those concerns were not dispelled when federal and state officials in South Dakota issued a statement that they were investigating alleged voter fraud in counties with significant Indian populations. The investigation, led by the state's Republican Attorney General Mark Barnett, was in response to a registration and get-out-the-vote campaign launched by the Democratic Party on the state's Indian reservations, where voters tend to be Democratic but where registration has historically been depressed.

Barnett, working with the FBI, announced plans to send state and federal agents to question two thousand new Indian registrants, many of whom were participating in the political process for the first time. County officials cooperated in the investigation and subjected Indian registration to a special level of scrutiny. No similar effort was made to investigate new registrations in the other counties in the state which had few Indian residents, even though these counties contained the overwhelming majority of all new registrations in the state.

Democrats charged that Republicans simply wanted to suppress Native American, and thus Democratic, turnout in the U.S. senatorial election involving Republican John Thune and Democratic incumbent Tim Johnson. Regardless of its purpose, the ballot security investigation may have actually energized Indian voters. In Shannon County, for example, which is more than 95 percent Indian, turnout in the 2000 presidential election was 38 percent. In the off-year election in 2002, it jumped to 44 percent. Moreover, the increased Indian/Democratic vote proved decisive for the senatorial election, which Johnson won by 428 votes.

Republican officials in Florida, New Mexico, Pennsylvania, Washington, Ohio, and Wisconsin made similar claims of widespread fraud and abuse in voting. But in April 2007, the *New York Times* reported that five years after the Bush administration had begun its crackdown on voter fraud, it had turned up virtually no evidence of any organized effort to skew or corrupt federal elections.[12] While there were a few instances of individual wrongdoing, most were the result of confusion about eligibility to vote. And most of those charged were Democrats.

Ballot security measures continue to be adopted around the country. In 2005, the Republican-dominated Georgia legislature, in a vote sharply divided on racial and partisan lines, passed a new voter identification bill which had the dubious distinction of being the most restrictive in the United States. To vote in person—but not by absentee ballot—a voter would have to present one of six specified forms of government-issued photo ID. Those without such an ID would have to purchase one, or swear they could not pay the twenty-dollar fee. The bill was entirely unnecessary. Not only were there laws already on the books that made voter fraud a crime, but there was absolutely no evidence of fraudulent in-person voting to justify the stringent photo ID requirement. The new requirement will also have an undeniably adverse impact upon minorities, the elderly, the disabled, and the poor.

The League of Women Voters and the American Association of Retired Persons estimated that 152,664 of the people over age sixty who voted in the 2004 presidential election did not have a Georgia driver's license and were unlikely to have other photo ID. Getting a photo ID would not only burden those individuals, but would place a special burden on those living in retirement communities, assisted living facilities, and in rural areas. According to the census, blacks in Georgia were nearly five times more likely not to have access to a motor vehicle than whites, and would thus be less likely to have a driver's license or access to transportation to purchase a photo ID. The disproportionate impact of the photo ID bill on African American voters was obvious, and that was apparently why some white legislators supported the measure. Representative Sue Burmeister, one of the sponsors of the photo ID bill, was quoted as saying if blacks in her district "are not paid to vote, they don't go to the polls."[13] If fewer blacks voted as a result of the photo ID bill, she said, it would only be because it ended voter fraud.

Then-Secretary of State Cathy Cox, a Democrat, wrote to Governor Sonny Perdue, a Republican, on April 8, 2005, and urged him not to sign the photo ID bill into law. "I cannot recall one documented case of voter fraud during my tenure as Secretary of State or Assistant Secretary of State," she said, "that specifically related to the impersonation of a registered voter at voting polls." She described the justification for the bill as a measure to combat voter fraud as "a pretext."

A recent survey sponsored by the Brennan Center for Justice at the NYU School of Law concluded that 25 percent of African-American citizens of voting age have no current government-issued photo ID, compared to 8 percent of white citizens of voting age.[14] Based on the 2000 census, this amounts to more than 5.5 million African American adult citizens without photo ID. Former President Jimmy Carter called the Georgia photo ID requirement a "disgrace to democracy," and said "it is highly discriminatory and, in my personal experience, directly designed to deprive older people, African Americans and poor people of a right to vote."[15]

The United States Elections Assistance Commission issued a December 2006 report in which it concluded that many of the allegations of voter fraud made in reports and books it analyzed "were not substantiated," even though they were often cited as evidence of fraud. Overall, the report found "impersonation of voters is probably the least-frequent type of fraud because it is the most likely type of fraud to be discovered, there are stiff penalties associated with this type of fraud, and it is an inefficient method of influencing an election."[16]

Georgia submitted its new photo ID bill for preclearance under Section 5 of the Voting Rights Act, and the Republican-controlled Department of Justice approved it, despite the recommendation of four out of five career staffers to object. The staffers' recommendation concluded "the state has failed to meet its burden of proof to demonstrate that [the photo ID requirement] does not have the effect of retrogressing minority voting strength."[17]

Joseph Rich, who served as Chief of the Voting Section of the department from 1999–2005, in testimony before a congressional committee, described Justice's failure to object as "the brazen insertion of partisan politics into the decision-making under Section 5."[18] Rich's comments were echoed by Bob Kengle, a lawyer who spent twenty years in the Civil Rights Division and served as Deputy Chief of the Voting Section. He left the section in 2005, he said, after reaching a "personal breaking point" precipitated by "institutional sabotage . . . from political appointees," "partisan favoritism," and the Administration's "notorious" Georgia Section 5 decision and its pursuit of "chimerical suspicions of vote fraud."[19]

THERE ARE OTHER notable examples of partisanship overriding career staff recommendations in Section 5 determinations. In Mississippi, the state legislature failed to adopt a congressional redistricting plan following the 2000 census. A state court then ordered into effect a plan favored by Democrats, which was submitted to the Department of Justice for preclearance. However, another lawsuit was filed in federal court by the Republican Party. The federal court adopted a plan drawn by the Republican Party, which it ruled would go into effect if the state court plan was not precleared by a specified date. The career staff unanimously recommended that the state court plan be precleared because it did not have a discriminatory purpose or effect. Department of Justice political appointees, however, delayed acting on the Section 5 submission so that the plan drawn by the Republican Party could be adopted. According to Rich, Kengle, and career section attorney Mark Posner, it was "perhaps unprecedented for the Division's political staff to override a unanimous staff recommendation to preclear a submitted change."[20]

Another example of partisan bias driving Section 5 decision-making took place in Texas in 2003. At the urging of U.S. Rep.

Tom Delay, then Republican House Majority Leader, the state legislature adopted a mid-decade congressional redistricting plan solely to increase the number of Republican-controlled districts. In doing so it diluted minority voting strength in several areas of the state. The career staff in a lengthy and detailed memo concluded the plan was retrogressive and violated Section 5. The political staff nonetheless precleared the plan.[21] The Supreme Court later invalidated the plan as diluting minority voting strength in violation of Section 2 of the Voting Rights Act.[22]

The Supreme Court has agreed to hear a challenge to a photo ID law adopted by Indiana in 2005, which is similar to Georgia's. The majority of the court of appeals upheld the law, but it nonetheless acknowledged there is "[n]o doubt most people who do not have photo ID are low on the economic ladder and thus, if they do vote, are more likely to vote for Democratic than Republican candidates," and that "the new law injures the Democratic Party."[23] In a dissenting opinion, Judge Evans said the "law will make it significantly more difficult for some eligible voters . . . to vote—and this group is mostly comprised of people who are poor, elderly, minorities, disabled, or some combination thereof." He described the photo ID law as "a not-too-thinly-veiled attempt to discourage election-day turnout by certain folks believed to skew Democratic."[24]

The stated rationale for the Indiana law—as for the Georgia law and numerous other restrictions on the right to vote—was "to reduce voting fraud."[25] But it was conceded by the state, and found by the lower court, that no one in the history of Indiana had ever been charged, much less convicted, of the crime of fraudulent in-person voting. A challenge to the Georgia photo ID law is also pending in federal court and will surely be affected by the outcome of the Indiana case.[26]

The right to vote is protected by more constitutional amendments—the First, Fourteenth, Fifteenth, Nineteenth, and Twenty-Sixth—than any right we enjoy as Americans, not to mention numerous federal and state statutes which guarantee and protect voting rights, as well as declarations by the Supreme Court that the right to vote is fundamental because it is protective of all rights. Despite these statements of constitutional, statutory, and judicial principles, one of the enduring, and unconscionable, ironies of our democracy is the willingness of those with the power to try to limit the right to vote for racial and partisan reasons.

We have surely learned in the South since the 1954 *Brown* school desegregation decision, which transformed the region despite the substantial white backlash it ignited, of the need for strong laws protecting civil rights. We have also learned that if our democratic principles are to have true meaning, the constitution and laws enacted to implement them must be strongly and fairly enforced untainted by racial and partisan bias. Unfortunately, the proponents of "ballot security" and partisan administration of voting rights laws are choosing to ignore those lessons, and in doing so are betraying American democracy. ❧

Lessons from the Bayou

Leading the Way Through the Storms

Frye Gaillard

In the days just after Hurricane Katrina, the people of Bayou La Batre, Alabama—those who had lost everything in the storm—crowded together in a local auditorium, sleeping on cots, eating the meals that were provided twice a day. Already, volunteers were pouring into this tiny fishing village on the Alabama coast, where a battered population of 2,300 souls extracted their modest living from the sea. They had lived through their share of hurricanes before, but never anything like this, never a storm surge of fifteen feet sweeping away everything in its path.

The people of Bayou La Batre were reeling.

On the auditorium stage, a local doctor had set up shop, tending to the maladies of the hour—the cuts and bruises of the early cleanup, infections acquired from contaminated water, asthma and allergies from the mold-infested homes. As she went about her work, it didn't take long before the volunteers noticed something extraordinary about the doctor, a round-faced woman with soft, dark eyes and a radiant smile, and a manner that seemed both gentle and direct. Regina Benjamin was African American, but her patients clearly came from every part of the town, from every spot on the racial and economic spectrum.

In 1990, Benjamin had opened her own health clinic on the Bayou, and in many ways it was a homecoming. She was raised on the shores of Mobile Bay, in the little town of Daphne maybe forty miles away, and she loved the easy rhythms of the coast—the subtle sunsets and changing color of the water and the way the people would look you in the eye. "These are warm-hearted people," she said, "and there is no pretense. They love you or they hate you."

In many ways, she decided, they were like the people in a lot of Southern towns—down-to-earth, hard-working—but in Bayou La Batre there was also a difference. The village was old by the standards of America, going back all the way to the 1700s when French explorers sailed into the Gulf and began building settlements from the Mississippi River to Mobile Bay. In the middle of the eighteenth century, they placed a battery of cannons at the mouth of a bayou just west of Mobile, and the area became known as Bayou La Batre. A Frenchman named Joseph Bosarge applied for a grant of more than twelve hundred acres on the swampy western shore of the bayou, and his descendants today are scattered up and down that part of the coast.

For more than two centuries, they have shrimped or fished, or helped build the boats for the people who do, and their oral history has been a living thing. Until his death in the spring of 2007, Floyd Bosarge, one of Joseph's fifth-generation descendants, held a fish fry every Monday afternoon in a boat-building shed out behind his house. His friends and family members would gather, as they had every Monday for more than forty years, swapping stories and memories of life on the Bayou. Some of the tales were irreverent and funny, while others shaded from legend into myth, and all celebrated life with the sea.

"We love it like a farmer loves digging in the dirt," said long-time oysterman Avery Bates. "You're feeding your family and the people around you. You know you're involved in something worthwhile."

BUT IF TRADITION runs deep in Bayou La Batre, it has been, for much of the current generation, an area bombarded by the forces of change. Almost certainly, the most dramatic change took shape in the 1970s when the war in Vietnam limped to an end, and a stream of refugees from Southeast Asia—Laos, Cambodia and Vietnam—began seeking sanctuary in the Bayou. Many arrived with memories nearly too gruesome to bear, stories they most often kept to themselves, of children gunned down by the Khmer Rouge or days they had spent at sea in leaky boats, trying to escape from Vietnam.

In Bayou La Batre, they quickly found work in the seafood shops, shucking oysters, cleaning crabs, and some eventually managed to buy their own boats, pursuing a life not altogether different from the one they had known in Southeast Asia. By the end of twentieth century, they made up a third of the local population, and for the refugees and the white and black families who were now their neighbors, the adjustment did not come easily at first. There were scattered racial slurs in the schools, verbal confrontations among many of the shrimpers, and a few white families simply moved away.

And yet whatever the undertow of mistrust, when Regina Benjamin came to the Bayou she saw fundamental reasons for hope. Despite the barriers of language and culture—and the Asians wanted to hold on to what they could—she could see the beginnings of a mutual respect. In the crab and oyster shops, the refugees' work ethic was beyond reproach, and as one old salt from the Bayou put it, "It made Bayou La Batre even more of a seafood production town. The Asian workers would pick one hundred to a hundred and twenty pounds of crabmeat a day. They doubled the production of American pickers. If they were shucking oysters, they sometimes worked twelve hours a day, and changed the whole complexion of

FRYE GAILLARD, writer-in-residence at the University of South Alabama, is co-author of the forthcoming *In the Path of the Storms: Bayou La Batre, Coden and the Alabama Coast.* This essay is adapted, in part, from that book.

oyster production. They shrimped also. They bought up old boats and worked hard and upgraded their boats. They were heavy producers, and people had to respect that about them."

By 2005, when Hurricane Katrina headed for the coast, Dr. Benjamin, among many others, saw in the live-and-let-live life of the Bayou a reproach to the curious xenophobia that was sweeping through the country—the new epidemic of national disdain for the refugees from Mexico and other places who were doing the work that no Americans wanted, but who were making more than they could ever have hoped to at home. That hostility toward strangers had long since faded in Bayou La Batre, and particularly in the wake of the catastrophic storm, Benjamin saw people now pulling together—white, black and Asian—in the uncertain struggle to rebuild the town.

Even in the middle of the hurricane itself, as the wind and water roared in from the Gulf, there were stories of color-blind heroism—of neighbors who turned to each other for survival. Sophol and Chandara Ngam, refugees who worked in the seafood shops, remembered the steady rise of the flood, filling their house, and still it wouldn't stop. They waded outside as the water kept coming, kept getting deeper, and they knew that soon they would have to swim. But they didn't know how, and neither did most of their seven children. They began to call out, "No can swim! No can swim!" and finally Ralph Harbison, a volunteer fireman who lived nearby, appeared with a boat. As the whole Ngam family scrambled on board, Harbison waded through the chest-deep water and pulled them to safety.

"All I could think of," he told a reporter for the *Mobile Register*, "was getting them out of there."

It was a story repeated many times in the storm and the difficult period of recovery that followed. "There's still room for improvement," says Dr. Benjamin, "but there's been a lot of sharing in a small-town way. If somebody needed help during the storm, they didn't stay within their own group. People helped each other regardless. They knew that we are all in the same state."

IF THAT REALIZATION, more and more, had become the new reality in the Bayou, most people said that Regina Benjamin was a part of the change. From the beginning, she was a reassuring presence with her cheerful smile, the crisp white coats that she wore in her office, and her manner of quiet and steady self-possession. She came to the village in 1990 and opened her storefront clinic near the water, and the word quickly spread among the people of the town that this doctor was different from many of her peers. The old-timers said she was like Mose Tapia, the family practitioner who served the community from the 1920s to the 1960s—in the days when doctors still made house calls. Working near the turn of the twenty-first century, Benjamin saw no reason why she shouldn't do the same. She would leave her office, which was, in fact, only a block or two from where Tapia's had been, and rumble through the town in her Toyota truck, dropping in on patients who couldn't come to her. Sometimes she would travel alone; other times she worked with Nell Bosarge Stoddard, her long-time nurse who was still going strong well into her seventies. Like the majority of people in Bayou La Batre, Nell Stoddard was white, but after a while nobody paid much attention to that—to the veteran nurse, who had lived in the Bayou for much of her life, working side-by-side with the young black doctor who felt right at home.

"She loves this community," Stoddard later explained. "She's very down to earth. There's nothing about her that puts people off."

So they made their rounds and treated everybody who came through the door—shrimpers with shark bites, middle-aged women who had never had a Pap smear, shipyard workers with carpal tunnel syndrome. One day a deep-water shrimper came to the clinic after three weeks at sea, sporting an ugly gash on his hand. He said it had happened a few days earlier, and lacking any way to stitch it closed, he had poured peroxide into the wound, then Super-glued it shut. To Benjamin's amazement, it was healing just fine.

As the years went by, she found she loved these people on the Bayou, the hard-working men and their children and wives, who sometimes worked alongside the men on the boats, or in the crab shops, or shucking oysters hauled in from the bay. "The most calming time for me is talking to a patient," she said, and it never mattered what their backgrounds were. It was clear from the start that the blue-collar poor—who couldn't afford insurance, but earned too much to qualify for Medicaid—deserved the same care as anybody else. And there were also patients who couldn't pay her at all, except perhaps with a bushel of oysters or homegrown pecans, or maybe five dollars at the end of the month. But she knew that all would pay what they could.

"These are proud people," she said. "They don't want charity."

In the early years, to supplement her clinic's meager revenues, Benjamin would work extra shifts in emergency rooms, or lecture sometimes to groups of physicians, and slowly but surely she began to develop a national reputation. The *Reader's Digest* did a profile, and so did Rick Bragg of the *New York Times,* and on his national newscast for ABC, Peter Jennings chose Benjamin as his "Person of the Week." In 1998, she won the Nelson Mandela Award for Health and Human Rights, while serving on the board of the American Medical Association (the youngest doctor ever chosen to do so) and the Board of Physicians for Human Rights.

But her focus remained her clinic on the Bayou. She was caught in the struggles of the people in the town, particularly when the hurricanes came through, which began in earnest in 1998. On September 28, a dwindling storm called Georges hit the Mississippi coast, and the still-potent winds on the eastern side pushed a wall of water into Bayou La Batre. Benjamin's clinic was flooded, and her insurance paid only $20,000 toward replacing the building and everything that was in it. But she found a new site in the heart of downtown, took out a mortgage, and built a new clinic on four-foot stilts—the better to avoid future flood waters.

Hurricane Ivan hit the town in 2004, damaging homes and blowing down trees, and then came Katrina. The massive storm made its first landfall on August 25, 2005, as it crossed the southern tip of Florida and entered the warm and inviting waters of the Gulf. Over the next several days, it strengthened to Category 5, sending a storm swell surging toward the coast. On August 29, the wall of water swept through the Bayou, where the town existed essentially at sea level, and two thousand people were driven from their homes.

WHEN THE WINDS subsided, Benjamin drove over from Daphne to check on her clinic as well as her patients. When she arrived at her office, she thought at first that it didn't look too bad; the walls and the roof seemed to be intact, and she wondered if she had been lucky this time. But when she opened the door, she was hit with a stench that nearly made her sick. As the *Reader's Digest* reported, "Seawater, old fish and dead crabs mingled with raw sewage. Chairs and tables were tossed about as if they'd been in a washing machine."

Benjamin and her nurse Nell Stoddard put on gloves and set out to salvage whatever they could, but they also knew that their patients were going to need them. In the chaotic week that followed the storm, they set up operations at the community center that doubled as a shelter. Grace Scire, one of the volunteers at the center, who later went to work in Benjamin's office, remembered the doctor with her reassuring smile ordering the medicines her patients had to have, but couldn't afford after losing nearly everything in the storm. Insulin, antibiotics; whatever it was, Benjamin arranged for nearby pharmacists to fill the prescriptions and then send her the bills. She said she would pay them somehow.

"After the storm," Benjamin recalled, "we saw everybody for

free for eight months. People didn't have their co-pays. But they needed care, and they needed their meds."

In Benjamin's mind, none of that was extraordinary, for it was part of a small-town way of life—distinctively Southern, some people might say—in which neighbors understood they were in it together. As a girl growing up on Mobile Bay, she had been raised on stories from the Great Depression—how her grandmother, a matriarch in Daphne's black community, would put out lemonade and sandwiches for the hoboes passing by on the highway. Her mother played a similar role, and when Benjamin graduated from Xavier University in New Orleans and entered Morehouse School of Medicine, she developed her own caregiver's obsession with somehow making a difference in the world. In 1982, she finished her degree at the University of Alabama at Birmingham, then spent her residency at a family practice clinic in Georgia before returning to the Alabama coast.

"It was like coming home," she told one reporter. "I hope my patients get something because I get even more."

Most of the time she doesn't say much more, doesn't engage in public introspections about the basic motivations of her work. She is more likely to deflect questions with a joke. She once told a reporter from *People* magazine that in recruiting another doctor for her clinic, she would simply pass along what the job meant to her. The help-wanted ad, she said, might read: "Long hours, low pay, great job satisfaction and all the shrimp and oysters you can eat."

Embedded in the essential good humor of her comment is an admission that life in Bayou La Batre has been hard—especially in the two years following Katrina. In the difficult autumn of 2005, Benjamin mortgaged her home and maxed out her credit cards to restore and rebuild her clinic. It was set to reopen on January 2, 2006, when, incredibly, a fire broke out the night before and burned the modest new building to the ground. When Benjamin arrived and stared at the charred remains of her work, all she could think of, despite the first wave of depression and shock, was that she had to find a way to push ahead.

"We'll rebuild it," she told a reporter from the *Mobile Register*. "This will give me an opportunity to try and maybe do it differently. While I like what we had, maybe I can do it better."

And in fact, she did. She applied for federal money, and after sorting through the massive bureaucratic confusion, arranged for a grant of $1.1 million—federal dollars routed through the state and then through Volunteers of America—to rebuild yet again. It was the kind of perseverance she saw all around her as the Bayou struggled against the odds to recover. And Katrina was not the community's only problem.

IN THE BRAVE new world of a global economy, there were changes in the local seafood industry—an $80 million enterprise in the Bayou, which represented 85 percent of the area's economy. Perhaps most urgently, higher fuel prices and the competition from imported shrimp, now cheaper than those caught closer to home, were squeezing shrimpers' profit margins. "It's been just devastating," said Robert Shipp, professor of marine sciences at the University of South Alabama. "The future of the shrimp industry is not good at all."

Crabs and oysters have been more stable, but in Bayou La Batre, shrimp production has been the biggest industry, and to complicate matters, there has been an ongoing conflict between the shrimping fleet and commercial sports fishermen in pursuit of red snapper. The snapper are often caught in the shrimp nets, which has produced over time an intricate set of environmental regulations. Oystermen, too, have been embroiled in environmental debates. Mechanical dredging has recently been legalized, as it was in the middle of the twentieth century, and many oystermen fear that despite the efficiency of the dredging process, it will do major damage to the oyster beds.

In addition to all these uncertainties, there has been the specter of high-end development—big-money builders who have their eyes on the Bayou if the area can make it through a few more years without being struck by another hurricane. Many people are ambivalent about this new possibility. On the one hand, the economy needs a boost, and developers might be able to provide it. On the other hand, people are afraid that everything will change if suddenly new condos are lining the waterfront, bringing higher taxes and perhaps new pressure on old-timers to move.

As one Alabama commentator put it, "the unanswered question, two years after the catastrophic storm, is whether the town can find the tricky balance between injecting new life and tearing out the old."

Regina Benjamin believes that it can, and she said she was happy to be a part of the attempt. For her part, she expects to expand her own clinic's work, hiring a physician's assistant and maybe two more doctors, and beginning a new cancer screening program to focus on the under-served parts of the community—particularly the Vietnamese. She knows that most of her patients are survivors, for indeed the whole community is that way—the whites, the blacks, the Southeast Asians, and now the Mexican immigrants coming in. Together, they have made their way through the storms, and are battling through the economic hard times. And they also share a sense of common ground—a feeling of community—in this battered, multicultural New South village with old-fashioned values springing from its core.

Somehow there is hope in that simple truth, and as Benjamin put it in a recent interview, "There's nowhere else that I'd rather be." ❧

Our Appointment with Destiny

A Cautionary Tale

Glenn Feldman

I see in the future a crisis approaching that causes me to tremble for the safety of my country . . . Corporations have been enthroned, an era of corruption in high places will follow, and the money-power of the country will endeavor to prolong its reign by working upon the prejudices of the people until the wealth is aggregated in a few hands and the Republic is destroyed . . . — Abraham Lincoln[1]

In November 2006 much of the country let out a sigh of relief that could be heard across the Atlantic, indeed the world. For the impossible happened. Democrats had won a majority on both houses of Congress, and the Republican lock on all three branches of government was broken—suddenly, decisively, and, potentially, with epic repercussions.

Since that time things have deteriorated rapidly for Republicans and more specifically for the presidency of George W. Bush. The one thing Karl Rove gambled would never happen, happened. Administration officials and their apologists, so fond of crowing that "elections have consequences" when Democrats were in the minority, have taken on the look of deer in headlights as they contemplated the results of an election that was a shock.[1] As Congress changed hands, and with it Democratic control over committees and subpoena power, bodies have begun to bob inconveniently to the surface.

At this writing, scandals continue to cascade . . . bad news upon bad news for Republicans . . . the words and names tumbling one on top of the other—some the focus of investigation, others the victims of misdeeds: Scooter Libby, Walter Reed, Alberto Gonzalez and his eight U.S. attorneys, Pat Tillman, Paul Wolfowitz at the World Bank, Larry Craig, a prostitution ring involving Bush's primary advocate for sexual abstinence, the forced silence of professional scientists on climate change . . . of professional prosecutors on official misconduct . . . of professional soldiers on colossal military blunder . . . of professional auditors on billions in tax money and military appropriations lost and unaccounted for. And always, always floating somehow above it is the name and visage of former chief political adviser Karl Rove, the Rasputin of our age. Compounding previous public relations disasters (Jack Abramoff, Duke Cunningham, Mark Foley, Pastor Ted Haggard, Abu Ghraib, Guantanamo, Donald Rumsfeld, Tom DeLay)—and the painful peeling back of the realization that our preemptive 2003 attack on another sovereign nation had nothing to do with finding Weapons of Mass Destruction that were not there, or Saddam Hussein's nonexistent role in 9/11—it seems clear the verdict on this administration will not be a kind one. Now, with a year remaining in office and approval ratings slipping lower and lower, distinguished historians have dispensed with protocol to weigh George W. Bush's certain occupancy in the deepest cellar of American presidents.[2]

With all of this happening at a blurring pace, it is tempting for that half of the American population that has always resisted Bush to get carried away. Denied a place at the table for so long, it is tempting for them to survey the smorgasbord of public scandal before them, the outrage and incompetence that are becoming daily more plain, and to stuff themselves with reckless abandon.

Sudden feasting like that is dangerous for a starving man. We, too, would do well to resist the temptation to binge. We would do well to remember that this has always been about more than one president—even a suit as simultaneously empty and dangerous as George W. Bush. The vehicle that brought so unimpressive a man to power—and us as a nation so close to actual ruin—is still largely intact. Bush's ascension was the culmination of a perfect storm of unchecked fundamentalist fervor, public sloth, communications and technological revolution, media cowardice, and a not-inconsequential amount of Democratic timidity. Yet this has also been about something more—something far darker within our national conscience: hyper-patriotism, jingoistic nationalism, moral chauvinism, hatred of "the other" (even among our fellow citizens), and the most unattractive combination of certitude that God is on our side with the most ungodly indifference to the weakest among us or the casualties of our imperial over-reach.[3] Surveying America today, the Southern experience should teach us that we should not assume the darkness has passed.

In critical ways this nation has declined. Three or four decades ago our media would have led the call for George W. Bush's impeachment instead of cheer-leading the parade into a carnival of blood we antiseptically termed "shock and awe." Rush Limbaugh and Bill O'Reilly would have been laughed off the public airwaves, recognized for the demagogic blowhards they are. Today these figures are lionized by a disturbingly large segment of our populace. They are rock stars. Perhaps more unsettling, they are treated as legitimate journalistic figures by people who know better. They appear in *Time* and on cable news instead of white-power, Aryan websites or *Thunderbolt* magazine.[4] Today a large part of the ink spilled on global warming is corporate-sponsored hack "science" designed to muddy the waters so that revenues from oil and auto-

---

Historian **GLENN FELDMAN** is associate professor and director of the Center for Labor Education and Research at the University of Alabama at Birmingham. He is the author or editor of seven books on Southern politics, religion, race, and economics. Feldman is a native of Birmingham, Alabama.

mobile production can be preserved. Fifty years ago, were we truly a nation at war, our people would have done more in the way of sacrifice to "support the boys" in Iraq than slap a yellow ribbon on our new, over-sized SUV as we refilled its gas tank. What is not clear is if the decline will be permanent or if we can recover, and what role the American South will play in the drama.

In large part the question will turn on whether the United States will choose to preserve the New Deal or jettison it for an earlier, more starkly divided time. In all of this the South will be critical, for it was the American South more than any other place that first led the revolt against the New Deal (after profiting from it more than any other region). It was Southern Democrats who met in Macon, Georgia in 1936 to plot against the FDR presidency, who issued the "Conservative Manifesto" in 1938 and rebelled openly in the "Dixiecrat Revolt" ten years later. And it was Southern Democrats who left the New Deal party in droves to become Republicans in the 1970s. Surveying our present situation, one is likely to get the slow, sickening feeling that much of today's status quo (and, certainly, the "conservative" agenda) looks, frighteningly, more like the Gilded Age than it does the New Deal. This is true in virtually every sector imaginable: free market fundamentalism, neo-imperialism, yellow journalism, Social Darwinism with its fixation on "personal responsibility" and its blindness to systemic causes and solutions, the robber barons and their modern parallels in CEO pay and corporate scandal, yawning income and wealth disparities, crushing pressure on the middle class, assaults on labor rights, environmental protections, and Social Security, and a willingness to do or say anything to "win." It is impossible not to note the similarities between George W. Bush and William McKinley, or Karl Rove and Marc Hanna. It is difficult to forget that the only thing the Bush Administration did quickly or decisively in the wake of Hurricane Katrina was to propose that the 1938 Davis-Bacon protection of prevailing wage rates be annulled so the Gulf

Coast could be rebuilt with suppressed wages. It is impossible not to notice that the target of much of this administration's domestic policies (Social Security, "card-check" union organization) are the children of the New Deal.[5]

I

The results of 2006, as significant as they were, do not erase our last two presidential elections which were characterized by blustering preachers, unrepressed homophobia, Supreme Court justices turning themselves into pretzels to annul a lifetime of states' rights decisions, and sabers, flags, and bibles rattled at any who would dare question the administration—even at a Georgia senator with only one limb remaining from his real (not imagined) war service in the jungles of Vietnam.[6] Yet even if the results of 2000 and 2004 are reversed in 2008, even if the Democrats can arise after Bush as the Republicans did after Goldwater, be cautious. [7]

Old South values still count, be they racial, supremely emotional, plutocratic, anti-federal, anti-"foreigner," anti-tax, anti-social service, romantically martial, blindly patriotic, and illiberal. Since the 1960s "the Southern way" on politics has become the national way. For the "Republican South," there was no great awakening and pull to the GOP. There was, rather, simply the almost wholesale substitution of the GOP for the Democratic Party that was finally lurching to the left on civil rights, Vietnam, and moral/social issues. People like former Labor Secretary Robert Reich like to say that pocketbook issues dictate how Americans vote.[8] Maybe. But not in the South, never in the South, and now less so in the nation. Once overt racism worked its magic, but increasingly it is a *politics of emotion* that has worked so well and been characterized by more subtle, coded references on race combined with what can be called *The New Racism*, meaning appeals to moral chauvinism, religious bigotry and authoritarianism, and an almost-gleeful kind of public, narrow-minded intolerance.[9]

As the Plains states, the Rocky Mountains, and the rest of the American Heartland picked up this kind of politics they have also become decidedly more "Southern."[10] Karl Rove did not invent this wheel. He simply rode—perhaps more ruthlessly and brazenly than ever before—the same one Lee Atwater, Harry Dent, and Strom Thurmond did before him; the one George Wallace and the Dixiecrats used before *them*; and one that looks an awful lot like the one Southern Bourbons used to suppress class consciousness during Reconstruction and the turn-of-the-century disfranchisement movement.[11]

There were undeniable problems with John Kerry's campaign (such as voting for war authority in Iraq, allowing Mary Beth Cahill to confront Karl Rove's brass knuckles with school-marmish civility, and an exasperating propensity to give convoluted answers to one-sentence questions). But the real problem was the opposition—hate/talk radio, the Internet, Religious-Right organization, and the $300 million-a-year think tank industry dominated by what reasonable people once considered to be the *far* right.[12] Clear Channel alone reaches 100 million Americans daily. What does the liberal Air America do?

Another electoral problem is structural. Diebold, ES & S, and other companies with close ties to the GOP program the voting machines that much of America uses to vote; secretaries of state in Florida and Ohio count and certify the votes while they oversee the Bush campaign in state; and these machines cannot produce a paper trail to reflect one's vote as any self-respecting ATM or gas pump can do. This is because somebody wants it so.[13] It benefits someone.

II

Old South politics still count. For those who have persisted in doubting whether the American South still exists as a distinguishable reality,[14] they need go no further than the Catholic vote—long the most accurate indicator of American presidential preference. In 2000 George W. Bush (a Southern Methodist) lost the Catholic vote 49-47 percent to Al Gore (a Southern Baptist). Four years later and a ceaseless drumbeat about gays, abortion, Hollywood, and a "culture of life" that curiously excluded a now-estimated 600,000 Iraqi dead—and Bush *won* the Catholic vote 53-47 percent over a *Catholic*, John Kerry. Among *Southern* Catholics of *all incomes*, he carried a whopping 67 to 33 percent.[15]

If anything, the biggest surprise of postwar American politics is the debunking of the assumption many people had that the South's worst traits would gradually be ameliorated by integration into the American mainstream. Instead of the Southern way on race, economics, and taxes being softened, the worst molecules of Southern society have been infused into the bloodstream of the nation—the actual reverse of what many expected after civil rights. Eighty years after the Scopes trial we have evolution on the defensive, ironically furnishing the best evidence we have to date *against* the theory that human beings advance.[16]

Yet it must be realized that very little of this happened by accident or in some natural stream of events. Around 1935 the economic conservatives who opposed the New Deal set out to fashion what can be termed a *Great Melding* with social conservatives. Above all its other sins, perhaps, the New Deal's most egregious offense was its challenge to the "near spiritual belief," as one analyst put it, that business "simply by pursuing profit, had the power to redeem society . . ." During World War II organized business interests increasingly realized that their cold war with social conservatives was a drag on their success. In response they launched a concerted propaganda campaign to redefine the traditional American suspicion of concentrated power.[17] The campaign registered success beyond its architects' wildest dreams, altering the basic composition of "government" in the public consciousness from something that gives to something that takes away, and paved the way for anti-federal animus to be the glue binding an economic and racially conservative alliance.[18] The U.S. South became the proving ground for this.

Today individuals like Ralph Reed, Richard Land, and Trent Lott profess to be great racial progressives and admirers of Martin Luther King. But they have a core commitment to economically and socially conservative values.[19] How did this happen? Did it simply occur in the natural order of things?[20] This melding happened because elite economic conservatives tapped into powerful emotional issues (race, sex, immigration, and religion) to help plain people forget their economic interests.[21]

"This alliance between religion and politics didn't just happen," Paul Weyrich explained with evident satisfaction. "I've been dreaming and working on this for years."[22] Indeed, a moment of indisputable import was Barry Goldwater's 1964 campaign, when the conservative wing of the Republican Party seized power from Old Guard liberal Republicans, and waged a campaign that netted just six states. In addition to Arizona, they were the former-Dixiecrat states: Georgia, Alabama, Mississippi, South Carolina, and Louisiana. George Wallace would take the same states in 1968 minus Arizona. Republican operative Richard Viguerie volunteered to raise funds for Wallace provided he get to keep the Alabamian's list of urban ethnics, blue-collar workers, and Southern Democrats alienated by their national party's leftward drift on race. After an ill-fated attempt to take over Wallace's American Independent Party, the Religious Right set its sights on one of the two major political parties. They chose the GOP and sealed the decision with a 1979 summit that merged Viguerie's organization with those of Falwell, Weyrich, and Howard Phillips.[23]

For decades race was the most reliable fuel for a politics that ran on emotion. In the Jim Crow South through the 1960s it was perfectly acceptable, even advantageous, to race-bait openly. With a growing black electorate and the maturation of a post-*Brown* generation of whites who reject segregation—at least in public and in principle—it is no longer acceptable to do this. More subtle race appeals still exist, of course, clever and thinly disguised references to "law and order," welfare, affirmative action quotas, and taxes to support "social programs." But, to a large extent, conventional race baiting has been supplanted by *The New Racism*'s religious-moral baiting of "character," "values," and the like. It is no longer acceptable to call an opponent a "nigger lover." It is acceptable, even commonplace and shrewd, to paint political opponents as moral reprobates of questionable integrity—basically, of being morally and religiously inferior human beings.[24]

III

What can Democrats do? Capitalize on the truth. The message of 2006 is that Democrats need to campaign on their honest beliefs and values—economically progressive for sure—but adapted to the particular "section" of the South where they are. If Harold Ford is pro-gun and more socially conservative than other Democrats, and is closer to the Deep South, so what? Ford didn't win—but his combination of social conservatism and economic progressivism (while not quite my cup of tea) allowed him to do better than anyone ever imagined a black man could do in Tennessee. And, in the end, the GOP resorted to old race and sex gutter politics to seal Bob Corker's win; but perhaps not next time.

While the rise of the modern GOP in the South is obviously about more than just race, just as clearly it is about race more than anything else. Several recent studies—especially those of Matthew Lassiter, and Byron Shafer and Richard Johnston—have emphasized the non-racial in this massive partisan shift. It would be unfortunate if others were also lumped into this rather myopic approach.[25] The South did not become Republican so much as the Republican Party became *Southern*. White supremacy was the first and most powerful wedge the modern GOP learned to use in Dixie, often to retard mass white class consciousness. But the party's skillful—

even masterful—manipulation of the other emotional issues has allowed Republicans to profit from recent Southern "changes," as in civil rights, while capitalizing on the powerful constants in the white Southern *cultural* experience that have been there since at least Reconstruction (anti-federalism, illiberalism, fear and dislike of "the other."

Sheldon Hackney has carefully considered a number of qualifiers to his solution of what he termed "Fermat's Last Theorem of Southern History"—the problem of whether the U.S. South is still a distinctive region. Hackney is right about a lot of things—first and foremost the reality and persistence of Southern distinctiveness—but also the idea that the South has long been both the "land of super-patriotism and the locus of dissent."[26] Hackney is right that there is a changing or molting quality to the South, but through all of these periods—Conservative Democratic and newly Republican—the white Southerners who dominated the region have been moved by emotional considerations bound up in prevailing regional notions of cultural regularity. After 1865 this dominant cultural ethos took the form of white supremacy and enmity to the federal leviathan. Later it took the form of a *politics of emotion* that distracted plain folks from their class interests. After the Second Reconstruction, it emerged in a *new racism* predicated on more muted racial themes but also on a cultural orthodoxy resting on moral and patriotic chauvinism, which has now become the modern Republican South. Hackney is also correct that white supremacy and the rise of the Religious Right have been prime factors in the ascendant GOP, but he has not yet discussed two others that are equally important: the technology revolution in cable, talk radio, and the Internet, and the rise of well-heeled conservative think tanks. Through these tools the less tolerant, less humane, and frankly less attractive side of the South's essentially dual personality has been popularized.[27]

Like a spurned and sometimes-scorned lover, the South has consistently been the region most susceptible to a demagogy that preys on its most primal and irrational fears, jealousies, prejudices, and emotions. Rejected by the whole like no other—militarily and decisively—the South and her people have been the most eager to prove their love (and worthiness) through self-conscious and grandiose exhibitions of patriotism, piety, and devotion to things martial. Like a jilted lover desperate for a second chance, Southerners have combined sectional defensiveness with something near desperation to be loved again. In all of this, the South's contribution to private power and individual wealth has been considerable. Its neglect of progressive, shared, and communitarian values has been serious. The ineluctable inequalities and imbalances that result from such a system have proliferated nowhere greater than in the American South. Sadly, the greatest lesson the South may be able to offer is a cautionary tale—a tragic example the country should watch closely, learn well, and then, by all means, avoid.

Yet to end here would be to give in to a type of despair. The same South also harbors more experience with confronting poverty, demagogy, military foolhardiness, and disaster than the other four-fifths of the Union combined. As C. Vann Woodward once hoped, this is worth something.[28] And there is something more. This same South has harbored—even birthed—some of the most thoughtful, committed, and resilient progressives that America has ever produced. And it has done so in every chapter of the South's history, even—yea, especially—in its darkest moments. It was present in abolition and in home-grown resistance to the Confederacy, in Reconstruction, Populism, biracial unionism, and the movement for civil rights. Such resilience, its very existence in the belly of the beast, cannot be dismissed—no matter how sporadic, uneven, or flawed. It might instead be cultivated and savored. And in so doing, perhaps this South can offer example and even inspiration to embattled progressives everywhere. ❧

Afterword

Reflections on the Future

Dan Carter

Principiis obsta; Finem respice: Resist the beginnings; Consider the end. Although my mother taught Latin, I'm not a Latin scholar; the phrase comes from a haunting 1955 book by Milton Mayer featuring interviews with ten Germans who looked back on the meaning of their nation's journey to the holocaust. As Heinrich Hildebrandt, a retired high school teacher of literature, told Mayer:

> What happened was the gradual habituation of the people, little by little, to be governed by surprise, to receiving decisions deliberated in secret; to believe that the situation was so complicated that the government had to act on information which the people could not understand, or so dangerous that, even if people could understand it, it could not be released because of national security . . . To live in the process is absolutely not to notice it . . .[1]

But how do we get our fellow Americans to resist those beginnings and consider what could be an end in which our own American version of the unimaginable has become the norm?

Today, according to studies undertaken by the Pew Foundation, eighty per cent of the American people say that they receive most of their information about politics and public policy from watching television and listening to talk radio.

In an effort to understand what this means, I spent some sixty to seventy hours in the summer of 2004 watching the evening news as produced by the fading networks and the cable news broadcasts of CNN, Fox, and MSNBC. I supplemented this by reading the transcripts of Rush Limbaugh and several of his ideological clones. Along with many other individuals, I have written about the rising impact of what David Brock has called the growth of the great right-wing "wind machine." The worst example, of course, is Fox cable news which is essentially the press arm of the Republican Party and the Bush administration. And there is concrete, verifiable social science data showing that all of the major television networks' political coverage has become considerably more conservative over the last twenty-five years.

But at the end of this extended exercise in masochism, I concluded the main problem was not the inherently conservative slant of the television "news"; it's not even the way that television news has become a business that is geared solely to raising audience share and increasing stockholders' returns by turning the language of civic life into sensation, melodrama, and amusement ("If it bleeds, it leads!"). No, the main problem is the sheer irrationality of the way television dispenses "information."

This from my notebook on the news from CNN in one ten-

DAN CARTER is the University of South Carolina Educational Foundation Professor Emeritus. The author and editor of more than forty scholarly articles and seven books including *Scottsboro: A Tragedy of the American South* and *The Politics of Rage: George Wallace, The Origins of the New Conservatism and the Transformation of American Politics,* Carter has received eight major literary prizes including the Lillian Smith, Bancroft, and Robert Kennedy awards as well as a special citation in non-fiction from the Mystery Writers of America.

minute time bloc in the summer of 2004:

- Segment 1: Two minutes and thirty seconds on the Scott Peterson trial.

- Segment 2: Forty-four seconds of President Bush before a group of veterans explaining that terrorists are out to destroy this nation because we love freedom.

- Segment 3: A voice over a picture of John Kerry and then eighty seconds of "debate" on the Swift Boat controversy in which John O'Neill, co-author of *Unfit for Command*, and a junior Kerry campaign staffer raise their voices higher and higher, talking over each other much of the time: "He's a liar"—"No he's not"—"He is so"—"No he's not"—"Is so" . . .

- Ad 1: A twenty-five second promotion for a drug promising to cure erectile dysfunction.

- Ad 2: A twenty second series of frenetic clips promoting the latest Toyota SUV.

- Ad 3: A fifteen second description of upcoming CNN programs.

- Ad 4: A twenty second promotional ad by the diamond sellers of America.

- Segment 4: An eighty-five second account from CNN's Baghdad correspondent describing the latest bombing in Iraq. At the end, the correspondent off-handedly mentions that a marine has been killed in Fallujah. Little time was devoted to this: no film footage.

- Segment 5: Twenty seconds of happy talk between the announcers.

- Segment 6: A fifteen second teaser about the upcoming weather forecast.

And then on to a new set of ads. (CNN, I should add, is no worse than most of what is now called television "news." In fact, CNN is a lot better than Fox, which consistently combines incoherence with crude right-wing propaganda.)

In this jumble of disconnected "facts" and screaming talking heads, logic, reason, sequence, and context disappear. One fact is as important as another—no, take that back, any "sensational" fact that can be presented with visual materials is far more important than something like growing economic inequality, global warming, or nuclear proliferation. For years, conservatives complained about "post-modernism" among academics and the loss of fixed standards of truth and factuality. But today's television news is the essence of post-modernism.

While this profit-driven entertainment industry focuses on the exploits of Paris Hilton and Britney Spears, the nation experiences a growing gap between rich and poor, a scandalous failure to guarantee health care for more than forty-five million Americans, the degradation of our environment, the resurgence of racial isolation and separation in our schools and communities, and the cancerous growth of what historian Jacquelyn Hall aptly described as a malignant "'prison-industrial complex,' which far outstrips apartheid-era South Africa in incarcerating black men." Abroad, the endless war in Iraq moves relentlessly on, threatening further escalation in the Middle East, while the Bush administration resolutely refuses to address the potentially devastating consequences of global warming, water shortages and the specter of worldwide struggles for dwindling natural resources, particularly energy resources.

I THINK IT is fair to say that, however depressed we are by the difficulties of breaking through this blizzard of infotainment, the writers in this collection cling to a belief that the written word can still make a difference; that we can somehow find the civic will to focus upon the many ways in which our future is threatened by our failure as a nation to confront these and a host of other problems.

In part, that means drawing upon our past as we face the future. Despite Carl Jung's cynical observation ("Man never learns from history, and, as a rule, in respect to a problem of the present, it can teach us simply nothing . . .") conservatives and liberals alike instinctively call upon history to help us understand what we should do (and to validate our actions and policies; that's why the past is always contested territory).

As I've read the essays included in this collection, I keep wondering: Does that Southern historical experience offer us a special insight into the challenges this nation faces? It's not that I believe American philosopher George Santayana's aphorism: "Those who cannot remember the past are condemned to repeat it." I've always been uncomfortable with that phrase, because it seems to suggest that the lessons of that past are easily transferable to the present. They are not.

As I followed the trial of former Serbian strongman Slobodan Milosevic some years ago, I was struck again and again by the parallels between Serbs and white Southerners; both victims of history, both in the thrall of manipulative demagogues who were able to transform their sense of victimization into a blindness for the sufferings of others. But I always saw these parallels as suggestive insights, not definitive explanations. During the late 1950s and early 1960s, as America edged toward greater involvement in Vietnam, the Munich analogy was accepted for the most part uncritically by Americans and there were constant comparisons between Ho Chi Minh and Adolph Hitler; Vietnam and Nazi Germany. Well, the Bay of Tonkin was not Munich; Ho Chi Minh certainly was not Hitler—and neither, I might add, was Saddam Hussein.

And whatever their shared sense of victimization, Serbs are not white Southerners.

So, I don't think history repeats itself, but I do think Mark Twain was onto something when he suggested that "it does rhyme a lot."

I've thought often of Twain's quote as I have followed the ongoing debate over the insistence of apologists for the Bush administration that our endless war with terrorism requires that we abandon two centuries of constitutional safeguards and grant the president almost limitless powers. There are many dimensions to this struggle. For me, however, the willingness of this administration to embrace torture, rendition, and permanent detention has become the canary-in-the-coal-mine of our national psyche, a dramatic symbol of the moral devastation wrought by a generation of cold-war rhetoric and half a decade of politically fomented public hysteria.

Even on this issue, I believe that our Southern past speaks to us.

Thirty years ago when I was working on a study of the aftermath of the Civil War, I encountered a forgotten episode in the history of the region. In early December 1865 as the first post-emancipation Christmas drew near, waves of hysteria swept through several dozen Deep South communities and occupying federal forces received frantic calls for help. White Southerners told Union officers and agents of the newly created Freedmen's Bureau that the emancipated slaves were preparing to rise up and slaughter their former masters and rape their former mistresses. To be sure, there have been slave uprisings in Southern history, notably the 1739 Stono Rebellion in South Carolina and Nat Turner's 1835 uprising in Virginia. But most of these so-called "rebellions" existed only in the feverish imaginations of fearful whites.

And the same was certainly true in 1865. As I read the accounts of the "proof" of these nonexistent uprisings—almost always based upon the extraction of confessions from freedmen and women through torture—I kept returning to one case in which a detachment of union soldiers had rescued three black men in Watkinsville, Georgia, who were accused of planning the slaughter of whites in the area. Blindfolded, roped together, and dragged a half-mile to the banks of a deep stream, they had been beaten for two hours and threatened with drowning. The first man later told a union army officer that he thought the "only chance of saving his life was to say what the white men evidently wanted him to say . . ." And so he described with ever-more elaborate details a grand scheme to kill, murder, and rape the white residents of the area. A second tortured freedman found (as he said), it was "useless to tell the truth" and so he too made "a lie up out of whole cloth."

Today there are "plots" and plans to attack the United States for reasons that we all know. But as I thought back to the 1865 accounts, I could see clearly how these episodes of whipped-up hysteria were made possible by the willful embrace of the image of slave (and the freedmen) as somehow subhuman. And I appreciated even more keenly how the mobilization of panic and fear conveniently allowed the strangling of dissent from skeptics (and there were skeptics) by creating a false sense of white unity in the face of the false threats of mass murder at the hands of diabolical ex-slaves.

HISTORIAN C. VANN Woodward thought Americans could learn from the Southern past when he published his famous 1960 essays, "The Search for Southern Identity" and "The Burden of Southern History." In particular, Woodward suggested that the white Southerners' "un-American" experience—their commitment to human slavery, their defeat in the Civil War, and generations of extended poverty in a land of relative plenty—could serve as a chastening lesson for a nation intoxicated with a self-image of itself as a virtuous, innocent, and all-powerful people moving inexorably on an upward path of progress at home and benevolent domination abroad. Unfortunately there is little evidence that we do learn anything from our past that is more than transitory. After all, neoconservative scholars and pundits are hard at work today promoting the argument that Vietnam was "winnable" had weak-kneed "sunshine patriots" not stabbed the military in the back by caving in to anti-war liberals.

Twenty years from now, we may look back upon the way in which the post-9/11 hysteria enabled the current administration's reckless and disastrous foreign and domestic policies and see them in the same light as President Lincoln's abuse of civil liberties during the Civil War, or our internment of the Japanese during World War II—a regrettable lapse in our nation's respect for law that was ultimately recognized and corrected. But I see little evidence that this is a short-term aberration.

To say this is to sound overwrought. If we have any sense of perspective on the past, we know that emotion can cloud our judgment. What seems critical one day is inconsequential a decade later; threats evaporate, circumstances change. And as the German schoolteacher Heinrich Hildebrandt learned, none of us enmeshed in the present can foresee the future clearly enough to know absolutely the connections between beginnings and endings.

So, what is the future? Where do we end? Are we on that slippery slope that Milton Mayer described so well? Or something in between?

What is certain is that our future depends upon what we do in the coming months and years. *Principiis obsta; Finem respice:* Resist the beginnings; Consider the end. ❧

Notes

To "Foreword"

1 Richard Freeman, *America Works* (Russell Sage, 2007).

2 For an elaboration of this point, see *New Commission on the Skills of the American Workforce, Tough Choices or Tough Times* (WDC: National Center on Education and the Economy, 2006).

To "To Rescue Our Heritage"

1 *New York Times*, December 15, 2002, "Bush Has Widened Authority of C.I.A. To Kill Terrorists."

2 *Arkansas Times*, "The War on Dissent," October 12, 2001.

3 "Two Wars and Two Presidents," Raleigh *News & Observer*, May 25, 2007

4 "Clinton Proposes Vote to Reverse Authorizing War," *New York Times*, May 4, 2007

5 "Bush Vetoes Bill Tying Iraq Funds to Exit Schedule," *New York Times*, May 2, 2007.

6 *New York Times*, May 2, 2007

7 *The Federalist Papers*, No. 69

8 *Elliott's Debates on the Constitution*, page 528

9 Putney, "Executive Assumption of the War Making Power," 7 *National U.L. Review* 5-6, (1927).

10 *The Papers of Thomas Jefferson*, 397 Boyd edition (1955).

11 Letter from Madison to Jefferson, April 2. 1798 reprinted in *Ideas, Congress, Constitutional Responsibilities and the War Power*, 17 Loyola (L.A.) L. Rev. 599, 616 1984.

12 Fullbright, "Congress, the President and the War Power," 25 *Ark. L. Rev.* 74 (1971).This talk of kings and executive power harkens back to biblical times. When the elders of Israel asked Samuel to give them a king "to go out before us and fight our battles," Samuel warned against a king: "He will take your sons and make them serve in his chariots, and some shall run before chariots. He will take your daughters for perfumers, cooks, and confectioners, and will seize the best of your cornfields, vineyards, and olive-yards and give them to his lackeys." I Samuel 8: 11-12. The people refused to heed Samuel's advice, and opted for a king. They got Saul, who conferred with the Witch of Endor (vice president and secretary of defense?), and led Israel into defeat against the

Philistines. 1 Samuel 28.

13 *Talbot v. Seaman*, 5 U.S. 1 (1801).

14 Ratner and Cole, "The Force of Law, Judicial Enforcement of the War Powers Resolution," 17 *Loyola (L.A.) L. Rev.* 715, 723 (1984).

15 A. Schlesinger, J. "The Imperial President," p. 42

16 *Ideas, supra* note 14 at 618.

17 Ratner and Cole, *supra* note 17 at 734.

18 87 stat. 555, 50 U.S.C. Sec 1541 ff.

19 Zablocki, "War Powers Resolution: Its Past Record and Future Promise," 17 Loyola (L.A.) L. Rev. 579, 583 (1984).

20 *Ibid.* at 591.

21 Crockett v. Reagan, 720 F2d 1355 (D.C. Cir. 1983); Sanchez-Espinoza v. Reagan, 770 F2d 202 (D.C. Cir. 1985); Conyers v. Reagan, 795 F2d 1124 (D.C. Cir. 1985).

22 Little v. Barrowe, 6 U.S. 170 (1804).

23 Youngstown Sheet and Tube Co. v. Sawyer, 343 U.S. 579 (1952).

24 Hamden v. Rumsfeld, 126 S. Ct. 1606 (2006).

25 Foreign Assistance Act of 1974.

26 The Lebanon Emergency Assistance Act of 1983.

27 A bill to authorize appropriations for fiscal year 1984 for intelligence and intelligences-related activities of the United States Government, Public Law 98-215.

28 *New York Times*, April 29, 1999, page 1.

29 Nicholas Kristoff, "The Soldiers Speak, Will President Bush Listen?" *New York Times*, February 28, 2006.

30 Dennis Rogers, "A Son is Home But All is Not Right," Raleigh *News & Observer*, June 2, 2007.

31 "The Despair Beneath the arab World's Growing Rage," New York Times, October 14, 2001. Robert M. Gates recently told the students at Kansas State that "the military alone cannot defend America's interests around the world" and suggested a "dramatic increase" in spending for "economic reconstruction and development." "Defense Secretary Urges More Spending for U.S. Diplomacy," New York Times, November 27, 2007.

32 "Bush Requests $30 Billion to Fight AIDS," *New York Times*, May 31, 2007

33 This is not the first time the government has used remote hideaways for the detention of its captives. In the Civil War it was Fort Jefferson in the Dry Tortugas. A young officer stationed there described the place in these words: "Situated at about an equal distance from Cuba, Key West, and the Florida mainland, it is seen rising from the depths of the Gulf of Mexico like a vessel riding at anchor. No other land is anywhere visible excepting a few small coral reefs scantily covered with a scrub growth of mango trees.Six walls enclose

the seven acres and no sound is heard except that of the waves beating against the stone breakwater. Never was jail more jail-like nor the bitter draught of imprisonment more undiluted." Confined within the sunbaked walls were court-martialed soldiers and civilians found guilty by military commissions. Among these was Dr. Samuel Mudd, who had tended the broken leg of John Wilkes Booth. After putting a bullet in the back of Abraham Lincoln's head, Booth leaped from the president's box at Ford's Theater, breaking his leg. He mounted a waiting horse, and rose east into Maryland. At 4:00 a.m., he came to the home of Samuel Mudd, who set his leg. Mudd and eight others were tried for conspiracy before a hastily assembled military tribunal of nine officers. Five of the conspirators were hanged; Mudd and three others were sentenced to life imprisonment at hard labor. Quickly and quietly they were sent to Fort Jefferson in the Dry Tortugas. An epidemic of yellow fever swept the fort in 1867, killing the medical doctor. Mudd assumed his duties and helped stem the spread of the disease. Volunteers of the 82nd United States Colored Infantry (who garrisoned the fort) petitioned the president to pardon Mudd because of his constant presence in the midst of danger and infection. Mudd was pardoned and returned home to Maryland and the practice of medicine, happily so, even knowing that "His name is Mudd" became common-place pejorative.

34 "Guantanamo Bay Faces Sentence of Life as Permanent U.S. Prison," *New York Times*, September 16, 2002

35 "Al-Qaeda Captives Cases Vague," Raleigh *News & Observer*, June 26, 2004.

36 "Officials Describe Secret C.I.A. Center at Guantanamo," *New York Times*, December 18, 2004.

37 "Afghans Freed from Guantanamo Speak of Heat and Isolation," *New York Times*, October 29, 2004.

38 "3 Afghan Youths Question U.S. Captivity," *New York Times*, March 12, 2004.

39 "Twelve Kuwaitis Challenge Guantanamo Detention," Raleigh *News & Observer*, October 16, 2002.

40 "Kuwaitis Press U.S. Over 12 Held at Guantanamo," *New York Times*, June 24, 2002.

41 *Time Stood Still*, A Brief History Detention, appendix.

42 "18 Are Sent Home From Guantanamo," *New York Times*, December 18, 2006.

43 "Despair Drove the Suicides," Raleigh *News & Observer*, June 18, 2006.

44 "Red Cross Finds Detainee Abuse in Guantanamo," *New York Times*, January 30, 2004.

45 Hamdi v. Rumsfeld, 542 U.S. 507, 124 S. Ct. 2633 (June 28, 2004).

46 "U.S. is Readying Review Panels for Cuban Base," *New York Times*, July 13, 2004.

47 Neil Lewis, "Guantanamo Prisoners Getting Their Day, But Hardly in Court," *New York Times*, November 8, 2004.

48 William Glaberson, "Guantanamo Detainees' Suit Challenges Fairness of Military's Repeat Hearings," *New York Times*, May 15, 2007.

49 Neil Lewis, *supra* note 71.

50 "Guantanamo Detainees Make Their Case," *New York Times*, March 24, 2005.

51 "Gitmo: A National Disgrace," *New York Times*, June 6, 2007.

52 "Guantanamo Bay Faces Sentence of Life Imprisonment as Permanent U.S. Prison," *New York Times*, October 10, 2002.

53 "U.S. Erecting a Solid Prison at Guantanamo for Long Term," *New York Times*, October 22, 2003.

54 "Gitmo Camp Marks 3 Years," Raleigh *News & Observer*, January 10, 2005.

55 *Ibid.*

56 "Navy Doctors Force-Feeding 2 Prisoners," *New York Times*, April 2, 2002.

57 "Some Guantanamo Prisoners Have Gone on Hunger Strikes," *New York Times*, July 22, 2005

58 "Guantanamo Hunger Strike Continues," Raleigh *News & Observer*, September 9, 2005.

59 "Hunger Strike Grows to 75 Detainees," Raleigh *News & Observer*, May 30, 2006.

60 "Force-Feeding at Guantanamo is Now Acknowledged," *New York Times*, February 22, 2006.

61 Luke Mitchell, *Notebook*, *Harper's Magazine*, August 2006.

62 "Hunger Strike by Detainees Goes to Court," *New York Times*, September 22, 2005.

63 "Striking Guantanamo Detainees Gain in Ruling," *New York Times*, October 27, 2005.

64 Luke Mitchell, *supra* note 64.

65 "Suicide Attempts at Guantanamo," *New York Times*, February 20, 2003.

66 "Prisoner's Ruse is Inquiry Focus at Guantanamo," *New York Times*, June 12, 2006.

67 "Saudis Skeptical: Some Suspect Torture," Raleigh *News & Observer*, June 12, 2006.

68 "Red Cross Criticizes Indefinite Detention in Guantanamo Bay," *New York Times*, October 10, 2003.

69 "Investigators for U.N. Urge U.S. to Close Guantanamo," *New York Times*, February 17, 2006.

70 "U.S. Should Close Prison in Cuba," *New York Times*, May 20, 2006.

71 *Ibid.*

72 *Ibid.*

73 "Try Detainees or Free Them, 3 Senators Urge," *New York Times*, December 13, 2003.

74 "New to Pentagon, Gates Argued For Closing Guantanamo Prison," *New York Times*, March 23, 2007.

75 "An Exit Strategy for Guantanamo," *New York Times*, May 3, 2007.

76 "White House Has Tightly Restricted Oversight of CIA Detentions," *New York Times*, April 6, 2005.

77 "C.I.A. Dismisses a Senior Officer Over Data Leaks," *New York Times*, April 22, 2006.

78 *Supra*, note 79.

79 "Terror Suspects Sent to Egypt By the Dozens, Panel Reports," *New York Times*, May 12, 2005.

80 "European Inquiry Says CIA Flew 1,000 Flights in Secret," *New York Times*, April 27, 2006.

81 "Rebellion Against Abuse," *New York Times*, November 3, 2005.

82 "Detainees Suit Gains Support from Jet's Log," *New York Times*, March 30, 2005.

83 "Canadians Fault U.S. For Its Role in Torture Case," *New York Times*, September 19, 2006.

84 *Ibid.*

85 "Canada Offers to Pay For False Accusation," *New York Times*, January 1, 2007.

86 "U.S. Defends Detention at Airports," *New York Times*, August 10, 2005.

87 "Rice Ordered Release of German Sent to Afghan Prison in Error," *New York Times*, April 23, 2005; "Disappeared But Not Silenced," Amnesty International, Spring 2007; "Civil Liberties," ACLU, Winter 2007.

88 "German Spy Agency Admits Mishandling Abduction Case," *New York Times*, June 2, 2006.

89 "Pilots Accused in CIA Rendition Case Traced to Johnston," Raleigh *News & Observer*, February 19, 2007.

90 "Federal Judge Dismisses Lawsuit By Man Held in Terror Program," *New York Times*, May 19, 2006.

91 "Suit Over CIA Program," *New York Times*, May 31, 2007.

92 "Inquiry in 2003 Abduction Rivets Italy," *New York Times*, July 8, 2006.

93 "*The CIA's Italian Job*," *The Nation*, April 9, 2007.

94 "Cleric Cites Torture, Shows Scars," Raleigh *News & Observer*, February 23, 2007.

95 "Italy Indicts 26, Many From CIA in '03 Abduction," *New York Times*, February 17, 2007.

96 "Italy Braces for Legal Fight Over Secret CIA Program," *New York Times*, June 8, 2007.

97 "Senate Committee Attacks CIA Detentions," *New York Times*, June 1, 2007.

98 Kent v. Dulles, 357 U.S. 116 (1958).

99 "Senator? Terrorist? A Watch List Stops Kennedy at Airport," *New York Times*, April 20, 2004.

100 "Minnesota: Terror List Delays Marines," *New York Times*, April 13, 2006.

101 *Supra* note 102.

102 "Infants Collared in No-Fly Confusion," Raleigh *News & Observer*, August 16, 2005.

103 "Terror List Casts Wide Net," Raleigh *News & Observer*, October 20, 2005.

104 "Watch List Dangers: Senator Edward Kennedy, Rep. John Lewis," Anthony Romero, *Newsletter of the National Committee Against Repressive Legislation*, September 2004.

105 "Inspection Notes Errors in Terror List," New York Times, September 7, 2007.

To "Politics and Religion"

1 *Washington Post*, May 28, 2007. On the reverse side was thoughtful reporting of the militarization of our foreign policy. A similar lot of advertisements appeared on Veterans Day.

2 See the Air Force's eight-page "advertising supplement" in the Washington Post, September 18, 2007. See too, "The Women's War," *New York Times Magazine*, March 18, 2007.

3 See *The Chronicle of Philanthropy*, 2006.

4 See, e.g., Chris Hedges's June 3, 2007, report in the *Philadelphia Inquirer*: "What if Our Mercenaries Turn On Us"; and *Washington Post* reports on July 1—"In Iraq, a Private Realm of Intelligence-Gathering," and on July 8—"Who Runs the CIA? Outsiders for Hire"; see the comprehensive accounts in the *Washington Post* of July 1, 2007; and in *Defense Horizons of the National Defense University*, July 2007. An excellent piece, too, was David Nasan's *Post* op-ed of September 23, 2007, "We Can't Rely on the Kindness of Billionaires."

5 *Divided America*, Simon and Schuster, 2007. Much can also be learned from Thomas F. Schaller, *Whistling Past Dixie*, Simon and Schuster, 2006.

6 The first quotation is from his essay on Self Reliance; the second from that on Compensation.

7 This was in his book, *Religion Within the Limits of Reason Alone*. The title represents well his thesis: religion is an invaluable aspect of human life, but only when bounded by reason. Translated by T. M. Greene and H. H. Hudson,

Harper and Row, 1960. Page 92.

8   *Ibid*, page 121.

9   *New York Times*, March 18, 2007; *Washington Post*, May 14, 2007. A headline in the February 4, 2007, *Washington Post* exclaimed, "War in Iraq Propelling A Massive Migration: War Creates Tension Across the Middle East."

10 It is the only "eye for an eye" legal norm; we do not punish theft with theft, rape with rape; only murder with murder.

11 There are many editions. The one I have before me is *Narrative of the Life of Frederick Douglass, An American Slave, Written by Himself*, Signet Classics, New American Library, 2005, pages 122-128.

To "Hospitality or Exile"

1   "Oedipus at Colonus," tr. Robert Fitzgerald in *The Complete Greek Tragedies*, vol. 2. *Sophocles*, ed. Grene, David, and Richmond, Lattimore (Chicago 1959) 108, lines 631-633.

2   David Carter, *Stonewall: The Riots that Sparked the Gay Revolution* (New York 2004), 39

3   *Time on Two Crosses: The Collected Writings of Bayard Rustin*, ed. Carbado, Devon W. and Donald Weise (San Francisco 2003) 288

4   Fitzgerald translation, 105, lines 556-566.

5   Fitzgerald translation, 108, lines 634-641.

To "Labor's Failure in the South"

1   This data is abstracted from excellent and more comprehensive research published by Barry T. Hirsch and David A. Macpherson in 2007.

2   The best sources on Operation Dixie and the arguments presented here are Barbara S. Griffith, *The Crises of American Labor: Operation Dixie and the Defeat of the CIO* (Temple University Press, 1988); Michael Goldfield, *The Color of Politics: Race and the Mainsprings of American Politics* (New Press, 1997); Robin D. G. Kelley, *Building Bridges: The Challenge of Organized Labor in Communities of Color* (NYU Press, 1999); Michael Honey, *Southern Labor and Black Civil Rights: Organizing Memphis Workers* (University of Illinois, 1993); and Robert Korstad, *Civil Rights Unionism: Tobacco Workers and the Struggle for Democracy in the Mid-20th Century South* (University of North Carolina Press, 2003).

3   Griffith, *Crises*, Chapter IV, "Case Study in Textiles," pp. 46-61

4   Robert Comeaux, the organizing director of HOP, has repeatedly expressed the lessons of the campaign in graphic detail, as have other participants. This section is based on conversations between Comeaux and the author in 1992 and 1993, as well as conversations with other organizers directly involved with HOP.

5   The public employee unions, AFT and AFSCME, felt that they did the best with HOP because they could simply sign up members. As the campaign progressed, adding new workers was at a premium even if they were not added through the private-sector process which would have required election and certification and perhaps collective bargaining

6   The cultural shift around jurisdiction that would come later to institutional labor was first manifest in these early fights and frustrations in Houston, and they presage the present arguments around "sectoral" emphasis and commitments to organizing that split the AFL-CIO and culminated in the creation of the Change to Win Federation. The problems of "organizing" unions versus "servicing" unions, between the building trades and just about everyone else, and the confusions over the clarity of roles between the AFL-CIO and its member unions on the life-and-death struggles around organizing methodology, and the mandate for organizational growth, all came increasingly to the forefront in the problems that beset and crippled the Houston Organizing Project.

7   All of us who were there heard Sweeney express just that commitment in his campaign speech in the AFL-CIO Convention held in New York. This was a personal passion of Ray Abernathy from Atlanta who ghosted many of Sweeney's speeches and rarely failed to make sure the pledge to organize the South was fully embedded in them.

8   More than twenty thousand area workers were employed directly by hotels and another thirty thousand by restaurants, bars, and other hospitality venues, according to Department of Labor statistics.

9   Disclosure: I was chief organizer of the HOTROC campaign and served as chief organizer of SEIU Local 100 headquartered in New Orleans, as well as ACORN, whose national office was also in New Orleans. During part of this seminal period I was also secretary-treasurer of the Greater New Orleans AFL-CIO and president of the SEIU Southern Conference, so I was in a position to know much of this information as a participant.

10 The cornerstone of such agreements was usually a "card check" of union supporters which would trigger an independently conducted certification process with the employer maintaining neutrality and expressing neither opposition nor support for the unionization effort, but instead allowing employees to choose without intimidation whether they wanted union representation.

11 The Service Employees, arguably one of the most progressive unions in the country and certainly the largest and fastest-growing union in the United States over the past two decades, is a good example of this political contradiction. I became the first executive board member elected from the South in 1996, when Andrew Stern became international president. The Southern Conference was also charted at the same time where previously the country was divided between East, West, and Midwest running from north to south. Eight years later when I left the board to organize the multi-union Wal-Mart campaign in Florida and elsewhere, all of the conferences were gone, there

were some more board members from the South, so this wider geographical reality had become institutionalized, but the membership percentage from Southern locals compared to what is now almost 1.5 million members in the union was miniscule for all practical purposes, and the voice within the overall union was similarly soft. The notion that a major U.S. union could be led by a labor leader from the South is about as farfetched as an international union being led by someone from Canada. But in fact that happens, so I guess it has become even more unlikely to imagine international unions leading such a movement in the South again.

12 This is demonstrated by the Service Employees whose most extensive growth has been among home healthcare workers, which was achieved in California and Illinois after commitments of fifteen- and twenty-years duration, based on constant organizing and adaptable strategies combing worker power and political leverage.

13 See Rathke on "Majority Unionism" in *Social Policy* (June 12, 2002) available via www.chieforganizer.org.

14 The successful experiment of the Wal-Mart Workers Association in Florida is indicative of this membership-based, non-collective bargaining methodology. Also see, Rathke, "A Wal-Mart Workers Association: An Organizing Plan" in Nelson Lichtenstein's edited volume, *Wal-Mart: The Face of Twenty-First-Century Capitalism* (New Press, 2006).

Resources, Notes to "Dixie Reaches the Boiling Point"

www.cleanenergy.org (Southern Alliance for Clean Energy—the latest developments, state-by-state updates)

www.fightglobalwarming.com (Get the facts on global warming, learn the dangers, calculate your impact, and make changes that matter)

www.energyguide.com (energy analysis)

www.energy-star.gov (ratings of high-efficiency products, store locator)

www.thinksouth.org (Center for a Better South)

www.gettinggreener.info (progressive environmental ideas from the Center)

1 The "minor" greenhouse gases can be more efficient light absorbers than CO_2. Methane, for example, absorbs light twenty-three times more efficiently than CO_2, and accounts for 25 percent of global warming, but its lifetime in the atmosphere is only ten years, as compared to carbon dioxide's one hundred years.

2 "The Threat to the Planet," *New York Review,* July 13, 2006.

3 November 3–9, 2006.

4 Leadership in Energy and Environmental Design (LEED) is a rating system for the design, construction, and operation of green buildings developed by

the U.S. Green Building Council.

5 November 6, 2006.

6 "Top climatologist warns global warming will hit Vermont hard," *Barre-Montpelier Times Argus*, August 22, 2006.

7 *Advocacy in Action*, newsletter, Spring 2007.

8 David Whitman reports in *Washington Monthly*, September 2005, "Burning Atlanta," that electric utilities are the biggest stationary source of carbon dioxide.

9 According to 2005 figures from the U.S. Department of Transportation, 14,398 for the average Mississippian; 12,508 for Georgians; 11,621 for South Carolinians.

10 *USA Today*, February 22, 2001.

11 "You've got to deal with forests if you're going to make any progress on climate change," Carter Roberts, World Wildlife Fund president.

12 According to new research by Tony Del Genio, a NASA scientist, the predicted stronger updrafts, when the wind moves vertically instead of horizontally, will mean more lightning and bigger hail. Harold Brooks, scientist with NOAA's severe storms lab in Norman, Oklahoma, describes the possibility of baseball-sized hail traveling at 100 mph, "falling like a major league fastball," he said.

13 "City of Asheville, Warren Wilson to combat greenhouse gases," *Asheville Citizen-Times*, August 7, 2007.

To "Ballot Security"

1 Frederick D. Ogden, *The Poll Tax in the South* (University of Alabama Press, 1958), 7 n.28.

2 *Democratic National Committee v. Republican National Committee*, Civ. No. 81-3876 (D. N.J. Nov. 1, 1982).

3 *Long v. Gremillion*, Civil Suit No. 142,389 (Rapides Parish, La., Oct. 14, 1986), p. 4.

4 *United States v. North Carolina Republican Party*, No. 92-161-CIV-5-F (E.D. N.C. 1992).

5 Remarks of Monica M. Goodling Before the Committee on the Judiciary, United States House of Representatives, May 23, 2007, p. 2.

6 *Cantrell v. Charleston County Election Commission*, No. 86-CP-10-4636 (9th Jud. Cir., Nov. 4, 1986).

7 *United States v. Charleston County, S.C.*, C.A. No. 2-01-01155 11) (D. S.C.), Trial Transcript, p. 2689 (Maurice Washington).

8 Id., pp. 473-74 (Truett Nettles).

9 *New York Times*, October 23, 2002; Gannett News Ser., October 25, 2002.

10 *Detroit Free Press*, October 30, 2002.

11 *Martin v. Beaufort County Election Commission*, C.A. No. 9 02 3732 23 (D. S.C.).

12 "In 5-Year Effort, Scant Evidence of Voter Fraud," *New York Times*, April 12, 2007.

13 "Georgia voter ID memo stirs tension," *Oxford Press*, November 18, 2005.

14 *Citizens without Proof: A Survey of Americans' Possession of Documentary Proof of Citizenship and Photo Identification*, Brennan Center for Justice at NYU School of Law, November 2006.

15 "Suit slams voter ID law," *Atlanta-Journal Constitution*, September 20, 2005.

16 United States Elections Assistance Commission, *Election Crimes: An Initial Review and Recommendations for Future Study* (Washington, D.C.; December 2006), 9, 16.

17 Section 5 Recommendation: August 25, 2005, p. 20.

18 Testimony of Joseph D. Rich, Oversight Hearing of the Civil Rights Division, House Judiciary Subcommittee on the Constitution, Civil Rights and Civil Liberties, March 22, 2007.

19 Bob Kengle, "Why I Left the Civil Rights Division."

20 Joseph D. Rich, Mark Posner and Robert Kengle, "The Voting Section," in *The Erosion of Rights: Declining Civil Rights Enforcement under the Bush Administration*, ed. William L. Taylor, et al. (Wash., D.C.; Citizens' Commission on Civil Rights, 2007), 37.

21 Id.

22 *LULAC v. Perry*, 126 S.Ct. 2594 (2006).

23 *Crawford v. Marion County Election Board*, 472 F.3d 949, 951 (7th Cir. 2007).

24 Id. at 954, 955.

25 Id. at 952.

26 *Common Cause/Georgia v. Billups*, 504 F.Supp.2d 1333 N.D. Ga. 2007).

To "Our Appointment with Destiny"

1 *Washington Times*, 19 May 2005. "Inhofe Finds Out 'Elections Have Consequences,'" www.cnn.com, 22 March 2007.

2 "Bush Impeachment on the Table, Hagel Says," *Los Angeles Times*, 26 March 2007, www.latimes.com, concerned Senator Chuck Hagel (R-Neb.). Sean Wilentz, "The Worst President in U.S. History?" *Rolling Stone*, 21 April 2006. Jay Tolson, "Ten Worst Presidents: Introduction," *U.S. News & World Report*, 16 February 2007, www.usnews.com. Catherine Dodge, "Bush Iraq Plan May Be Last Chance to Avoid History's 'Dustbin,'" www.Bloomberg.com, "Politics," 22 January 2007. Eric Foner, "He's the Worst Ever," *Washington Post*, 3 December 2006, p. B1. Rick Shenkman, "George Bush's Misplaced Hope

that Historians Will Rank Him Higher than His Contemporaries," *History News Network*, http://hnn.us, 1 January 2007.

3 These tendencies have been amply demonstrated by some of America's finest scholars. See Richard Hofstadter, *The Paranoid Style in American Politics and Other Essays* (New York: Alfred A. Knopf, 1965), Seymour Martin Lipset and Earl K. Raab, *The Politics of Unreason: Right-Wing Extremism in America, 1790-1970* (New York: Harper and Row, 1970), and David Brion Davis, *The Fear of Conspiracy: Images of Un-American Subversion from the Revolution to the Present* (Ithaca: Cornell University Press, 1971).

4 On the "rock star" reception given to extreme-right incendiaries, see Ben Adler, "Why Liberals Should Keep Complaining About Ann Coulter," *New Republic*, www.tnr.com, 16 March 2007 and Sherie Gossett, "Ann Coulter 'Raghead' Comments Spark Blogger Backlash," *Cybercast News Service*, www.cnsnews. com, 13 February 2006. An important reason extremist right comment has enjoyed entrée into mainstream venues is that modern radical right media is extraordinarily successful at playing as if there are two co-equal sides to every question and they are simply taking one, legitimate if differing, viewpoint that deserves to be treated with seriousness and heard in an open society. Every now and then a member of the extreme-right chattering class lets the open secret slip. Matt Labash, a young writer for Rupert Murdoch's *Weekly Standard* and, formerly, *American Spectator*, admitted that the modern right-wing media simultaneously rejects the conventional "standards of fairness, accuracy, and unbiased coverage that they [simultaneously] demand from the 'liberal media.'" As Labash himself put it: "We've created this cottage industry in which it pays to be un-objective . . . It's a great way to have your cake and eat it too. Criticize other people for not being objective. Be as subjective as you want. It's a great little racket." David Brock, "The Mighty Windbags," www.salon.com, 11 May 2004 (quotations). The aggregate effect of this, of course, has led to extreme timidity on the part of the mainstream media (the so-called "liberal media") who do not want rightist charges of bias to stick. A corollary is widespread confusion over what the word "conservative" really means. Since modern rightists have described their extreme positions as "conservative"—and been allowed to get away with that from a mainstream media more enamored with "balance" than actual reality—the actual word "conservatism" is headed toward "becoming totally meaningless altogether." Bill Zide, "The 'C' Word," www.truthout.org, 13 June 2006 (quotation). Or, as Andrew O'Hehir put it: "the mainstream media's fetish for journalistic 'balance,' regardless of its relevance to reality." "The Know-Nothings," www.salon. com, 14 September 2005 (quotation). Nor is this unintentional. As Donald Devine, a lecturer at a "conservative boot camp" in Santa Barbara that schools its college-age recruits on F. A. Hayek, Milton Friedman, Frank Meyer, and William F. Buckley, explained: Four decades ago "we had to make the term 'conservative' respectable. Now 'conservatism' has become such a popular word it doesn't mean anything." Jason DeParle, "Passing Down the Legacy of

Conservatism," *New York Times*, 31 July 2006 (quotation).

5 Interview with Grover Norquist in Pablo Pardo, "In Twenty Years, the American Welfare State Will No Longer Be Needed," *El Mundo*, 12 September 2004, reprinted in *E Messenger: The Electronic Newsletter of the Florida AFL-CIO*, www.flaaflcio.org, 8 October 2004. Yoshi Tsurumi, Bush's Harvard Business School MBA professor for economics, remembers that the future-President made the statement that "The government doesn't have to help poor people," including people on fixed incomes who needed heat, "because they are lazy." Tsurumi recalls that Bush sneered at him for showing the film *The Grapes of Wrath*, based on the John Steinbeck novel of the Great Depression. He also called FDR's New Deal policies "socialism," and "denounced labor unions, the Securities and Exchange Commission, Medicare, Social Security, you name it. He denounced the civil rights movement as socialism. To him, socialism and communism were the same thing." See Mary Jacoby, "The Dunce," www.salon.com, 16 September 2004 (quotations). Paul Krugman, "Gilded Once More," *New York Times*, 27 April 2007.

6 This refers to Republican attack ads that linked incumbent U.S. senator Max Cleland with Osama bin-Laden and Saddam Hussein that helped a candidate hand-picked by Karl Rove (Saxby Chambliss, who did not serve in Vietnam due to a knee injury) to unseat the Georgia senator who lost three limbs in Vietnam. "Ad Uses Saddam, bin Laden to Question Cleland's Record," *Associated Press*, 11 October 2002. Mary McGrory, "Dirty Bomb Politics," *Washington Post*, 20 June 2002, p. A23. Eric Boehlert, "'The President Ought to be Ashamed,'" www.salon.com, 21 November 2003. "Commander-in-Chief Lands on USS Lincoln," www.cnn.com, 2 May 2003. "'Mission Accomplished' Whodunit," www.cbsnews.com, 29 October 2003.

7 Joshua Kurlantztick, "Democrat Lessons," *Prospect*, www.prospect-magazine.co.uk, December 2004. Josh Marshall, "It's Tough to Have a Goldwater Moment When You're So Close," www.thehill.com, 4 November 2004. George F. Will, "A Goldwater Revival," *Washington Post*, September 2, 2004, p. A23. For a variation on this theme, see John Fund, "Internet Rules," *Wall Street Journal*, www.wsj.com, 31 October 2005. "What Now for Democrats?" *Washington Post*, November 9, 2002, p. A25.

8 Robert B. Reich, "Who Really Picks the Next President," 26 August 2004 and "The Real Battle in the Battle Ground," 22 September 2004, Public Radio's Marketplace Commentaries, www.robertreich.org; D. Stephen Voss, "Strength in the Center," www.digitas.harvard.edu, ca. 2004.

9 I have discussed concepts such as the "Reconstruction Syndrome," a "politics of emotion," 'neo-Kluxism," and "The New Racism" in various places. See, e.g., Glenn Feldman, "The Status Quo Society, The Rope of Religion, and The New Racism," 287-352 in *Politics and Religion in the White South*. Edited by Glenn Feldman. Lexington: University Press of Kentucky, 2005, and Glenn Feldman, "Ugly Roots: Race, Emotion, and the Rise of the Modern Republican

Party in Alabama and the South" 268-309 in *Before* Brown: *Civil Rights and White Backlash in the Modern South.* Edited by Glenn Feldman. Tuscaloosa: University of Alabama Press, 2004.

10 Michael Lind, *Made in Texas: George W. Bush and the Southern Takeover of American Politics* (New York: Basic Books, 2003). Peter Applebome, *Dixie Rising: How the South is Shaping American Values, Politics, and Culture* (New York: Harvest Books, 1997). David Herbert Donald, "The Southernization of America," *New York Times*, 30 August 1976. John Egerton, *The Americanization of Dixie, the Southernization of America* (New York: HarperCollins, 1974).

11 On this final topic, see Glenn Feldman, *The Disfranchisement Myth: Poor Whites and Suffrage Restriction in Alabama* (Athens: University of Georgia Press, 2004).

12 Laurie Goodstein and David D. Kirkpatrick, "Conservative Group Amplifies Voice of Protestant Orthodoxy," *New York Times*, 22 May 2004. Nicholas Confessore, "Welcome to the Machine: How the GOP Disciplined K Street and Made Bush Supreme," *Washington Monthly*, www.washingtonmonthly.com, July/August 2003. Don Hazen, "The Right-Wing Express," www.alternet.org, 7 February 2005. Michael Dolny, "What's in a Label?" *Fairness & Accuracy in Reporting*, www.fair.org, May/June 1998. Paul Krugman, "Supply-Side Virus Strikes Again: Why There is No Cure for this Virulent Infection," *Slate*, http://web.mit.edu, 15 August 1996. Eric Alterman, "How We Got Here," Center for American Progress, *Think Again*, www.cfap.org, 28 August 2005. David Callahan, "$1 Billion for Conservative Ideas," *Nation*, www.thenation.com, 26 April 1999. David Brock, "The Mighty Windbags," www.salon.com, 11 May 2004 and *The Republican Noise Machine: Right-Wing Media and How it Corrupts Democracy* (New York: Crown, 2004). Jessica Clarke and Tracy Van Slyke, "Making Connections, *In These Times*, www.alternet.org, 27 April 2005. Kim Campbell, "A Call to the Right," *Christian Science Monitor*, 25 July 2002. In fact, among right-wing media managers the inability of liberals to reduce complex issues down to the level of black-and-white sound bites in misleading and moralistic terms is actually lampooned as a "weakness" that, they are confident, should ensure conservative dominance in talk-radio for years to come. See comments about Al Franken's liberal talk show on "Air America," in Leonard Pitts Jr., "Just What We Need: More On-Air Yahoos," *Miami Herald*, 24 February 2003, p. 1B (quotation).

13 Gregory Korte, "Blackwell Revels in the Hot Seat: Promoting Bush—and Himself," *Cincinnati Enquirer*, 25 October 2004. Jo Becker, "Behind the Scenes, Officials Wrestle Over Voting Rules," *Washington Post*, October 10, 2004, p. A1. Robert F. Kennedy Jr., "Was the 2004 Election Stolen?" *Rolling Stone*, 1 June 2006. Bob Fitrakis and Harvey Wasserman, "Why is the man who stole Ohio campaigning with a white supremacist?" www.freepress.org, 9 October 9, 2006. Harold Meyerson, "The GOP's Shameful Vote Strategy," *Washington Post*, 27 October 2004, p. A25. Art Levine, "Salon's Shameful Six," www.salon.com, 15 August 2006. Richard Byrne Reilly, "Election Day Has its

(Dirty) Tricks, Too," *Pittsburgh Tribune-Review*, 28 October 2004. Historian Dan T. Carter has also made the important point in a number of places that our current "rotten borough" system of gerrymandered congressional districts disproportionately favors Republicans. For example, Carter reports, over the last 6-year Senate election cycle, Republican candidates actually won less than 47 percent of the total vote but occupied 55 of the chamber's 100 seats. Carter, "Is There Still a Dixie? The Southern Question and the Triumph of American Conservatism," p. 3, (Paper delivered at the University of Sussex, October 2006.) I am grateful to Professor Carter for making a copy of this paper available to me. Also Dan T. Carter to author (email), 9 November 2004. Email in possession of the author. "The Long Shadow of Jim Crow: Voter Suppression in America, 2004," A Report by the People for the American Way and the National Association for the Advancement of Colored People (NAACP), www.pfaw.org, 2004.

14 The two most notable recent books to do this are Matthew D. Lassiter, *The Silent Majority: Suburban Politics in the Sunbelt South* (Princeton: Princeton University Press, 2005) and Byron E. Shafer and Richard Johnston, *The End of Southern Exceptionalism: Class, Race, and Partisan Change in the Postwar Period* (Cambridge: Harvard University Press, 2006).

15 Glenn Feldman, "Unholy Alliance: Suppressing Catholic Teachings in Subservience to Republican Ascendance in America," *Political Theology* 7 (April 2006): 137-79, see esp. pp. 138-39.

16 One of the few studies that has recognized the irony of the nationalizing of Southern thought and culture, especially the worst aspects of it, is George Lewis, *The White South and the Red Menace: Segregationists, Anticommunism, and Massive Resistance, 1945-1965* (Gainesville: University Press of Florida, 2004).

17 On traditional deference toward business and the New Deal challenge, see George A. Steiner and John F. Steiner, *Business, Government, and Society: A Managerial Perspective* (Ninth edition. (Boston: Irwin, McGraw-Hill, 2000), 88-89, 124 (quotation), 373 and Robert L. Heilbroner, *The Worldly Philosophers: The Lives, Times, and Ideas of the Great Economic Thinkers*, revised 7th edition (New York: Touchstone Books, Simon and Schuster, 1999), 277.

18 After the legal victories of the modern civil rights movement, "personal responsibility" soon became the common coin for *The New Racism*, with its coalition of economic and social/religious conservatives, that largely replaced the anti-federalism coin of the old racism and its alliance between economic and racial conservatives.

19 Garry Wills, "Fringe Government," *New York Review of Books* 52 (October 6, 2005): 46-50. See the formal statement with a list of original signatories, "Evangelicals & Catholics Together: The Christian Mission in the Third Millennium," *First Things* 43 (May 1994): 15-22. Tom Strode, "Land: Religious Right Has Won Fight With Secular Fundamentalists," *Baptist Press*, 26 January

2005. Ralph Reed, *After the Revolution: How the Christian Coalition is Impacting America* (Dallas: Word Publishing, 1996), 230-40. For the Orwellian use of abortion by the far right as the new civil rights, see e.g., Greg Pierce, "Inside Politics: Civil Rights Award," *Washington Times*, www.washingtontimes.com, 5 December 2006, John-Henry Westen, "Pastor Warren, Would You Permit a White Supremacist to Speak at Your Church?" *Christian Post*, www.christianpost.com, 6 December 2006, and Stode, "Land." Comments of Richard Land at the conference "Role of Religion in Public Life," James Madison Institute, Princeton University, Robert P. George, presiding, C-SPAN, www.c-span.org, 24 December 2005. Of course, Lott's newfound and professed racial tolerance ignores a long personal history of intolerance, beginning with his apprenticeship to Mississippi Dixiecrat congressman William Colmer and continuing at the University of Mississippi and in the U.S. Congress. See Nicholas Lemann, "What is the South?" *New Republic*, 29 January 2007, pp. 24-28.

20 *Engel v. Vitale*, 370 U.S. 421 (1962). *Roe v. Wade*, 410 U.S. 113 (1973).

21 David Brooks, "Dollars & Sense," *New York Times*, 26 January 2006, p. A23. Jason L. Riley, "President Bush Needs to Lead His Party on Race," *Wall Street Journal*, 16 January 2003, p. A12. Richard Benedatto, "GOP: 'We Were Wrong' to Play Racial Politics," *USA Today*, www.usatoday.com, 14 July 2005, regarding RNC chair Ken Mehlman. Shankar Vendatam, "Study Ties Political Leanings to Hidden Biases," *Washington Post*, 30 January 2006, p. A5. Reed, *After the Revolution*, 236 and 237 (quotations).

22 Ricca, "The American Right," 15 (Weyrich quoted).

23 Ricca, "The American Right," 8-9. Rick Perlstein, *Before the Storm: Barry Goldwater and the Unmaking of the American Consensus* (New York: Hill and Wang, 2001), 374. Of course George Wallace was too shrewd to be taken in by any of this. On one occasion, Wallace mused, "You know, I should have copyrighted all of my speeches. If I had, the Republicans in Alabama, throughout the South, and all over the nation would be paying me hundreds of thousands of dollars. They owe everything they have to my kind of Democratic thinking." Glenn Feldman, "Ugly Roots," 286 (Wallace quotation). See also Jason Sokol, *There Goes My Everything: White Southerners in the Age of Civil Rights* (New York: Knopf, 2006), 252 (Wallace quotation).

24 Ricca, "The American Right," 11 and 15 (Weyrich quotation). See David B. Smith, "You're Talking About Them, Not Me, Right God," *Voice of Prophecy*, www.vop.com, 27 July 2004. John Gallagher and Chris Bull, "Perfect Enemies: The Religious Right, the Gay Movement, and the Politics of the 1990s," *Washington Post*, ca. 1996.

25 Lassiter, *The Silent Majority*. Shafer and Johnston, *The End of Southern Exceptionalism*. A more complex work is Joseph Crespino, *In Search of Another Country: Mississippi and the Conservative Counterrevolution* (Princeton: Princeton University Press, 2007). Two recent works have not followed the lead of Lassiter, and Shafer and Johnston. See Sokol, *There Goes My Everything* and

Kevin M. Kruse, *White Flight: Atlanta and the Making of Modern Conservatism* (Princeton: Princeton University Press, 2005). See Glenn Feldman, "Review of Shafer and Johnston" *Journal of Southern History* 73 (August 2007): 746-48 and "Review of Sokol," *Journal of American History* 93 (September 2007): 647-48.

26 Sheldon Hackney, "The Ambivalent South," 385-95 in *Warm Ashes: Issues in Southern History at the Dawn of the Twenty-First Century.* Edited by Winfred B. Moore Jr., Kyle S. Sinisi, and David H. Whyte Jr. (Columbia: University of South Carolina Press, 2003), esp. pp.387, 390, 392 (quotations).

27 James C. Cobb, "An Epitaph for the North: Reflections on the Politics of Regional and National Identity at the Millennium," *Journal of Southern History* 66 (February 2000): 3-24.

28 C. Vann Woodward, *The Burden of Southern History* (1960 reprint. Baton Rouge: Louisiana State University Press, 1968).

To "Afterword"

1 Mayer, *They Thought They Were Free: The Germans, 1933-1945* (Chicago: University of Chicago Press, 1955), pp. 166-169, 200.

Acknowledgments

The authors acknowledge and give thanks for the inspiration provided by John Egerton, Paul Gaston, Sheldon Hackney, and Connie Curry, all contributors to our preceding volume, *Where We Stand: Voices of Southern Dissent,* who for good reasons—typically other pressing writing commitments—could not participate in this project. Fortunately, all nominated other writers qualified to take their places and gave important guidance in the shaping of this book. It is also our good fortune that eight of the original contributors returned.

This book would not have appeared without the support of NewSouth's publisher, Suzanne La Rosa; managing editor, Brian Seidman; and financial manager, Lisa Emerson. Nor could it have been presented in such readable and, we hope, intelligent style without the masterful craftsmanship, practiced editorial hand, and devotion to well-expressed ideas concerning all things "Southern," of editor Randall Williams.

A. D.

www.ingramcontent.com/pod-product-compliance
Lightning Source LLC
Chambersburg PA
CBHW020843270326
41928CB00006B/523